THE
END
OF
GREATNESS

THE
END
OF
GREATNESS

Why America Can't Have

(and Doesn't Want)

Another Great President

AARON DAVID MILLER

palgrave
macmillan

First published in 2014 by PALGRAVE MACMILLAN® TRADE in the
United States—a division of St. Martin's Press LLC, 175 Fifth Avenue, New
York, NY 10010.

Where this book is distributed in the UK, Europe and the rest of the world,
this is by Palgrave Macmillan, a division of Macmillan Publishers Limited,
registered in England, company number 785998, of Houndmills, Basingstoke,
Hampshire RG21 6XS.

Palgrave® and Macmillan® are registered trademarks in the United States, the
United Kingdom, Europe and other countries.

ISBN: 978-1-137-27900-2

Library of Congress Cataloging-in-Publication Data

Miller, Aaron David.
    The end of greatness : why America can't have (and doesn't want) another
great president / Aaron David Miller.
       pages   cm
    ISBN 978-1-137-27900-2 (hardback)
    1. Presidents—United States—Evaluation. 2. Political leadership—United
States—Evaluation. I. Title.
JK516.M477   2014
320.973—dc23
                                                                    2014009441

A catalogue record of the book is available from the British Library.

Design by Letra Libre

First edition: October 2014

10 9 8 7 6 5 4 3 2 1

Printed in the United States of America.

CONTENTS

PART III

What's So Great about
Being Great, Anyway?

ACKNOWLEDGMENTS

WRITING A BOOK IS NO EASY ENTERPRISE. AND IT can be an isolating, even a lonely experience. In my case, I had a few advantages that made it much less so.

First, I had the full support of the Woodrow Wilson International Center for Scholars and its terrific president and CEO the Honorable Jane Harman. The Center is the living memorial to our twenty-eighth president, our only PhD president, and the only president buried in Washington, DC. It is an extraordinary place, a truly unique community of scholars rich in expertise and knowledge and yet steeped in the ways of Washington too. I owe a special debt to Haleh Esfandiari, the Center's remarkable and irreplaceable head of the Middle East program, who provided constant support and encouragement.

Second, a number of historians and experts on the presidency offered wise counsel and guidance. David Greenberg, a friend, wonderful historian, and visiting fellow at the Wilson Center, was an invaluable sounding board and teacher. Robert Dallek, James Pfiffner, Mel Leffler, Steven Hess, Norman Ornstein, and CNN's John King spared a good deal of their precious time and wisdom. Doris Kearns-Goodwin encouraged me from the beginning to take on the project despite its breadth and complexity. And my brother Richard Miller, a terrific historian in his own right, put up with and answered my many annoying questions.

Third, I had wonderful research assistants during the course of this project. Thanks to Rebecca Lund, Amanda Robinson, Alexandra Neal,

Yevgenya Kutepova, Alexandra Billings, William Swadley, Chelsea Biggs, and Alexander Fullman. To Adam Barnhart, Ryan Blackwell, Jennifer Jones, Mike Habashy, Josh Cox, Shervin Taheran, Amy Parker, and Mitchel Hochberg, I owe special thanks. Josh Nason found himself in the unenviable position of being at the Wilson Center during the final stages of the project. His efforts were invaluable to the completion of the book. I'm not sure I could have finished it without him.

Finally, to my wife, Lindsay, daughter, Jennifer, and son, Danny, there are no words that can express my appreciation for your constant love and support.

INTRODUCTION

The End of Greatness?

A COUPLE YEARS BACK, I GAVE A TALK TO A GROUP of Princeton graduate students and faculty on the indispensable role leaders play in successful Arab-Israeli negotiations. Having worked on the Middle East peace process for over twenty years, I had come to the conclusion that, far more than any other factor, it was willful leaders—masters, not prisoners, of their political houses—who produced the agreements that endure.

It proved to be a pretty tough crowd.

One graduate student insisted that I had been taken hostage by Thomas Carlyle and his "Great Man" theory of history. Another critic, a visiting professor from Turkey, protested that I had completely ignored the broader social and economic forces that really drive and determine change.

I conceded to both that the debate about what mattered more—the individual or circumstances—was a complicated business. But I reminded the professor that she hailed from a land in which one man, Mustafa Kemal—otherwise known as Ataturk—had fundamentally changed the entire direction of her country's modern history. We left it at that.

History, to be sure, is driven by the interaction between human agency and circumstance. Based on my own experiences in government and negotiations, individuals count greatly in this mix, particularly in matters of war, peace, and nation building. Historian John Keegan made the stunning assertion that the story of much of the twentieth century was a tale, the biographies really, of six men: Lenin, Stalin, Hitler, Churchill, FDR, and Mao.[1] Wherever you stand on the issue of the individual's role in history, its impact must be factored into the equation, particularly when it comes to explaining turning points in a nation's history.

Nonetheless, the professor from Turkey had a point. Today we are consumed with leaders and leadership as the solution, if not the panacea, to just about everything that ails us. We admire the bold transformational leader who seeks fundamental change, and value less the cautious transactor who negotiates, triangulates, and settles for less dramatic results. And we tend to forget too that great leaders almost always emerge in times of national crisis, trauma, and exigency, a risk we run if we hunger for the return of such leaders. Still, Holy Grail–like, we search for some magic formula or key to try to understand what accounts for great leadership. And we hungrily devour the lessons from the careers of those in business, media, or politics whom we deem to be effective leaders. Indeed, we seem nothing short of obsessed with the L word.

Micah Zenko, my fellow columnist at *Foreign Policy,* notes that if you type "leadership books" into the Amazon search engine you get 86,451 results.[2] Want to study leadership, or better yet become a leader? There is certainly a program for you. The International Leadership Association lists over 1,500 academic programs in the field.[3] Yale University alone has a Leadership Institute, a Women's Leadership Initiative, a Global Health Leadership Institute, and an MBA on Leadership in Healthcare.[4]

This focus on leaders is understandable, particularly during times of great uncertainty and stress. It is only natural and even logical to look for leaders when our fate and future appear driven by impersonal and unforeseen forces beyond our control. The psychologists and mythologists tell us that the need to search for the great leader to guide or even rescue us is an ancient—even primordial—impulse. This strong need for great leadership exists also in America, though it seems in conflict with an American creed that places a premium on self-reliance and independence, is suspicious of power and authority, and, as we will see, expresses ambivalence about the very idea of powerful leaders. In fact, an exaggerated and misplaced need for heroes and heroic leadership seems particularly incongruous and even inappropriate in a political culture that celebrates effective leadership even while constraining it, and especially at a time when there seem to be so few outstanding political leaders to be found. To complicate matters further, we misunderstand how leaders actually lead. Indeed, today we have a far too idealized, even cartoonish, view of this matter. We have a notion that the best leaders are those who are elected promising high principles, lofty visions, or big agendas and then impose them through the power of persona and persuasion. And when leaders cannot play the hero's role, we attribute their failure to an inability to communicate and articulate a narrative so powerful and compelling that followers rally to the cause, and doubters and opponents have no choice but to comply or somehow melt away.

In a Shakespearean line Jack Kennedy loved, Glendower boasted to Hotspur in *Henry IV* (act 3) that he could "call spirits from the vasty deep"; "So can any man," Hotspur replied, then, reflecting the leader's predicament in our age, added, "But will they come when you do call for them?" This "call and they will come" conception of leadership is more appropriate to Hollywood and to a gauzy, idealized view of our history than it is to real life in the political world. "The Titanic," Democratic strategist Paul Begala quipped in reference to charges that Barack Obama had failed to craft a compelling narrative, "didn't have a communications problem, it had an iceberg problem."[5] A president's words matter, but there must be context to give them real meaning and power. But such context is often a matter of uncontrollable circumstances; leaders cannot create them out of whole cloth, whether it is crisis, opportunity, or both. Writing in the nineteenth century, Karl Marx famously observed: "Men make their own history, but they do not make it just as they please; they do not make it under self-selected circumstances, but under circumstances existing already, given and transmitted from the past."[6] For the aspirational leader who loves to focus on tomorrow, yesterday is ironically at least as important. More often than not, effective leaders intuit what the times make possible and then, if truly skillful, exploit and enlarge that opportunity and help shape the politics that sustain it.

Indeed, these days those who favor and align with the Carlyle crowd and the "Great Man" view of history—myself included—have a serious problem.

We are now well into the twenty-first century, a full 70 years after Keegan's six transformers either tried to take over the world or to save it. Look around. Where are the big heroes, the bold, breakthrough leaders, those who do not simply react to events but shape them too? Where are the giants of old, the transformers who changed the world and left great legacies? Plenty of very bad leaders have come and gone—Pol Pot, Idi Amin, Saddam Hussein, Muammar Qaddafi, Slobodan Milošević— and some larger-than-life good ones too, like Charles de Gaulle, Konrad Adenauer, Anwar Sadat, Mikhail Gorbachev, Pope John Paul II, and Nelson Mandela.

Leaders, to be sure, can emerge from the most unlikely places and at the least expected and most fortuitous times. Think only of Abraham Lincoln, Mahatma Gandhi, and Martin Luther King Jr. And who knows what kind of leaders history's long arc might produce in the future?

That said, betting on the future is at best an uncertain business. Today things don't look that bright. We face a leadership deficit of global proportions. In fact, we seem to be pretty well along into what you might call the post-heroic leadership era.

Today, 193 countries sit in the United Nations, among them 88 free and functioning democracies.[7] The five permanent members of the United Nations Security Council, the so-called great powers—the United States, Britain, France, China, and Russia—are not led by great, transformative leaders. Nor do other rising states such as Brazil, India, and South Africa boast leaders with strong and accomplished records. We certainly see leaders who are adept at maintaining power and keeping their seats—some, like Russia's Vladimir Putin and Turkey's Recep Tayyip Erdoğan, for many years. Germany's Angela Merkel is certainly a powerful leader and skilled politician; and the recently elected Indian Prime Minister Narendra Modi may well prove to be a leader to watch.

But where are those whom we could honestly describe as potentially great, heroic, or inspirational? And how many are not only great, but *good*—with compassion and high moral and ethical standards—too? How many will author some incomparable, unparalleled, and ennobling achievement at home or on the world stage, an achievement likely to be seen or remembered as great or transformational? Today, if I were pressed to identify a potentially great leader, I might offer up not a traditional head of state at all, but rather a religious figure: Pope Francis I, whose greatness as well as goodness may well be defined by the irony of his anti-greatness, commonness, and humility.

Nor do great events or crises these days seem to be leader friendly. Once rightly considered crucibles for emerging leaders, neither rebellion nor revolution seems capable of producing historic leaders befitting these historic circumstances anymore. The most sweeping transformation since the fall of the former Soviet Union, the so-called Arab Spring—now into its fourth year—has so far failed to generate a single political leader of consequence, certainly none with the power and capacity to transition from authoritarianism to democratic reform. Those who remain in an unsettled Arab world—largely the aging kings, emirs, and sheikhs—seem too busy looking in the rearview mirror to consider anything like future-oriented, bold, or transformative reform. Forget about historic transformations. Do today's leaders even have what it takes to be good transactional leaders, that is to say, to manage the more mundane problems and challenges at hand and to deliver good governance?

How do we explain the absence of great leaders on the world stage? There is no simple or single explanation, certainly not a one-size-fits-all answer. Part of the answer surely rests on the rather simple fact that greatness—if it is defined generally as incomparable and unparalleled achievement that is nation- or even world-altering—is by definition rare, not just in politics but in any aspect of human enterprise. And an appreciation of this caliber of achievement also requires time, the ultimate arbiter of what is of value in life, along with the perspective that only time can bring to judge an achievement's worth or quality. Unlike individual accomplishment in art, music, literature, or even sports, politics has far too many moving parts and a wider variety of factors beyond a politician's capacity to control. There is a terrifying complexity and contingency to political life, particularly in democracies where electoral politics, public opinion, interest groups, and bureaucracies conspire to frustrate even the best laid plans. And if this is true at home it is doubly so for those who seek foreign policy success in the cruel and unpredictable world beyond their borders.

Contemporary leaders aspiring for unparalleled, unprecedented achievement also face a "been there, done that" problem. Nations, like individuals, pass through foundational trials and existential threats and crises early in their histories. The nations and polities that survive likely never pass that way again, largely because they had the right leaders at the right time to guide them through these challenges. As nations mature, the need and opportunity for heroic action to preempt or deal with these existential challenges diminishes, along with tropes and narratives that define both the myth and reality required for great achievement.

Perhaps more telling in explaining the modern leadership deficit is that the world today has become a much more complex place for those who want to acquire, hold, and use power effectively, let alone produce historic change. Some argue that we've reached the end of leadership, others the end of power, or at least its decay and dissolution. Power, Carnegie's Moises Naim tells us, now faces off against fast-paced changes that have made people, goods, and ideas more kinetic, mobile, and connected, ideas that have unleashed expectations and aspirations much harder to manage and control. That certainly is the case for the autocrats who, as a veritable class of leaders, have fallen on hard times. In 1977, authoritarians controlled 89 countries in the world. By 2011, that number had dwindled to 22.[8] In Egypt and Tunisia, two authoritarian leaders who had ruled for decades were removed from power in a matter of months. Even in democracies, where today half the world's population resides, a globalized, technology-driven information age has made governing much more challenging. An intrusive 24/7 media that recognizes and accepts no boundaries, conflates celebrity with serious accomplishment, and strips away the distance, detachment, and the aura and mystique required for great leadership. Proximity, as Ben Franklin opined, produces contempt and children. And for politicians, too much exposure and familiarity diminishes the public's willingness to think of the leader as special or great. Today's media culture opens up a veritable window through which to observe and identify leaders' imperfections and flaws.

At the same time, the leveling and globalizing of the traditional playing field has imparted to the small a much greater power to compete with and influence the big. To a certain extent, this has always been the case. The power of a single individual to act has always been a terrifying one. The assassination of Austria's Archduke Ferdinand by a Serbian anarchist set into motion a chain of events that led to world war. The murder of Israeli prime minister Yitzhak Rabin helped kill the Oslo peace process and plunge the Israeli-Palestinian relationship into a crisis of confidence from which it has yet to recover. Still, today's smaller actors, freed from what Naim describes as the "size, scope, history, or entrenched tradition," increasingly challenge big ones in ways that few might have imagined possible.[9] On 9/11, attacks by nineteen al-Qaeda terrorists would set the stage for the two longest wars in American history and a fundamental reorientation of America's national security policy. In 2013, the revelations by a single US government contractor of a vast NSA intelligence collection effort at home and abroad triggered the biggest debate in a half century on finding the right balance between security, privacy, and individual rights in a democratic society. Like modern day Gullivers, aspiring and ambitious leaders are tied down by an army of constraints and challenges that make effective governing hard and frustrating.

— —

Nowhere is this leadership vacuum more acutely felt than in the politics of the United States, the world's greatest and most consequential power. Greatness is certainly not missing in the American story. Despite talk of decline, America remains the world's sole superpower, with a better balance of military, political, economic, and soft power than any other nation in the world. With 5 percent of the world's population, the United States accounts for a full 25 percent of the world's economic output, nearly half of its military expenditures, and has the best capacity to project its educational, cultural, and social media soft power resources.[10] We surely have no shortage of great athletes, actors, entrepreneurs, and scientists. Since 2000, Americans have won 21 out of 37 Nobel prizes in physics; 22 out of 33 in chemistry; 18 out of 33 in medicine; and an incredible 27 out of 31 prizes in economics.[11] Still, great nations are supposed to have great political leaders too, right? And yet today in America we hear very little talk of greatness in our politics. Instead, the focus is on the leadership deficit, on America the ungovernable, and on the sorry state of its dysfunctional politics. In 2011, the approval rating of the US Congress actually fell into the single digits and has hovered in the low twenties ever since.[12] One 2013 poll revealed that the public's view of Congress was significantly less positive than its view of root canal operations, NFL replacement refs, colonoscopies, France, and even cockroaches.[13]

Today, great lions no longer roar in the Senate. Indeed, what was once considered the world's greatest deliberative body is now populated by what congressional scholar and analyst Norman Ornstein calls "ideologues and charlatans."[14] The first branch of government is indeed what Ornstein and Thomas Mann call the "Broken Branch"[15]—polarized and partisan with few in either chamber willing to transcend narrow party differences or risk the wrath of their bases by reaching out across the aisle to do deals on the big issues. Republicans seem to be the most divided, dysfunctional, and, at their fringe, the most extreme, with a veritable "wacko bird" wing according to Arizona senator John McCain.[16] But the dirty little secret and truth on Capitol Hill is far more complex: neither party has the will or the capacity to address the truly core issues, such as breaking the Gordian fiscal knot of how to reduce debt by raising taxes and controlling entitlements. Far from looking at compromise as a virtue, in America's tribalized political world, it is seen as a liability or, worse, a betrayal. How many members of the House or Senate today would want to be described as the Great Compromiser, a title bestowed on Kentucky's representative and senator Henry Clay for his artful negotiating skills in the efforts to head off and defuse the crises over slavery before the Civil War?

Worried about our leadership deficit, we often look to our history for the comfort and security we cannot find in the present. And we don't find much of either there. After all, historians remind us, if thirteen colonies, and then states in a fledgling republic, perched precariously along the eastern edge of a vast continent and totaling a mere 4 million souls could produce leaders the likes of George Washington, Thomas Jefferson, James Madison, Benjamin Franklin, Alexander Hamilton, and John Adams in roughly the same political space and time, why, out of a population of more than 300 million, is it impossible for us to generate just a few great ones today?

Steven Spielberg's 2013 Hollywood film *Lincoln* was brilliant and inspirational. In portraying our sixteenth president as a visionary but practical politician who was ready for compromise in passing the Thirteenth Amendment to abolish slavery, the film clearly tried to offer up a counterpoint to the dysfunctional politics of our own time and perhaps raise the hope too that we might have such leaders again. But the movie was also a veritable poster child for Lincoln's idiosyncratic greatness and his unique times, and as clear a statement as any of why such a transformative president could simply never appear today.

We really have lost any real-time connection to greatness in our national politics. And how do we know to appreciate, let alone understand, what we cannot see? Last year, while briefing a group of US military officers, all roughly in their fifties and sixties, I asked them to identify one American political figure in their lifetime whom they deemed worthy of the term *great*. Complete silence. When I offered up my candidate—Martin Luther King Jr.—one officer immediately shot back: "That's not fair. He died in 1968." Precisely, I responded. King has been gone now for nearly half a century. And despite his flaws, a leader of his stature—or anyone close to it—has not appeared again.

It should come as no surprise that the concern about the leadership deficit in our political class also extends to the presidency itself, an institution that has become, both for better and worse, the central element in our political system. The British and Continental Europeans had, and in some cases still have, their kings and emperors; the Russians had their tsars; and the Vatican its popes. We have the presidency and our presidents. And despite the imperfections of both, the office and those who have held it have maintained a remarkable resiliency, prestige, and practical saliency these many years.

The very centrality of the presidency in our governmental system and our political culture guarantee its endurance. The presidency is the only national office all Americans help to select; the symbol of our government to the nation and to the world; the most dynamic change agent in our political system. And because it is occupied by a single individual, not the 535 or the 9 that represent the Congress and the Supreme Court, it is much easier to relate to and personalize.

Yet the centrality of the presidency must be reconciled with the limitations of the office and the constraints that bind it. All presidents disappoint in some fashion. The job description includes a structural impediment to high performance. "No man will ever bring out of the Presidency the reputation which carries him into it," Jefferson observed four years even before his own presidency began.[17] The powers at their disposal—no matter how great—are vastly exceeded by the responsibilities, challenges, and expectations they face. "All the President is," Harry Truman famously quipped a century and a half after Jefferson, in 1947, "is a glorified public relations man who spends his time flattering, kissing, and kicking people to get them to do what they are supposed to do anyway."[18] And then, finally, the act of governing almost always means disappointing constituencies and angering opponents.

Even so, the American public—and the political elites too—have always aspired to much more in this uniquely personalized American institution, and they continue to do so today. We continue to expect more, demand more than any president could possibly deliver. Writing 50 years ago, historian Thomas Bailey observed that Americans "are prone to place their Presidents—especially the dead ones—on a pedestal rather than under a microscope."[19] And this is confirmed by Gallup Polls revealing that once out of office and separated from the political and media fray, presidents' ratings are usually better than they were upon leaving office.[20]

Consider only the popular reaction to John F. Kennedy's tragically abbreviated 1,037-day presidency and the way his short time in office has resonated through the years.[21] Kennedy's dynamic, youthful image, beautiful wife, and idealized Camelot story, and the profound sense of loss that traumatized the nation in the wake of his assassination, left a "what might have been" mystique that has given his presidency enduring power far beyond its actual accomplishments. Public opinion polls often rank JFK (one of only three presidents instantly identified by his initials) ahead of both Washington and Roosevelt in presidential ratings. Indeed, on the occasion of the fiftieth anniversary of his assassination, a November 2013 Gallup poll revealed that of the ten presidents since Eisenhower, Americans judged Kennedy to be the best.[22] And as Larry Sabato argues in *The Kennedy Half Century,* Kennedy remains the ideal conception of a president, influencing his successors in ways that only a few presidents have and seemingly forgiven for his imperfections and transgressions.[23]

And all of this for a president that historians do not judge as a great, his tenure simply too abbreviated to be evaluated fairly. JFK's charismatic image, frozen forever in time, holds out the elusive promise of the idealized president: young, handsome, well spoken, aspirational in word and deed. His presidency—the last before the proverbial fall and the onset of almost two decades of diminished status and respect for the office—reflects something else too: the gap between the great presidents we want and aspire to and the ones we simply can no longer have. That we have a presidency-dependence, perhaps even an addiction, in America is clear. That might not be so bad if our addiction could be satisfied. But it cannot.

The presidency has always been an implausible, some might even say an impossible, job. But the mix of challenges and constraints—some old, some new—that we will follow through the course of this book has made the post–World War II presidency harder still: constitutional and practical constraints on the office itself; the president's expanding reach and responsibilities; the expanding role of a government we trust less, even when we demand more from it; America's global role; and an intrusive, omnipresent, and nonstop media.

These challenges have created the ultimate presidential bind. On one hand, we have become presidency-dependent in a president-centric system; on the other hand, our expectations have risen while the president's capacity to deliver has diminished. In essence, we are lost in a kind of presidential Bermuda Triangle, adrift between the presidents we still want and the ones we can no longer have.

That bind is the subject of this book. And three elements define and drive the core argument:

First, greatness in the presidency may be rare, but it is both real and measurable. Three undeniably great presidents straddle the American story: Washington, the proverbial father of his country; Lincoln, who kept it whole through the Civil War; and Franklin Roosevelt, who shepherded the nation through its worst economic calamity and won its greatest war. Their very deeds define the meaning of greatness in American political life. So let me be clear about my definition of that greatness: each of the undeniably great presidents overcame a truly nation-wrenching challenge or crisis; each used his crisis moment to fundamentally alter the way we see ourselves as a nation and the way we govern ourselves too, and in doing so changed the nation forever for the better; and each in the process transcended narrow partisanship and in time came to be seen even by critics as an extraordinary national leader.

In addition to these three undeniable greats, perhaps five others whom historians and the public judge favorably too—their own legacies secured through great accomplishments at critical moments in the nation's story—round out the group of top performers. The operative point is that this greatness club has created a frame of reference, a high bar really—and a problematic one at that—against which we have come to judge and evaluate our modern presidents and they have come to judge themselves. Part I defines greatness in the presidency and looks at who gets admitted into this elite presidential club and why.

Second, historic greatness in the presidency has gone the way of the dodo. And it is unlikely to return any time soon. The presidents we judge to be great are very much with us still, everywhere really. They are on our money and monuments, stars of our HBO specials and Hollywood movies, and subjects of best-selling presidential biographies. They are everywhere, that is, except in the White House. As we will see, what I describe as "traces of greatness," both real and perceived, have appeared in several of our more contemporary presidents. But those "traces" are not to be confused with the performance of the three undeniables or the handful of other top performers we hold in high esteem. The greatness I described earlier belongs to an America of a different time and place, to a different country really. If you measure the time span from the end of Washington's last term to Lincoln's first, then on to FDR's and forward to the present, we have now gone the longest stretch in our history, roughly 70 years, without an undeniably great president. Sure, this can be seen as a cute and meaningless piece of presidential trivia. But it also reflects the increasing challenges and constraints that limit the truly big things a president can do. Indeed, in a consensus-driven democracy, change is rarely speedy and transformative and those presidents who manage to drive it are rarer still. Part II explains why the history of the post-FDR presidency has been such a challenging tale, and why the times and circumstances have narrowed the prospects, the need, and the opportunity for sustained heroic action in the presidency.

Third, and there really is no other way to say this: we need to get over the greatness thing and stop pining for the return of leaders we can no longer have. Like the ghosts in Charles Dickens's *A Christmas Carol,* great presidents continue to hover, to teach, and to inspire. And we have much to learn from their successes and failures. But there is a risk in thinking, let alone succumbing to the illusion, that we will see their likes again, even in an altered contemporary guise. The world and country have changed and so have we. And besides, we should not want to see them again. Greatness in the presidency is too rare to be relevant in our modern times and—driven as it is in our political system by big crisis—too risky and dangerous to be desirable. Our continued search for idealized presidents raises our expectations and theirs, skews presidential performance, and leads to an impossible standard that can only frustrate and disappoint. To sum up: we can no longer have a truly great president, we seldom need one, and as irrational as it sounds, we may not want one, either. Part III explains why.

So what do we do about our seemingly insatiable presidential addiction? The conclusion offers some modest suggestions. But be forewarned in advance, it will be a hard sell and a tougher challenge to overcome and to let greatness go. Americans will always aspire to more. And we can no more give up on our presidents than we can on ourselves. So let's get started. Our story is really a journey through time and a period of presidential greatness once revealed and now gone. Perhaps along the way we can find a way out of our presidential predicament, maybe even begin to reconcile our expectations of presidential performance with the realities that constrain it. And perhaps at journey's end we can even begin to discover a way to narrow the gap between the presidents we want and the ones we can realistically have.

PART I

Greatness Revealed

AT THE CORNER OF ROCK CREEK PARKWAY AND Virginia Avenue, the ghosts of presidents past consort. The place is not mentioned in any Washington, DC, guidebook. Nor was it on the route of the ubiquitous Tourmobiles that once shuttled visitors around the nation's capital.

I first noticed it early one beautiful spring morning driving through the park, verdant and fresh from the previous night's rain. As I turned east away from the river, I saw a small piece of the presidential greatness puzzle captured in a single frame.

Up ahead, rising straight and strong, much like the man it honored, was the Washington Monument, dedicated in 1885 by one of our less renowned nineteenth-century presidents, Chester A. Arthur, to one of our greatest.

To my right, cantilevered over the Parkway, was the Kennedy Center for the Performing Arts, opened in 1971, only eight years after the president's assassination in Dallas, perhaps the most speedily erected major structure to honor any of our presidents.

And finally, brashly and inelegantly lording over several blocks on my right along Virginia Avenue was the Watergate Apartments complex, an infamous monument of sorts, a crime scene really, to a president whose name instantly evokes anything but greatness.

That small corner of the nation's capital holds memories of three American presidents, all profoundly different in style and accomplishment but each with a claim to a piece of greatness in the presidency worthy of attention.

In George Washington, after whom the office was fashioned by admiring and trusting compatriots, we have an undeniably great president whose quarter-century career spanned every momentous turn in the birth of the American Republic. John Fitzgerald Kennedy was not in office nearly long enough to be seriously judged a great president; yet his charisma, crisis diplomacy with Cuba, and tragic death continue to place him high in the public's mind and imagination, often ahead of both Washington and Franklin Roosevelt in public polls. And finally, there is Richard Milhous Nixon, a failed and unredeemable president to many, whose actions during the Watergate scandal undermined the very constitutional system he had sworn to protect; yet by any fair measure, for his diplomacy toward China and Russia and the Middle East, he may be America's most accomplished, if not one of its greatest, foreign policy strategists.

Trying to define and measure greatness in our presidents across political time and space is no simple matter. Indeed, I was warned by presidential historians, political scientists, and journalists not to get into this subject for that reason and others too. And here's why.

We have had presidents whose greatest career deeds preceded their less-than-great presidencies (Ulysses S. Grant, Dwight D. Eisenhower); presidents who failed abysmally in one area only to rise to great heights in another (Lyndon B. Johnson, Richard Nixon); others who were surely not undeniably great presidents, but who were great at being president (Bill Clinton; Ronald Reagan); a handful who have been judged by historians as top performers but whose challenges and legacies were not nearly as momentous as the undeniable greats (Thomas Jefferson,

Andrew Jackson, Theodore Roosevelt, Woodrow Wilson, Harry Truman); and finally, those I call the three indispensables (George Washington, Abraham Lincoln, Franklin D. Roosevelt) who guided the nation through calamity and crisis when America's fate, even its existence, hung in the balance, and who in the process left legacies that profoundly transformed the nation's story forever—and profoundly for the better, leaving the mark of undeniable and true greatness on the presidency.

For almost 60 years now (a quarter of the nation's history), presidential scholars, historians, and journalists—along with history buffs of varying persuasions—have been playing the presidential rating game. The game is subjective, flawed, and silly to some, because it obscures the complexities of the office and the broad range of factors that constitute successful presidential performance.

Some contend it is simply impossible to compare an eighteenth-century executive to one from the twenty-first century. George Washington presided over a fledgling nation of 4 million souls, including several hundred thousand slaves. Two centuries plus later, Barack Obama was inaugurated president of a country of well over 300 million with a sprawling government bureaucracy and vast global power and responsibilities that would have been unrecognizable to most of his predecessors, even many of those in the twentieth century.

Others claim the game is too politicized and now, like so much of our history, has been hijacked by liberals and conservatives alike in the ongoing game of political gotcha. Some conservatives argue that Calvin Coolidge, who presided over very prosperous times but who has received consistently low ratings from historians, deserves better. Many diehard Reagan supporters—and a few historians, some on the liberal side—see the refusal to regard Ronald Reagan as a great, or at least as our last transformative president, as just willful liberal bias. Others argue that the high rankings go only to presidents who saw big and active government as the answer to fixing the nation's problems. Historian Alvin Felzenberg makes the case in a wonderfully heretical book, *The*

Leaders We Deserved (And a Few We Didn't): Rethinking the Presidential Rating Game. The Bill Clinton lobby argues that he should move up the presidential ladder too because he led America through such prosperous times and left office with a budget in the black.

There is also a compelling argument that the passage of time provides context, perspective, and the opening of archival records that are vital to any serious evaluation of a president's performance. To journalist and one-time Lyndon Johnson aide Bill Moyers, there are no final judgments on presidents, only "interim reports."[1] Indeed, sometimes, as is the case with the rising stock of both Truman and Eisenhower, a former president can get a boost in popularity as a result of the mood of the times and the public's unhappiness with his successors.[2]

Views on Andrew Jackson—a driving force behind the democratization of American politics and yet a man who held racist views on blacks and Native Americans—has fluctuated greatly over the years. His most recent biographer, John Meacham, superbly chronicles Jackson's greatness, as well as his flaws.[3]

In 1921, when future senator Arthur Vandenberg, then a Michigan newspaper editor, polled a hundred prominent citizens to identify the "Greatest American," Thomas Jefferson received one lonely vote from James Cox, who had just lost the presidency to Warren G. Harding.[4] Jefferson would later get a big boost from Franklin Roosevelt (Cox's running mate in that unsuccessful presidential bid), who promoted him big-time and dedicated Jefferson's monument in 1943, 117 years after his death. Democrats clearly needed a patron saint on the mall too, to balance out Washington the Federalist and Lincoln the Republican.

Harry Truman left office with one of the lowest approval ratings in the modern presidency and yet has been resurrected by historians and the public alike as a tough and decisive president (especially given the poor performance of some of his successors).

Dwight Eisenhower too has benefited from the opening of new archival material and has shed his image as an affable golfing president for that of a more skillful behind-the-scenes leader, prudent and wise when it came to avoiding and getting out of costly Asian wars.

Nor do historians and the public always agree on who was a great and well-remembered president and who was not. How presidents manage to communicate with the American people, their likeability, image, and capacity to connect bear on presidential performance in real time and over time too. Historians regard Washington as an undeniably great president; yet his distance from our own time and stiff and formal persona has cost him in the public rankings. He wasn't just "one of the guys," Mount Vernon's former curator remarked on the bicentennial of his death.[5]

When we elect a president, it is not just about smarts and experience; it is also about whether we feel comfortable enough, figuratively speaking, to invite him into our homes for at least four years, maybe eight. Indeed, neither Reagan nor Clinton is on most historians' greats lists; yet they were brilliant politicians who left office well liked and remain even more popular today.

There is a much better chance of being remembered as a success if you can stick around for a full eight years, and even more so if the White House remains in your party's hands after you have served two complete terms. That is no mean feat and has only happened twice in the twentieth century (FDR and Reagan), though presidents have served out the terms of their predecessors and won reelection. Remember we have never had a truly great one-term president. Over the years historians have made the case for James Polk, on his election a self-declared one-termer who actually carried out all the goals he identified for his presidency, including acquiring California from Mexico, tariff reform, bringing the Oregon Territory into the Union, and creating a more independent treasury. But Barack Obama's quip to Diane Sawyer in 2009 that he would rather be a good one-term president than a mediocre two-termer seems disingenuous and just does not compute in the real world of politics and presidents' expectations.[6] Tragically abbreviated presidencies, particularly due to an assassin's bullet—for example, Lincoln and Kennedy—can prove to be exceptions and guarantee durability in the national consciousness too.

Getting reelected is usually necessary but not sufficient for admission into the presidential hall of fame. We have reelected enough average presidents to demonstrate that another four years isn't a ticket for admission. Even election landslides will not get you in. Since 1860, only four presidents have succeeded in gaining more than 60 percent of the popular vote in one of their elections (Harding, FDR, LBJ, Nixon), and only one is considered a great president.[7]

Maybe we should just accept the fact that the evaluation of our presidents, like history itself, will remain at best what Dutch historian Pieter Geyl described as "an argument without end."[8] I do not see things quite that way. What is so stunning about the results of the historians' rankings these many years are their consistency and seeming imperviousness to change, at least when it comes to the very top and bottom. There are some rough edges and anomalies—what to do with Ronald Reagan?—and a few presidents whose reputations have aged well with time—Truman and Eisenhower in particular. But since 1948, when historian Arthur Schlesinger Sr. launched the rating game's modern version, only a handful of presidents have moved up significantly and, not surprisingly, none from mediocrity to the very top.

So if you correlate our two-term presidents (and those who served out their predecessor's term and then won reelection) together with those who had singular accomplishments, you are well on your way to identifying the small group that comprise America's greatest presidents and most consequential performers (Washington, Jefferson, Jackson, Lincoln, Teddy Roosevelt, Wilson, FDR, and Truman). The relatively few top-ranked presidents drive the main point: sustained excellence in presidential performance, let alone undeniable greatness (as I have already defined it), is rare. The story of the post–World War II presidency is not what you would call an entirely happy one. As we will see, that saga is many things—a story of much talent, ambition, tragedy, scandal, and even, at times, extraordinary accomplishment—but one thing it is not is a record of undeniably great performance in the presidency.

Measuring greatness is not a science. But neither, as Justice Potter Stewart observed in his famous 1964 opinion on pornography, is it strictly a matter of personal preference either—an "I know it when I see it" kind of thing. The achievements of our undeniably great presidents are real, measurable, and defined by crises overcome and legacies that endure. Their greatness is not an abstraction and does not transcend history, though myth and legend contribute to and enhance it. To the contrary, greatness is situated in fact and rooted in stunning and incomparable achievements that come to be appreciated not just by their partisans and supporters but by their opponents too.

These presidents' deeds are all the more impressive because they occurred in a political system stacked against the kind of accretion of power and authority necessary to achieve them, so that big changes are always hard and slow, and because there was no inevitable or inexorable happy ending to their story, certainly not in the cases of Washington and Lincoln. In these early years, the nation's fate was up for grabs and dependent on wise decisions. Such decisions were not always made. But fortunately, through a combination of will, skill, and luck, the greats, including Roosevelt, got most of the big issues right. And during national crisis and challenge, getting most of the big decisions right is in itself a hallmark of a great president.

ONE

The Indispensables

GREATNESS WITH A CAPITAL G

ON FEBRUARY 14, 1933, A MONTH BEFORE HIS IN-auguration as president of the United States, Franklin Roosevelt went fishing, or to put it more precisely, he embarked on an eleven-day cruise aboard the *Nourmahal,* the 263-foot yacht belonging to his good friend and Hyde Park neighbor Vincent Astor.[1] Imagine any contemporary president, particularly against the backdrop of a severe economic crisis (America was three years into the Great Depression), pulling that off today without causing a scandal. Indeed, measured against today's presidential protocol, it is remarkable that Roosevelt would spend as much as half of his presidency outside of Washington.

At the end of the trip, the *Nourmahal* docked in Miami where the president-elect was scheduled to make remarks at the annual outdoor encampment of the American Legion at Miami's Bay Front Park. FDR delivered his brief remarks, and then he chatted with Chicago mayor Anton Cermak. Having supported Al Smith for president, the mayor had come to Miami looking for Roosevelt's political forgiveness and federal money for the city.

Suddenly, five shots rang out. FDR later recalled that they sounded like firecrackers. One hit Cermak in his side, grazing the liver and lodging against his spine. The shooter, Giuseppe Zangara, an unemployed Italian immigrant bricklayer, had fired at Roosevelt from between 25 and 40 feet away and would probably have hit him (five shots hit five different people, seriously wounding three, including Cermak) had it not been for an intrepid Miami housewife who jostled the shooter's arm.

Roosevelt's chauffeur began to speed away, but FDR told him to stop, twice countermanding Secret Service orders to leave the scene, and had Cermak placed in his car, where Roosevelt cradled and consoled the mortally wounded Chicago mayor en route to the hospital.

Initially, there was an assumption, including by Roosevelt, that Zangara was a Mafia hit man out to kill Cermak for his crackdown on the Capone crime syndicate in Chicago. Interrogation of Zangara, however, left little doubt that Roosevelt was the intended target. The Italian immigrant, clearly emotionally unbalanced and physically unwell, carried an intense hatred of big money, capitalism, and apparently presidents. He had wanted to kill Herbert Hoover too. On March 6, two days after listening to the radio broadcast of Roosevelt's swearing in from his hospital bed, Cermak died. Within two weeks, in what had to be the quickest judicial process in twentieth-century America, Zangara had been tried, convicted, and executed in the electric chair.

FDR's preternatural calm and coolness in the face of the assassination attempt buoyed the nation and sent a powerful message that the American people had chosen the right man with the right temperament to deal with a crisis. "The president-elect feeling that the bullets were intended for him," the *New York Times* reported, "straightened up, set his jaw and set unflinching with the calm courage in the face of danger which would be expected of one of his family."[2] Raymond Moley, a Columbia University political science professor recruited as a Roosevelt adviser, remarked that he had never seen anything "more magnificent" than FDR's calm that evening.[3]

But the assassination attempt against Roosevelt also raises a fascinating aspect of leadership and presidential greatness: the question of indispensability. French president Charles de Gaulle reportedly once observed that the cemeteries of France were filled with indispensable people. Most people, even those with the highest-ranking cabinet jobs, are probably replaceable, though they hardly look at themselves that way. The same might even be said about some of our presidents, especially a few of our nineteenth-century ones who came and went without leaving much of a legacy behind.

The argument is a familiar one. How important are individuals in the broader current of history? How much do they matter in comparison with the broader forces that shape their times? Had Adolf Hitler never been born, would someone like him have emerged to lead Germany in a similar direction? Had Al Gore been elected president in 2000 instead of George W. Bush, would America have gone to war in Iraq? Some people really do make a difference, a big difference. There may well be moments in history in which certain individuals were so essential to the course of events that to take them out of the story would change it dramatically. De Gaulle would certainly have considered himself one such person (and he probably would have been right).

Had Zangara's bullets killed or seriously wounded Roosevelt instead of Cermak and the others that evening in Miami, the arc of America's story might have changed profoundly. The Texan John Nance Garner ("Cactus Jack"), the vice president–elect, would have gone to the White House. Although Roosevelt's Depression-era economic policies were not nearly as effective as his supporters claimed in getting America out of its economic straits, would Garner have had the political skills, the reassuring and buoyant personality, the capacity to attract the right advisers, and the confidence to lead and calm the public during those dark days? Back then, it was very much a confidence game in the best sense of the phrase. And FDR was the master. Would any of FDR's Democratic challengers or Republican opponents in 1936 or 1940 have been able to prepare America for war, let alone provide his skilled and decisive wartime leadership?

And if the answer is no, then what is true for FDR—or any later American president in the twentieth century governing an established, stable country more than a century and a half old—is doubly true for earlier presidents presiding over a much more precarious enterprise. In June 1789, three months after his inauguration, Washington almost died from what was most likely anthrax. Was there another of his contemporaries with the authority, prestige, and sense of judgment to lead a young republic through perilous times? What if Stephen Douglas, who seemed prepared to reconcile with the South over slavery, had been elected president instead of Lincoln in 1860? Would the Civil War have been averted through yet another compromise (like those in 1820 and 1850), and slavery preserved? Would Lincoln's notion of the scorpion's sting[4]—by which slavery, contained in the South and unable to expand westward, would have destroyed itself—have come to pass? And how long would this have taken? As it is, it took more than a century after Emancipation to pass historic civil rights legislation, and even then, racial equality remained elusive. And it remains so even today.

The imponderable *what ifs* of history go on and on. And we will never know the answers. In his *Pensées,* Blaise Pascal whimsically posed the philosophical problem that if Cleopatra's nose had been shorter everything in the world would have been different.[5] There is no rewind button on history; counterfactuals are, at best, a guessing game. And leaders can certainly emerge unexpectedly from the most unlikely of quarters.

Still, I suspect that without a Washington, Lincoln, or FDR, especially in the early years, the American story would have changed, and much for the worse. History is not guided or directed by some prearranged master plan. It is a dynamic and pretty chaotic process driven by the interplay between human agency and circumstance that shapes events as they unfold.

We assume inevitability to the American enterprise because of where we now sit, a kind of inexorability that everything was destined somehow to turn out the way it did. We should not. For the first hundred years of our history there was very little certainty and no tradition of strong union or much civility in our politics. We had our bipartisan and collegial moments to be sure. But the American story was also filled with intrigue, conflict, and a variety of centrifugal forces (the Aaron Burr conspiracy, Shays' Rebellion, the Whiskey Rebellion, the Nullification Crisis, the Civil War) that threatened to pull the country apart. It is remarkable to think about it now, but the existence of the United States as a unified polity was probably not guaranteed until after the Civil War, almost a hundred years after the nation's founding.

In 1962 the American novelist Philip K. Dick wrote a counterfactual novel called *The Man in the High Castle* in which Zangara actually succeeds in killing Roosevelt. A series of weak American presidents beginning with James Nance Garner succumb to the country's isolationist impulses and do not try to stop German or Japanese aggression. By 1947, the Germans and the Japanese, attacking from both coasts, force the United States to surrender. We need to be careful about pushing this argument too far. After all, by the 1930s America was already established and stable. The country would have certainly survived without Roosevelt. Some argue that the talented Republican internationalist Wendell Willkie, who challenged Roosevelt in 1940, could have led the country to victory too. In a telling comment, historian H. W. Brands wonders how essential FDR really was and questions how the United States could have sat out the war.[6] But can there be much doubt that in Roosevelt's first seven years the country would have been much worse without FDR? During the 1930s, the world was a very grim place. The ascendancy of right wing and fascist ideologies put the very idea of liberal democracies in doubt and jeopardy. Hitler had come to power two months before FDR's swearing in. And despair, extremism, and violence were brewing in America too. In March 1932, a confrontation erupted between unemployed workers (participating in a Communist Party–organized hunger march) and management at the Ford River Rouge factory in Detroit.[7] Police and company security personnel killed 4 demonstrators and wounded 50. Days later at the funerals, 40,000 marched as the band played the communist "Internationale."

Roosevelt mattered. Add Winston Churchill to the mix, a man whose country would soon face a truly existential threat, and you begin to see the central, even indispensable, role leaders can play at critical moments. There is no way to prove it, but without these early greats getting the big decisions right, the hinge of history might have easily swung another way.

All of these challenges put a premium on the kinds of leaders who had the skill, the drive, and the purpose to devote to strengthening and preserving the fledgling American enterprise. The issue is not whether leaders can make a difference; of course they do. The issue is the degree of difference they make. What is so extraordinary is that during these critical times, leaders emerged who not only aspired to lead but also had the necessary qualities to do so. More than 30 years ago historian James Flexner dubbed George Washington "the indispensable man"; you might as well add Lincoln and Roosevelt too.[8]

By any conceivable measure, the legacies Washington, Lincoln, and Roosevelt left us were profound ones. Their greatness has stood the test of time, perhaps the ultimate arbiter of what any society values. And these three have also resisted history's power to destroy and deconstruct their reputations. Today their claim to greatness is made without much argument or debate among historians, presidential scholars, political analysts, and journalists. There is just no reason, or for that matter, no margin, for running any of them down.

They were certainly not perfect men. Nor were they one-man wonders. They had plenty of help from talented advisers, political parties, circumstances, and luck. And we should have no stake in idealizing them. Washington owned slaves and pursued runaways; Lincoln would have willingly accepted chattel slavery in the Old South had he been able to preserve the Union without war; and Roosevelt clearly overreached in trying to pack the Supreme Court. And for all his extraordinary wartime leadership, FDR interned thousands of loyal Americans of Japanese descent at home, and could have done more to help save European Jews. In the end, Washington could not prevent the fractiousness that marked his second term and beyond; Lincoln's freedom agenda could not prevent the racism and suppression of blacks during Reconstruction; and FDR couldn't end the Depression.

That two of the three died on the job expanded their emotional reach into American hearts and minds and linked their legacies to sacrifice, duty, and, literally in the case of Lincoln, to martyrdom; they became larger-than-life figures. Washington's stoic and grim death from infection at Mount Vernon (as was the medical practice at the time, they bled and blistered him, draining an estimated five pints of blood, or half his body's total volume) might just as well have taken place on the job, given the way he was regarded even after he left the presidency. Adolf Berle, a key member of FDR's Brain Trust, observed shortly after Roosevelt's death that great men have two lives: the first that ends with their death, the second that continues as long as their ideas and concepts remain powerful.[9] These three remained alive politically long after they physically passed on. Their legacies define much of the American story to this day.

The three indispensables—one in each century—spanned the breadth of the American story, governed under vastly different circumstances, and each occupied a presidency that changed radically over the years. Indeed, they could not possibly present a more diverse (even odd) trio: an ambitious Virginia planter from a pretty good (but not the very best) family, with no formal education but plenty of practical experience in agriculture, surveying, and military matters; a driven and very successful railroad lawyer, born in Kentucky, raised in Indiana and Illinois, eager to leave his mark on state and national politics; a Hudson Valley patrician with access to the best schools (Groton, Harvard), summers at Campobello, and a resume (much like his distant cousin Teddy) almost unparalleled in the history of the presidency, and like his two great predecessors, a very physical and commanding presence, even though after the age of 39 he would never walk or stand unassisted without the help of crutches, leg braces, or a friendly arm. Ambitious men all, driven men really, each in his own way committed to the American enterprise and determined to play a central role in its success.

It would be a mistake to stretch comparisons too far or to pigeonhole them into some clever paradigm or box. We would lose the sense of difference and distinction that made them unique and special, that separated each from the other, and that separated all of them from presidents of our own day. The particular sense of time and place for each president is important because it situates them and explains their actions and motives within the right context. You might easily argue that each led in three different Americas. The beginnings of their presidencies are separated by almost 70 years or so, roughly three generations.

Washington presided over a fledgling nation of farmers, artisans, and traders whose capital (then in New York, America's second-largest city behind Philadelphia) was about 30,000 souls, and where loyalty to individual states still trumped a strong national affiliation.[10] Lincoln governed a nation coming apart, the only president whose first and last days in office were dominated by both the prospect of civil war and war itself. Roosevelt, a man closest to our own times, presided over an industrialized nation and an established world power that had already fought and helped win a world war. Lincoln and Roosevelt seem close to one another as brilliant politicians, and nearer to our time, which make them more accessible than the often wooden and distant eighteenth-century Washington. Lincoln's ordeal was greatest, even though Roosevelt would be a nonstop crisis president for almost twelve years. Unlike

Washington, both were deeply hated from the beginning of their presidencies; like Washington, they were very private men. This reserve and
detachment, the mystique of leadership, was essential to preserve the
image of the lonely, even suffering, great man. And that is simply no
longer possible, perhaps not even desirable, in today's hyper-connected
and intrusive media world. Still, that detachment may well be a necessary part of the greatness image.

TWO

The Three Cs of Greatness in the Presidency

DESPITE THESE DIFFERENCES, THREE COMMON elements bind the performances of Washington, Lincoln, and Roosevelt and account for their achievements and success. I call them the three Cs of presidential greatness: most important, a *crisis* that severely threatens the nation for a sustained period of time and sets the stage for historic change; a president's *character,* comprising unique public and private aspects that drive effective leadership; and *capacity,* the know-how and ability to choose the right advisers, manage Congress, the party, the press, and above all, see in crisis how to create the basis for transformative change. Each would also catch very lucky breaks (right time and right place) and would benefit immensely from unforeseen and unanticipated forces. This kind of alignment that merged man, moment, and mission in a relatively seamless mix is rare. And it is rarer still because each man achieved great things in a political system designed to constrain the accretion of power by requiring political consensus for rapid change.

CRISIS: NO PAIN, NO GAIN

Of the three Cs, crisis is undeniably the most important. Without it, there is little sense of urgency or opportunity for even the most gifted leader. And without urgency, our consensus-driven system moves slowly, awkwardly, and much of the time not at all.

Writing in his classic *The American Presidency,* Clinton Rossiter, himself a proponent of the idea of greatness in the presidency, could not have been more on the mark: "We have no right to consider a man for membership in this exclusive club [of great presidents] unless he too presides over the nation in challenging years."[1] Later, Rossiter would also include "in great times."

But challenging years, as we know, can occur in different ways and give rise to different degrees of crisis and calamity. Woodrow Wilson's challenge in World War I was huge, but not nearly as nation-encumbering or as transformational as FDR's in World War II. In 1941, America was one country; by 1945, you might argue that it had become another. George W. Bush's crisis on 9/11 altered American foreign policy, drove the country into the two longest wars in American history, and created a vast Homeland Security network that has raised critically important questions— about the balance between freedom, liberty, security, the Constitution, privacy, and individual rights—that remain unresolved still.

But America's changed world after 9/11 would not be nearly as nation-altering as World War II or the Civil War. In 1861, the South possessed the world's largest chattel slavery enterprise. By 1865, it had ceased to exist; two quite distinct regions would be forced to become one, out of which would begin to emerge a more unified nation, a truly national polity and a second American revolution that would over time reshape the nation's politics, economy, and identity.

And so first-order crisis offered the three indispensables an opportunity to have their moment, leave their legacy, and step into history in ways that eluded all of their successors. Nation-encumbering crisis, and

I am choosing my words carefully here, constitutes an ongoing challenge for months or years that affects the nation as a whole; to use Richard Neustadt's notion, it is both an out-of-government as well as an inside-the-government crisis that affects everyone in some fashion. Few want to or can sit it out. Indeed, in some way, nearly everyone is drawn in. It is the American Revolution and the Civil War, not the Whiskey Rebellion; it is the Great Depression, not the Great Recession; it is World War II and not Iraq, Afghanistan, or even 9/11. The crisis is so comprehensive and enduring that it alters the country's institutions, reshapes mind-sets, and creates memories, myths, and narratives that influence a generation. Beginning in 1941, an astounding 16.1 million Americans in a country of 130 million put on a uniform.[2] And that experience would shape the values, outlook, and collective memories of an entire generation.

Take the Cuban Missile Crisis, on the other hand, the most serious challenge the United States faced during nearly six decades of Cold War with the former Soviet Union. For a dozen days in October 1962, the nation sat at the edge of its collective chair as President John F. Kennedy had to deal with the very real possibility of nuclear war over the stationing of Soviet nukes in Cuba. However terrifying the moment, it was just that. No matter how momentous and consequential those twelve days were for the president and America's Cold War policies, they cannot be compared to the twelve-year crisis of Depression and the world war Roosevelt confronted. The former may have changed Kennedy and the US-Soviet relationship; the latter changed the country.

No military conflict since the Second World War has been as beneficial to an American president, as consequential to the country, or as nation-encumbering. Our two Asian wars—Korea and Vietnam—turned into prolonged and difficult stalemates that the United States could neither win decisively nor easily walk away from. Unlike Korea, Vietnam did engage the nation largely because of the draft, the generational divide, and the changes, tensions, and conflicts in the broader social fabric the war created and reinforced. But the war itself offered few opportunities for heroic presidential action, though as we will see the social ferment it brought and reflected would offer Johnson other opportunities at home for great acts in the presidency. On the contrary, the Vietnam policies of both the Johnson and Nixon administrations would undermine the credibility of both of their presidencies and weaken the institution too.

The attacks on September 11, 2001, were different and potentially nation-encumbering. The Cuban Missile Crisis conjured up visions of unimaginable nuclear horrors; Vietnam entered the lives of most Americans through television coverage. The 9/11 attacks were a very real and immediate horror, the first large-scale terrorist attack on the continental United States by foreigners, and the second-bloodiest day in American history on American soil, exceeded only by one day during the battle of Antietam in September 1862.[3]

But while tragic and devastating in so many ways, 9/11 proved not to be a nation-encumbering crisis that would profoundly alter the character of American life, values, or institutions. The attacks shocked and jarred America's complacency about physical security and set into motion the two longest wars in America's history. But did it profoundly or permanently alter Americans' views of the world, reshape our daily routines, transform our sense of national identity, and impel us to alter the way we look at or govern ourselves? More than a decade out, it is not at all clear just how transformative 9/11 has been. Color-coded security threats quickly became meaningless; security lines at airports, annoying but manageable. Indeed, more Americans are traveling by air now than ever before, their sense of security seemingly restored.

The fact that the country could transition so quickly from George W. Bush, a president whose administration embodied the War on Terror, to one who was even more active on the counterterrorism front yet was reluctant to even use the term and was eager to find an expeditious way out of Afghanistan and Iraq, suggests the public's strong desire to move out of 9/11's fateful shadow and American interventions abroad. According to a Pew Poll in 2013, 52 percent of Americans say the United States should mind its own business internationally; whether this reflects a new isolationism, a cyclical pattern of retrenchment following both world wars, or simply a tendency to follow the lead of a risk-averse president when it comes to foreign policy remains to be seen.[4]

Paradoxically, the one area where the impact of 9/11 would prove most enduring grew out of government efforts to prevent another attack. From the Patriot Act to the revelation of the National Security Agency's vast effort to collect and monitor information in the name of combating terrorism, the United States has faced a difficult balance between national security and individual rights. Supporters of these measures point to the necessity of preventing another attack, and argue that all of these measures take place within the limits of the law and uphold appropriate levels of oversight. Opponents argue these measures have been a vast overreach into American's privacy, and have given certain government agencies far too much power given the degree of threat, without the necessary checks and balances. In an era of continuing terrorism challenges, the fundamental moral, legal, and political questions about security, privacy, individual rights, and the Constitution will likely be with us for years to come.

Unlike more limited crises, such as Cuba and 9/11, that played out largely within the federal government, the nation-encumbering challenges that made great presidents opened up the potential for enduring change. First, the crisis shakes the system. And if the threat is acute enough (southern secession, Depression-era 25 percent unemployment, the attack on Pearl Harbor), it creates new realities that allow presidents to consider dramatic actions that in ordinary circumstances would simply not be possible. Presidents take advantage of these changed circumstances not simply to save the system, but to change it. Indeed, urgency produces action and sometimes consensus and unity too. During Roosevelt's first 100 days, Congress did not so much pass fifteen pieces of

New Deal legislation "as salute them as they were sailing by."⁵ FDR, aided by the Japanese attack on Pearl Harbor, was able to create an even greater consensus on war than on domestic matters. Only sustained national emergency opens the door to sustained greatness in the presidency.

Lincoln's greatness was rooted almost entirely in the crisis of a fragmenting Union (brought about, to be sure, by his election), but it was something his predecessors did not face. It is easy to argue that the absence of consequential, even great, presidents for much of the pre–Civil War period resulted from leaders who were either unable or unwilling to confront the question of slavery. In the face of this bitter and emotional debate, the only possibilities for presidents were drift or expedient compromise, neither traditionally associated with historic greatness. It is no coincidence that those years were dominated not by strong presidents but by dominant legislators, like Henry Clay, who drove both the 1820 and 1850 compromises over slavery.

It says a great deal about Lincoln's own temperament that Clay (who never made it to the White House) was his idea of a hero. It also reveals a sharp contrast with our own times, in which partisanship is lauded over deal making—and in which legislators are not nearly as well known or well regarded as they were then or, frankly, at few other times in our history.

First-order crisis also offers the right leader an opportunity to forge a new consensus in public opinion as well as in a political system that is traditionally more often divided than not. Leaders are riding the turbulent waves and changes during these crises. Lyndon Johnson deserves enormous credit for the historic civil rights legislation he ushered through Congress in the mid-1960s. But would he have been able to succeed, including marshaling the necessary Republican support, without the broader civil rights movement and the passion, intensity, and tragic violence that accompanied it? A fragmenting Union and the possibility of an economic collapse sets into motion surges of fear, hope, and insecurities. The test of great presidents is whether they sense what publics need and want, and whether they can intuit what is necessary and, above all, act.

Our modern-day challenges—including debt and deficit, dependence on hydrocarbons, decaying infrastructure, and the new structural challenges to reducing unemployment—tend to divide rather than unite us. These challenges are acute but not relentless; they affect the nation as a whole but not in a way that necessarily forces action. Much of this is due to increasing polarization between Democrats and Republicans and the tribal nature of our current politics, particularly the ideological consensus within each party that reduces prospects for cross-party deals and the general disagreement over issues such as the role of government. Still, a crisis that is dire enough has the potential, under the direction of skilled leaders, to turn the "me" into "we." The good news is that we've been spared these wrenching crises. The bad news is that without them we seem incapable of producing any real sense of shared sacrifice, obligation, and responsibility, let alone the hot molten urgency required for historic change.

We should not lose perspective on this point. The crises Washington, Lincoln, and Roosevelt confronted did not unite the country in some mindless display of national purpose and consensus. Theirs were no golden ages of bipartisanship. Washington's time witnessed political invective, intrigue, and character assassination, including dueling to the death, which went far beyond even our own uncivil times. Lincoln's crisis tore the nation asunder. In 1856, South Carolina representative Preston Brooks caned his Massachusetts colleague Charles Sumner so violently on the Senate floor that it nearly fully paralyzed him. The 1863 New York City draft riots and racial violence that followed remain the single bloodiest act of domestic violence in American history, leaving up to 500 dead (though death totals vary widely).[6] And Roosevelt's New Deal policies made him one of the most hated men in America, a man perceived by many as, in the words of historian H. W. Brands in a wonderfully titled volume on the FDR years, a "traitor to his class."[7]

Lincoln and FDR were polarizers and party men; they drove change situated in strongly held partisan views based on what they believed was necessary to address the country's ills. Historian Jean Smith calls Roosevelt a divider, not a uniter, who "unabashedly waged class war." American business and organized labor fiercely opposed various aspects of his New Deal legislation, which passed with significant bipartisan support but over opposition of a "deeply entrenched minority."[8] But both men sold that change in ways their own politics would allow, in Roosevelt's case with the support of conservative southern legislators whom he courted and at the expense of any progress on civil rights. At the same time, however imperfectly and even hypocritically, they tried to package it in terms of broader values, such as freedom, liberty, security, personal rights, even economic security, that they believed were rooted in and consistent with American traditions drawn from founding documents. The change was sold as part of a broader national purpose designed to strengthen the American enterprise. And because their times were disruptive enough, their leadership compelling, and the need for change so clear, much of the public accepted and acquiesced. Indeed, the sacrifices Americans were asked to make in the Civil War and World War II were made easier by the sense that their generations were caught up in a great national endeavor and struggle and in a purpose broader than themselves. And the great presidents used their words to both create and reflect that national commitment and spirit. Washington's Farewell Address, Lincoln's address at Gettysburg, and FDR's first inaugural and his "Rendezvous with Destiny" speeches all highlighted this sense of national unity and purpose. When was the last presidential speech that came close to reaching toward and inspiring a common national purpose? You know the answer: Kennedy's "Ask Not" inaugural address. And that was more than a half century ago.

Finally, crisis of this caliber offers a chance for rare transformative change in a way that really does fundamentally alter the nation's story forever. We can argue about whether Roosevelt's leadership produced a true transformation of the country in the way that Lincoln's did. But these presidents, including Lyndon Johnson, created legacies that altered the way millions of Americans lived and looked at one another; they altered the role of their government and society. And their changes endured. Such change simply is not possible and would not work in more normal, noncrisis situations. This requires a president who has a broader vision, a set of realistic goals, and a capacity to understand how and when to try to achieve them. The ideas that made them great— Washington's conviction that the early Republic needed a strong central authority anchored in constitutional authority; Lincoln's view that the perpetuation of slavery was incompatible with the fundamental prosperity and democratic values of the country; and Roosevelt's commitment to an activist government pursuing relief and reform—were evident in their thinking well before their presidencies. But bringing them to fruition, making them real and legitimate and part of the American system, could only occur in the unfolding logic and dynamic of a major challenge or crisis in which those views would both crystallize and evolve in response to changing circumstances.

CHARACTER: ALL THE WORLD'S A STAGE

Crisis only opens the door to the possibility of leadership, transformative change, and greatness; it certainly does not guarantee or mandate its inevitability. The expression "cometh the hour, cometh the man" reflects more hope than experience, and very much depends on who the individuals really are and what kind of hour they are called to confront. Clearly, the hour and the man did not align for presidents James Buchanan and Herbert Hoover, but did for presidents Washington, Lincoln, and Roosevelt. The question is why for some and not others. The answer lies not only in the objective circumstances presidents inherit— the luck, so to speak, of their particular draw—but also in their own characters, for want of a better word. And there may not be a better one.

The challenge of sorting through the definition and meaning of character as applied to presidents and politicians is a complicated business. What is character? Is it the capacity to do the proverbial right thing, and the discipline to avoid doing the wrong one because of some preexisting moral and ethical code that keeps you in bounds? Indeed, is it defined by moral or ethical virtue of a personal nature, or driven by a more formalized religious, ethical, or secular code? Franklin Roosevelt was an adulterer; perhaps Eisenhower and Kennedy too. Are they disqualified in the character department because of their transgressions? Washington and Jefferson owned slaves—a respectable practice and sign of status and wealth in their day. Washington was at times a very tough slave owner, splitting families and on occasion authorizing whippings. Did they have good character?

Can character be compartmentalized? In public life, can character pertain only to civic accomplishment? Are presidents' personal lives their own as long as their habits remain private and do not interfere with their capacities to govern effectively? If you are engaged in policies that benefit the nation and improve the lives of millions, can you philander in your personal life or dissemble and even lie in pursuit of the public good and the national interest? Indeed, one of the oldest questions in politics is: How much bad should or can we tolerate in a politician, or president for that matter, in the pursuit of their doing good? Lyndon Johnson was crude, a philanderer, and, when it came to Vietnam, a liar; yet he had extraordinary courage and conviction when it came to fighting for civil rights legislation, and genuine compassion for the poor and disadvantaged in pushing his Great Society programs. And what do we do with Bill Clinton, who presided over prosperity at home and relative peace abroad? To what extent should his performance as president be judged by the Monica Lewinsky scandal? Americans may have already answered that question. Clinton left office with one of the highest approval ratings of any modern president, and he rates high on the list of presidents the public would like back.[9]

Then there is the question of how we actually know a person's character, how much we really know and understand about how and why individuals behave the way they do. John Adams, a man who would have taken pride in his own high character, famously observed that the people "have a right, an indisputable, unalienable, indefeasible, divine right to that most dreaded and envied kind of knowledge—I mean of the character and conduct of their rulers."[10]

The one small problem with Adams's requirement, of course, is that it is truly impossible to meet. People are complicated; they compartmentalize their personalities and are compartmentalized by forces often beyond their control. All kinds of behaviors can coexist in the same individual, tugging, pulling from a variety of different directions, sometimes integrated, at other moments working at cross purposes. What face or aspect a person shows at any given moment might be purposeful and calculating or reveal itself as a consequence of an uncontrolled emotion or need. Trying to explain a president's behavior while in office based on early and formative life experiences is at best a complex puzzle in which all the pieces are just not available. It is really more a guessing game, informed by the observations of friends and colleagues, and by the words and deeds of the individuals themselves.

Our three indispensables, particularly Lincoln and Roosevelt, present difficult challenges. They may have been the three most observed and studied men in American history, but they had few if any confidants and left very little in the way of revealing private notes, diaries, or memoirs. Lincoln's law partner William Herndon described him as "the most shut-mouthed man who ever lived."[11] Washington left a vast sea of correspondence, but as an eighteenth-century man when reputations were carefully guarded and expectations of self-revelations nil; he did not share much of his own personal introspections and was rarely emotional in public, even referring to himself in the third person. Indeed, to discourage visitors to Mount Vernon, Washington made sure there was inadequate signage pointing the way.[12] Roosevelt loved to be in the company of others—indeed needed to be. But he kept his interior space closed. We can always speculate of course how Lincoln's humble origins influenced his desire to succeed, or what impact his "hypo," or depression, if that is what it was, had on his presidency; or we can ruminate on what impact FDR's polio had on his character; but it remains just that—rumination and speculation.

So perhaps character needs to be approached from a slightly different angle. When it comes to presidents (and probably the rest of us too) there is a public and private dimension of the way we orient ourselves to the world. The word *character* is originally from the Greek, meaning engraved, stamped, or marked. Each of the greats had both a public persona and a private one, an unseen dimension much harder to define. Their characters as presidents represented the full package—a physical, intellectual, temperamental whole that made each an extremely effective leader. They were all characters in the literal sense of the word: they presented themselves not in a theater (though Washington did act in plays) but on a bigger stage at critical moments in the life of a nation. And they all had the actor's sensibility, the capacity to impress, to move, to inspire, and to intuit what their audiences felt and needed. It is no coincidence that Washington and Lincoln (tragically to a fault) loved theater and performance. And Roosevelt, the consummate performer, was acutely aware of his audiences and tailored his presentations accordingly: fireside chats, speeches, or public appearances. All presidents do this. Few are as masterful as Roosevelt.

Each also had a physical persona and image inseparable from the character role he played, which has become indelibly etched in the American memory. Washington (shoe size thirteen) and Lincoln (size fourteen) were large and imposing men, certainly much larger than American males at the time. Washington's height was a commanding six-foot-two and he weighed between 175 and 220 pounds at a time when the median height for an American male was five-seven and the median for European-born males in the colonies was five-four.[13]

Lincoln, though a couple of inches taller, was somewhat less imposing, with a high tenor voice and long arms and legs that could make him appear awkward and gangly. But Lincoln was nonetheless a striking and memorable figure, never quite as unattractive and ugly as he often joked about himself. By 1865, his lined, weary, cadaverous face and frame had taken on the image of suffering and death of a nation's ordeal. Lincoln's physical persona literally embodied his times.

Roosevelt too was a special case because of his polio, which seemed to reflect the nation's broken body but also its resilient spirit. Given the extent of his disability, there is no precedent for what Roosevelt accomplished. To lead a nation through a decade or more of nonstop crisis without the ability to stand or walk unassisted defies the laws of political gravity and history to boot. The fact that FDR could still be such a commanding presence in a society that puts such a premium on physicality, and in a political culture whose vocabulary is filled with phrases like "she's a woman in good standing," "stand up for what you believe in," or "what do you stand for?" is a reflection of his own charismatic persona.

Roosevelt himself was not ashamed or embarrassed about his polio. He purchased the land and buildings for a polio treatment facility in Warm Springs, which he patronized, organized the Warm Springs Foundation, and founded the March of Dimes. Some argue that FDR's wheelchair became like Lincoln's log cabin and contributed to his image as a man who had overcome tremendous odds and could identify with a people suffering in hard times. But Roosevelt's illness was likely more insignificant (most Americans knew he was "lame" but probably not the extent of his paralysis) to most of the nation than it was inspirational. What people saw—that cocked head and buoyant smile—and what they heard (the lustrous voice, one of America's greatest on radio) reassured and captivated. Roosevelt was never a man to be pitied. And he rarely referred to his polio, making clear that a "childish disease" would never defeat him.[14] On balance, you would have to wonder, as do many historians, whether FDR's polio meant less to him or to the public. Both seemed to ignore it.

F. Scott Fitzgerald wrote in *The Great Gatsby* that personality (and by implication, character) was really an unbroken series of successful gestures. He was onto something important. A leader's persona comes to embody a series of actions, physical gestures, words, and phrases that take shape into a personalized image. Today, we might call it a brand. The three indispensables were all quite consciously dramatists. They understood that to be president it was not enough to *have* character; you needed to *be* a character in order to lead and to use the presidency as a leadership tool, particularly in times of crisis. And like all great stage performers, they read their audiences, intuiting their moods, reflecting the moment but always looking for ways to inspire and reach beyond. The public wanted action characters, and so Washington projected authority; Lincoln, humanity and iron will; Roosevelt, confidence and faith in the future. "There have been times in this office," observed Ronald Reagan, perhaps our most effective public president since FDR, "when I've wondered how you could do the job if you hadn't been an actor."[15] To be a great president in momentous times means to be the character in chief.

So much for their exteriors. What mix of traits actually defined their internal, emotional landscapes? What were the interior strengths that enabled them to meet the enormity of the challenges they faced? What gave them the will to continue in the face of great odds and to hold up emotionally? Family? (Washington had no children of his own, though he cared deeply about those he adopted; Lincoln lost two of his four to illness—one before his presidency, and one during; and Roosevelt clearly enjoyed his children when he had the time for them.)[16]

What about their wives? Washington had a close companionlike relationship with Martha, who spent winters with him in the field during the war years. But both Lincoln and Roosevelt had very difficult marriages. Mary Todd Lincoln was combustible, demanding, and, while very protective of her husband, also emotionally unstable.[17] In Roosevelt's case, politics demanded that he work out a relationship with his remarkable wife, Eleanor, on whom he relied as a political asset more than a romantic one.

What about religion? None of these three seemed to ascribe to a rigid form of Christianity or religious doctrine. Washington never mentioned Jesus Christ in his writings, but he did become an officer in his church and attended religious service, albeit irregularly. When it came to religion, he seemed more focused instead on the more detached notions of providence or the "Great Author," concepts that reflected the Enlightenment views of his time. Lincoln would find great comfort in reading the Bible, although he did not affiliate with any organized church. His wife would say he was "not a technical Christian."[18]

Lincoln did have a powerful sense of fate, believing that his actions were somehow shaped by some greater force or power beyond his capacity to intuit, let alone to comprehend. And this must have given him some comfort, in light of the fateful decisions he had to make and the violence and death he saw. Only Roosevelt seemed to identify with an organized church and would remain committed to the Episcopal faith until his death. Roosevelt's optimism seemed situated in that faith, but like Washington and Lincoln, it was less a question of commitment to any sort of organized dogma. Once asked by Eleanor what he had learned in church, Roosevelt responded, "I think it just as well not to think about things like that too much."[19] I suspect that in all of their worldviews there was a distinct and a unique sense that they were caught up in something far greater than themselves and that, without putting a formal religious label on it, it involved some fated or directed plan.

With regard to their motives and character, I would suggest five elements common to all three that account for their capacity to achieve and accomplish what they did. First, they had *ambition*. These were driven men who from an early age put success, particularly public service, at the top of their agendas. They started young, though their generations died young too. At 23, George Washington was already the most well-known military figure in Virginia; at 25, Lincoln was elected to the Illinois state house; and at 28, FDR had won a seat in the New York state senate. Their drive to compete in the public arena and search for fame and recognition was critical. None would have been content to be spies or secret agents serving the Republic; they wanted to be known to the world.

Second, each possessed tremendous *physical courage* and seemed impervious to danger. During the 1760s, Washington demonstrated his bravery during the French and Indian Wars and endured physical hardship and illness throughout his life. In 1864, while watching a Confederate attack on Fort Stevens in northeast Washington, Lincoln had to be warned repeatedly to step down off the parapets, even after a Union surgeon standing near him was hit by enemy fire. That next year, soon after Richmond had fallen, he would fearlessly walk the city (James Madison and Lincoln remain the only two sitting presidents fired on in wartime situations). Roosevelt demonstrated his cool and his risk-readiness in Miami. Both Lincoln and FDR had also acquired a toughness, the former from his rough and tumble upbringing, the latter as a result of the challenges in overcoming his polio. Among other things, physical courage reflects willingness to risk and perhaps a nonchalance and fatalism so critical to entering the arena and surrendering to the uncertainties of the struggle there. And this risk-readiness was critical to the crises they weathered and political transformations they wrought.

Third, each had powerful *discipline* and *self-control*. Washington and FDR were individuals of a certain station in life who were conditioned to ascribe to certain standards (in Washington's case, an actual set of rules of etiquette that he would internalize) and expectations that governed their behavior. Roosevelt reacted to his illness with the stoic stiff-upper-lip character his class expected of him. Lincoln's emergence out of Illinois (the nineteenth-century equivalent of nowhere) without formal education, family connections, or wealth was a study in willful self-control, self-study, and self-advancement. If they had demons, they kept them under control. Lincoln, in particular, had the added burdens of coping with depression of some kind, an unstable wife, and the deaths of two of his four children. And yet they all were able to maintain an emotional balance and self-control in the face of extraordinarily trying circumstances.

Today the fashionable phrase for this kind of balance might be emotional intelligence. Leaders cannot lead without followers, and emotional intelligence—in those who have an awareness and understanding of themselves, a capacity to read others and to intuit how they see you—is vital to that goal. Being confident about who you are—being comfortable in your own skin—makes it easier to inspire, motivate, and direct others. And all three presidents were instrumental personalities in that they knew how to use and manipulate others. At the same time, they also had engaging personal skills: in Lincoln's case, his humor and compassion; in FDR's, an infectious vitality that connected him to others. When it came to Roosevelt, Churchill was no objective observer, but his description captures that capacity: "Meeting Franklin Roosevelt was like opening your first bottle of champagne; knowing him was like drinking it."[20]

Fourth, and closely related, Washington, Lincoln, and Roosevelt were *men of balance* with a sense of proportionality in their public lives. They avoided extremes. More than anything else, this sense of moderation in their views of the world anchored their judgments and allowed them to operate in circumstances where both a functional, middleground pragmatism and commitment to principle were required for success. They managed to find the vital center that made change possible while avoiding the dead center that would have precluded it.

Washington operated in a political culture wary of the concentration of power. And yet navigating carefully and respectfully without giving ground, he managed to sell the idea of what was required to create a strong central government. Lincoln pursued his central war aim—restoring the Union—with an iron will but with the flexible hands required to co-opt, defuse, and accommodate the political pressures arrayed against him, especially keeping the border states from secession while managing with remarkable skill to work in evolutionary fashion toward a revolutionary goal: the Emancipation Proclamation and the passage of the Thirteenth Amendment abolishing slavery. And FDR was able to find the right balance that allowed him to create huge innovations in domestic and foreign policy while legitimizing those changes and carefully balancing and bringing along key political constituencies.

Finally, each had an enormous degree of *self-confidence,* not just in themselves or their political philosophies but also in the future of the American enterprise. This sense of optimism came easier to Washington and FDR as men of privilege; Lincoln had more of a tragic sensibility, driven as he was by losses he experienced throughout his life and by the sheer volume and magnitude of death that marked his presidency. All were partisans and party builders with narrow concerns: Washington was perhaps the least narrow of the three, opposed as he was to factions but still very much a Federalist; Lincoln, who built the Republican Party; and FDR, who created a Democratic coalition that would last more than 40 years.

Each had a strong sense that there was a broader purpose in their labors and careers. It was never just about them and their own ambitions, though fiercely ambitious they were. More than that, each was tied in his own mind to a cause of immense historical importance, and each believed that he had been somehow chosen (fate/providence/fortune) to be an agent, even *the* agent, in its unfolding and design. Only this broader commitment to the American enterprise could have kept them focused, above the noise and confusion of the moment, and steeled them for the decisions they would have to make. Perhaps in the end, the real source of their faith and resolve—and what kept them going through the darkest of times—was this powerful commitment to the American experiment and the faith in its future. Given their central role to the enterprise, how could it have been otherwise?

THREE

Capacity

GETTING THINGS DONE

"HISTORY IS CONCERNED WITH THE THINGS Accomplished"—so President Warren Harding spoke about Lincoln while dedicating his memorial in 1922.[1]

Crisis and character go a long way in explaining great presidents, but not far enough. A president needs the capacity to get things done. And in the case of the greats, this means getting big things done. This requires an intuitive understanding of how to work the system, to use the office, to manage the press, the Congress, the cabinet, and, of course, the public.

Each great president surrounded himself with great advisers, whether it was Washington's all-star cabinet, Lincoln's team of Republican superstars, or FDR's Brain Trust plus wife Eleanor, who became invaluable as his eyes, ears, and envoy to the country at large. And getting big things done also means understanding how to use the emergency and circumstances at hand to set the stage for longer-range change, to be able to see in the near term what might be possible at the horizon. It is the latter ingredient, the ability to identify a broader, more distant goal—in the din and confusion of the moment—and to move the system toward that end, that defines the point of possessing this capacity. Without it, we would have crisis management without the broader horizon and vision that changes the nation and makes the crisis worth the pain and suffering it has caused. Getting there requires a blend of principle, political opportunism, and luck.

WASHINGTON: PRESIDENTIAL IMPROV

One of the knocks against George Washington, and the one that he least deserves, is that his record as president was more a result of who he was rather than what he actually accomplished—that, in effect, our first president lent his name and prestige to the presidency but little more.

The reality of his presidency was quite different. Washington was unique among our presidents for his ability to lead and inspire others, to see clear strategic objectives and priorities, to keep himself as free as possible from petty rivalries and jealousies, to rise above the clutter and noise, and in effect to legitimize a strong presidency, centralized government, and constitutional system when there were no precedents, traditions, or conventions to guide him. Jefferson may have been the Renaissance man, but Washington was the Renaissance president. During his two terms, from 1789 to 1796, and in his dramatic decision to leave office willingly after two terms when he could have had a third, Washington may well have influenced the presidency and America's system of governance more than any of his successors.

Unlike Lincoln or Roosevelt, Washington's crisis was not civil war, world war, or economic calamity. In a way, it was an even more daunting challenge. Even in extremely threatening circumstances, Lincoln and certainly Roosevelt had inherited an established country to govern.

Consider that America had yet to demonstrate it could exist and function as a unified polity. There was no formally established capital with a government center. There were no established bureaucracies or government departments, no precedents or conventions apart from an untested Constitution. In fact, when Washington was sworn in, that document had not yet been ratified by all thirteen states. Washington had already shepherded the fledgling American enterprise through a war of independence and the creation of a republic. But the pressures on him to now make it all work were even greater.

Having won independence, Washington was now expected to help create a nation de novo—a republic, no less, for which there was no real precedent—and to fashion it out of a group of former colonies lacking a strong center and without a tradition of central authority. As early as 1780, Washington had identified the problem: "I see one head gradually changing into thirteen."[2] When the phrase "United States" was used in the Declaration of Independence, it meant thirteen separate states, maybe not as disconnected as separate countries, but certainly not part of an organic, encumbered, or united confederation. And to add to his woes, Washington presided over a young republic very vulnerable to foreign powers (Britain, France, and Spain) that were not oceans away in Europe but actually had military and colonizing presences in North America.

Washington faced a systemic crisis (and opportunity): how to create a legitimate national government by navigating between a new and untested set of constitutional principles on one hand, and a strong opposition to centralized authority on the other. The notion of operating in uncharted territory applied not just to an unexplored west (another of Washington's passions) but to the terra incognita of the untested and yet to be legitimized presidency and political institutions. "I walk on untrodden ground," Washington wrote a year into his presidency.[3]

Washington's seminal achievements lay in three areas: setting precedents, strengthening central authority, and reducing the young republic's vulnerability in a dangerous world of European powers and conflicts whose own rivalries with America threatened its territorial and political interests. Through it all, his realism, sense of balance, and good judgment gave him a capacity to get most of his big issues right.

Since he had no predecessors, what Washington did and did not do would shape the office in profound ways. From the beginning, like any good CEO, he realized he needed help. Congress created three executive departments—one for foreign affairs, one for military matters, and a third for fiscal affairs. He ensured that these department heads reported directly to him, not to the Congress. By maintaining this important precedent, he protected executive authority. Picking the right advisers was critical. Never again would a president be surrounded by such an array of talent (and egos) than by this original team of rivals (especially Jefferson vs. Alexander Hamilton): Jefferson at State; Hamilton at Treasury; Henry Knox at War (Washington did not need much help there); and James Madison in Congress, who supported him on legislative matters.

Ever the balancer, Washington sought to create good relations with Congress and to respect both its independence and authority. (He did not use his veto until 1792, three years into his first term.)[4] But he also drew the line when it came to limiting Congress's role in foreign affairs and protecting the president's executive authority. In August 1789, with Knox in tow, Washington went to the Senate in person to consult on the matter of an Indian treaty. He became so exasperated with Senate procedures and delay that he left abruptly; he would return a few days later, but that would probably be the last time a president would appear personally on a matter related to the conduct of treaty negotiations. He would be forceful as well in protecting the executive's right to withhold information from Congress on certain matters involving diplomacy and negotiations. When Congress requested private diplomatic correspondence on negotiations with Britain over the Jay treaty, Washington held firm.

Washington proved as forceful and wise on matters of policy as he was farsighted on precedent, particularly when it came to maintaining the credibility of the national government in the face of challenges to its authority. In 1794, three years after Congress had imposed an excise tax on whiskey, armed resistance against federal officials broke out in western Pennsylvania. Washington biographer Ron Chernow describes the so-called Whiskey Rebellion as the single most serious show of armed force against the federal government until the outbreak of the Civil War.[5]

In early August, a force of some 6,000 protestors carrying their own flag actually assembled near Pittsburgh threatening to take the federal garrison in the city. The next day Washington convened the cabinet, ordered up the militia of 13,000, and sent out a delegation to talk the dissidents down. He gave them until September to disperse. In the only example of a sitting president leading troops to a potential battle, Washington rode out (with Hamilton) at the head of the force. The so-called Whiskey Rebellion dissolved quickly without confrontation. In the process, Washington's actions had boosted the credibility and power of the federal government.

It was with the same kind of realism and judgment that Washington responded to the administration's other great challenge—keeping America out of Anglo-French conflicts of the 1790s. The last thing the Republic needed was a major confrontation with Britain over residual issues from the 1783 Paris treaty, or worse, to be drawn into an Anglo-French confrontation on the high seas. Despite American commitments to France under the terms of their 1778 agreement, Washington quickly established a policy of strict neutrality. And later he dispatched Chief Justice John Jay to London to cut the best deal he could with Great Britain. War was averted; the British evacuated forts in the Northwest Territory, and the Americans got limited trade with the West Indies. But on the sensitive issue of neutrality on the high seas, the British reneged on a commitment that American ships could carry goods to either the British or French belligerents.

Given the prevailing power balance and America's priorities, it is hard to fault Washington's pragmatism and realism. But many did. The depth of anti-British sentiment created one of the most poisonous and polarized periods in American history. The announcement of the treaty led to some of the worst personal attacks against Washington. If the president was contemplating a third term, the nasty public battle over the Jay treaty, and the attacks on him, personally, doubtless reinforced his desire to retire to Mount Vernon. When he did, voluntarily giving up a third term that easily could have been his, Washington created a two-term precedent in the presidency that would be broken, only temporarily almost a century and a half later, by Roosevelt's four. But more than that, in giving up power in a republic that many doubted could survive, he demonstrated a selflessness and respect for America's system and a willingness to abjure power. In doing so, Washington drove home the point that the well-being of the many is more important than the needs of the one, and that it was indeed possible for a leader to be both strong and respectful of freedom and liberty—a situation without precedent in the eighteenth century.[6]

Washington had no distinct ideology or political philosophy of governance. Given who he was and the task at hand, he really did not need one. He despised factionalism, though his own sentiments clearly lay with the Federalists. And he failed to understand that, in a country as large as the United States, proliferating interests and political parties were inevitable, most assuredly volatile, but in fact necessary for the health of an emerging democracy. But he can be forgiven for not appreciating that. And to be sure, creating those politics would not be his legacy. Instead, his remarkable legacy lay in protecting America's independence, creating the political, economic, and security institutions of the state—including a mint, a national bank, a budget, a fiscal system, a coast guard, a navy—and legitimizing a strong presidency, respecting the Constitution and Congress, and all the while maintaining peace at home and avoiding war abroad. Washington's greatness lay in helping to fashion out of little more than a set of untested ideas and theories a system of governance that would prove unique, enduring, and inspirational to not only millions of his own countrymen, but for millions more around the world.

LINCOLN: ASHES AND BLOOD

Criticisms of Abraham Lincoln abound. He was an ambitious and calculating politician who tailored his antislavery views to fit the racism of Illinois politics; he was a bigot whose solution to the race problem in America was colonization outside the United States; he was against the abolition of slavery, was prepared to let it exist in the South so long as it did not spread, and as late as 1864, would have paid compensation if the South would have agreed to rejoin the Union; he undermined the Constitution by suspending habeas corpus; and finally, had it not been for the Civil War, he might have been a pretty insignificant president. True on most counts, maybe even the latter.

But against all Lincoln's imperfections there is also this: he was our greatest and most beloved president. Lincoln's accomplishments and his greatness are incomparable, and seem even mythical. But they are very real, anchored in the greatest calamity in the life of any nation—civil war—and in this case, one that cost almost a million Americans dead and wounded. Preserving the Union would have been an extraordinary achievement under any circumstances. Understanding that the sacrifice of war and the nation's future required that it be reconstituted on a different basis took Lincoln's achievements to a new level. Both the Emancipation Proclamation and the Thirteenth Amendment formally ending slavery provided that new foundation and, together with the Declaration of Independence and Constitution, now given new meaning, constituted new foundational documents. That Lincoln was able to achieve all of this in a national career that lasted barely seven years (from 1858, when he started speaking nationally on the slavery issue, to his death in 1865) makes what he achieved even more surreal and extraordinary.

Today we grapple with serious and debilitating polarization both in our politics and media; we lament the red state versus blue state map; and we worry about conflict-laden terms such as target states, battlegrounds, or political hit lists. And still our red-versus-blue political wars do not even begin to approach the calamity of Lincoln's blue-versus-gray problem. In response to his election, eight states seceded from the Union. The day after his inauguration the issue of what to do about resupplying Fort Sumter in Charleston Harbor lay on his desk.

Lincoln's crisis was defined by the secession itself and the realities of a divided nation. In 1861, he presided over a North whose finances were in tatters and whose standing army consisted of only 16,000 men, a quarter of whom would soon resign.[7] He led a cabinet of rivals, egos, and superstars who were all much more experienced in national government than he was. And he sat in a vulnerable capital, sandwiched between Virginia, which had seceded, and an openly hostile border state, Maryland. One half of the country did not recognize his authority; and half the North had voted for other candidates.

In light of the North's divisions and weakness, Lincoln faced a united and highly motivated Confederacy of eleven states with about 9 million people, roughly a third the population of the Union. The Confederacy comprised an area of roughly 800,000 square miles, about the size of Spain, Italy, Germany, and Poland, combined with a 3,500-mile-long coastline, natural rivers, and mountain barriers. Lincoln also squared off against the most powerful slave system the world had ever known. In 1861, that system produced three-fifths of the nation's total exports; its estimated value exceeded that of all the nation's factories and railroads combined. And what did Lincoln have to accomplish in the face of these odds? Keep the border states loyal, the North unified, prepare for war, keep the Republican Party and cabinet together, and bring the South back into the Union. There were few who believed Lincoln could do any of it. "Wanted," the *New York Times* wrote in April 1861, "A Policy."[8]

So how did Lincoln do it? What enabled such a man to defy the odds, to overcome challenge and adversity, and to get so many of his decisions right?

From the beginning to the end of his short presidency (one four-year term and several months), Lincoln was a wartime president. No other chief executive in the nation's history inherited such circumstances. Eisenhower inherited Korea; Johnson and Nixon, Vietnam; Obama, Iraq and Afghanistan—all difficult challenges but with ample time to ponder and plan. Barack Obama had months to decide on the surge in Afghanistan. Lincoln had weeks to decide what to do about resupplying Fort Sumter. At times Lincoln's war was only five miles from the White House. The politics and strategy of waging war consumed him.

Because of his generals' deficit, Lincoln had no choice but to be involved in almost every aspect of war making, and the war's relationship to Congress and politics. Even after he discovered Ulysses S. Grant, the president still exercised a close management style, even monitoring Grant's activities clandestinely through the *New York Times* journalist Charles Dana.[9]

The president took a personal interest in firearms and weaponry, including the test firing of the main types and meeting with the occasional inventor. Lincoln made repeat visits to the various fronts and battle areas, including Antietam, Chancellorsville, Gettysburg, and even walked the streets of a captured Richmond. The first and only president to hold a patent (number 6469, granted in 1849 for a device to lift boats over shoals[10]), Lincoln took an intense interest in technology too. Not surprisingly, it was the telegraph, which Lincoln had first seen in 1857, that gave him the ability to monitor and lead the war effort the way he did. There was no telegraph set up in the White House, which meant the president had to use Washington's commercial facility; later one was installed at the War Department.

This kind of electronic oversight, what historian Tom Wheeler cleverly calls "Mr. Lincoln's T-mails," became a critical component of Lincoln's wartime leadership.[11] It gave him access to battlefield information and some freedom from dependence on his generals. In the first fourteen months of his presidency, Lincoln sent fewer than twenty telegrams. On May 24, 1862, as Stonewall Jackson threatened Washington, he sent nine. From that point on, he spent more time at the telegraph office than anywhere else but the White House. According to Wheeler, during great battles Lincoln would "even sleep in the telegraph office."[12]

Grant, William T. Sherman, and Philip Sheridan may have won the war for Lincoln, but it was the president who set and guided the overall strategy. That strategy, like most in wartime, had to be altered and revised at times, not necessarily because it was inherently flawed but because of events beyond Lincoln's immediate control. What soon became painfully clear was that the destruction of the Confederate armies would not occur easily or quickly; it might (and did) take years. Nor would Lincoln's strategy of a multipronged, comprehensive set of offensives designed to encircle the entire circumference of the South produce results quickly. In the end, it would require the focused, concentrated, hard war of 1864 and 1865, designed to break the morale and will to fight of the Confederacy's civilian population. Waging this kind of hard war was perhaps Lincoln's most painful decision. As Grant famously said (in a statement occasionally misattributed to Sheridan) when Union forces finished the campaign in the Shenandoah Valley, "Even the crows would have to pack their provender (lunch)."[13] Lincoln knew how much blood would flow from such a strategy and how much harder it would be to pursue postwar policies of reconciliation.

But it was the slavery issue and how it figured in Lincoln's conception of war and peace that reflected and produced the biggest changes in his overall strategy.

Lincoln's early views on slavery bore all the hallmarks of an aspiring politician seeking to make a name for himself on the local, state, and ultimately national level. Lincoln may have found slavery repulsive, but his relevance and viability as a politician required a gradual and pragmatic approach. And Lincoln sought to find a balance, the inhabitable political space if you will, between the founders and compromisers who had kicked the slavery can down the road and the abolitionists who sought its immediate eradication. Moreover, regardless of Lincoln's personal views of slavery, the Constitution had legitimized it. As president, Lincoln had sworn to uphold the Constitution. That made Lincoln's political space even smaller. The ground he would occupy at least until 1862 was pretty firm in his own mind: slavery could not be allowed to spread to new territories and states. But, he believed, if confined to where it already existed, it would eventually die out. In 1861 and as late as 1864, Lincoln seemed prepared to accept this as a basis for compromise to avoid or end the war.

How much Lincoln's own views actually changed on slavery during the course of the war is a fascinating question. We know he abandoned his commitment to colonization, and by 1865 was probably even contemplating a more expansive view of voting rights for freed blacks. But in a way, the president's attitude on the question of emancipation—his most fateful wartime decision—had been shaped by a combination of principle and pragmatism long fixed in his mind.

First, slavery was wrong, a stain on the founders' vision and an obstacle to American democracy, economic growth, and development; second, there was no way that slavery, sanctioned by the Constitution, could be ended quickly or easily, particularly given his need to keep wavering proslavery border states in the Union. At the same time, Lincoln was coming under increasing pressure from northern abolitionists to take some action. And with the war effort stalled, Lincoln began to look for ways to pressure the Confederacy and shorten the conflict. Emancipating slaves might work to further undermine the South's morale, weaken its labor force, mobilize former slaves as soldiers, and accelerate the war's end.

Balancing these conflicting pressures proved to be Lincoln's genius. What he came to understand clearly was that if he could sell emancipation (as a wartime expedient) he could also shorten the war, justify the sacrifices made, strengthen the nation, and lay the basis for the war's broader purpose: a "new birth of freedom" that might finally reconcile the principles of the Declaration of Independence with the realities of governance contained in the Constitution. Not moving against chattel slavery during the war years would have missed a unique moment to eradicate it; moving prematurely in the direction the abolitionists wanted him to go might have lost the border states and undermined the war effort. Lincoln's Goldilocks approach on slavery (not too hot, not too cold, but just right) showed his capacity to understand how a transactional measure, rationalized and marketed with narrower goals, could become a transformational policy with extraordinary implications. With a foot in the past (wrap emancipation in the values of the founders and the Declaration), one in the present (sell emancipation as an important war aim in his role as commander in chief), and another in the future (lay the basis for a nation, freer and more morally sound), Lincoln found and secured his greatness.

Emancipation, with the political reality of its then geographic limits, would free no slaves. Even a year after it was issued, the war was far from over and Union victory far from assured. Indeed, even though the Supreme Court might have upheld Lincoln's executive action, there were no guarantees. There was great concern that emancipation might somehow be revoked, modified, or derailed. As Lincoln knew, the Constitution sanctioned chattel slavery; if things were to change, the Constitution itself would need to be amended and somehow brought into line with the Declaration of Independence. One founding document would have to be reconciled with the other.

It is critical to keep in mind that Lincoln's capacity to accomplish what he did was intimately tied to his relationship with the Republican Party, which he helped to found in 1860 and helped strengthen as president. Unlike Washington or Jackson, Lincoln had no personal base outside of the party. He was neither a war hero nor a widely recognized statesmen or politician. The party became a way to marshal support in the North for his wartime policies, for the Union, for emancipation and for the Thirteenth Amendment. And Lincoln used the tools at his disposal—patronage in an expanding government, harnessing a cabinet reflecting diverse views in the Republican Party, and a relationship with the press to build the party and its base.

No piece of legislation got more of Lincoln's attention and his selling skills than the passage of the Thirteenth Amendment. The Senate had adopted the measure in April 1864. And while Lincoln may not have offered to buy votes, he worked hard with key representatives to secure passage in the House. The Constitution had not been amended in 60 years, and there was tremendous opposition to passage from northern states rights activists. Still, with eleven southern states out of the Union and unable to influence the debate, Lincoln's campaign prevailed.

On January 31, 1865, roughly two years after Lincoln signed the Emancipation Proclamation, the House passed the measure abolishing slavery and involuntary servitude. The impact of the actual amendment to the Constitution (not ratified by the states until December 6, 1865) would be limited in practical terms. It may have ended slavery as an institution, but it did little to promote racial equality or end discriminatory policies that would remain institutionalized and legitimated as accepted practice in both the North and South. Nor did the amendment lead to the emergence of strong political movements to work toward ending discrimination and promoting equality and civil rights—certainly not in 1865, nor for decades after.

Historian Theodore Lowi's claim that in 1875 you "would never have known there had been a war or a Lincoln" may be a bit hyperbolic.[14] But certainly when it came to quick or easy change on the race issue, the power of entrenched racism, the independence of state and local governments, and the strong tradition of limited federal government prevented anything like a transformation. What the amendment did accomplish, together with the Fourteenth and Fifteenth Amendments, was to lay the foundation for a future based on racial equality and civil rights under the law. In preserving the Union, abolishing slavery, and opening up the Constitution for change and interpretation, Lincoln provided future generations with the tools to achieve equality. One of the many tragedies of Lincoln's presidency was that he would not live to see its ratification.

Lincoln's other great achievement lay in consolidating a greater sense of nationhood out of the conflict that had threatened to tear it apart. The sheer magnitude of the death (2 percent of the country's population, roughly 7 million people by today's proportions) and destruction created a new relationship between the federal government and the public, certainly in the North, where the soldiers' sacrifices were now declared the nation's.[15] The war strengthened immensely the power of the federal government and the industrialized and manufacturing base of the northern states, perhaps even sealed us as a nation.[16] The South's devastation was the North's triumph; the shift of power and wealth would be irreversible. Civil war accelerated the United States' transition to an industrialized power by creating a dramatic expansion in railroads, manufacturing, and the telegraph. During Lincoln's administration, the nation's tax system was overhauled, the first income tax institutionalized; the Morrill Act, which created the great land grant universities, was passed, as well as the Homestead Act, which facilitated land acquisition and expansion westward. It might be an exaggeration to credit Lincoln and the war with laying the basis of a durable American nation-state. But not by much. And so, having shepherded the nation through its cruelest trials of civil war, and having preserved its unity on a sounder, freer foundation, Lincoln remains its greatest president.

ROOSEVELT: TRY SOMETHING

No president can serve even a four-year term, let alone eight years, without making serious mistakes. And Franklin Delano Roosevelt, who was into his fourth term when he died, made his fair share. FDR lacked Washington's strict ethical standards or Lincoln's humility; he carried on his affair with Lucy Mercer Rutherford years after he promised Eleanor it had ended. His economic policies couldn't end the

Great Depression, and in 1937 he overreached badly with a Supreme Court–packing scheme and an attempted purge of his political rivals that would shatter the illusion of his invincibility and weaken him politically. His wartime decision to set up detention camps for thousands of Americans of Japanese descent was perhaps the most abominable act of his presidency.

Yet with the exception of Lincoln, no American president faced greater nonstop challenges over a longer period of time, managed them as adroitly, and got most of the big issues right. In the process, Roosevelt set a standard for greatness in the presidency that none of his successors has rivaled, let alone surpassed.

Even against the backdrop of America's recent economic recession, it is hard to appreciate the depth of the economic and social catastrophe of the Great Depression that Roosevelt inherited. There was no massive starvation. But the Great Depression witnessed genuine hunger and malnutrition and organized looting, primarily by those in need of food. A thousand homes were foreclosed each day in America's cities. Scenes of grown men and children, hoboes and vagrants haunting garbage dumps and trash heaps were all too common. Suicides tripled. And the potential for violence and confrontation loomed large. In March 1930, a thousand New Yorkers standing in a Salvation Army bread line charged two bakery trucks; in 1931, Arkansas residents used guns to force Red Cross officials to hand out food.[17] In April 1933, hundreds of Iowa farmers stormed the courtroom of a district judge who refused to prevent foreclosures. He was later found by the roadside stripped and covered with axle grease.[18]

By the winter of 1932–1933, the economic crisis had deepened. Five thousand banks had failed and $9 million in savings accounts had been wiped out. The half a million home mortgages foreclosed, 12 million workers who had lost their jobs, and many more underemployed highlighted the dangerous trends.[19] America was certainly not in a pre-revolutionary state, but there were clear indications that unless the new president came up with a policy to help turn things around, the nation would sink deeper into despair and the ever-increasing potential for violence and extremism might come to fruition.

As FDR biographer Jean Edward Smith reveals, the two crises FDR would weather—the Depression and World War II—gave him a giant stage to test and demonstrate who he was, what he stood for, and how he actually conceived of the presidency in practice. Besides his name and political talents, Roosevelt also had huge majorities in the House (3:1) and in the Senate (2:1).[20] Borrowing a page from Cousin Ted's presidential playbook, he also understood that the purpose of the presidency, certainly in times of crisis, was partly about drama. Against the backdrop of a crisis this severe, FDR knew that in addition to making a difference (actually bringing relief from a depression), he also had to make an important psychological point (buoying the nation's confidence). If things were not improving, people at least had to have real hope that they would.

Roosevelt's self-confidence was at the core of his character. It was easy to see where it came from. A golden boy youth with a doting mother, no siblings, summers at Campobello (an island in New Brunswick between Canada and Maine of sublime beauty and serenity), the best schooling at Groton and Harvard, and personal memories of three presidents would go a long way to convince anyone that he was close to the center of the universe. Roosevelt had his share of failures, including a long shot bid as James Cox's vice president in 1920, but even that had helped his national reputation. In fact, FDR remains the only man to accede to the presidency having lost a vice presidential bid. Talk about self-confidence. As Smith stunningly notes: "At the age of fifty, Franklin Roosevelt had become president. He would remain president for the remainder of his life."[21]

Critics of FDR and the New Deal are correct to point out that none of FDR's economic policies (or certainly Hoover's, for that matter) broke the back of the Great Depression. At the end of the day, it was

World War II that rescued America. Only in 1943 did average unemployment drop below its 1929 level. Still, in addition to the A grade FDR gets for keeping the nation's confidence level high and believing in itself, his hodgepodge of New Deal policies actually did begin to create an upward arc of recovery. Except during the 1937–1938 recession, unemployment fell every year of the New Deal. And GDP grew at an annual rate of 9 percent during Roosevelt's first term, and after the 1937–1938 dip, around 11 percent.[22]

Roosevelt's inherited crisis had the potential to do serious damage to America's social fabric, its free market economy, and its democracy. The country was clearly adrift, leaderless, and needed direction. What FDR provided in the First New Deal was really limited reform and relief. It was not a coherent economic philosophy or doctrine, but it sought to generate answers to problems through experimentation and action. Historian Richard Hofstadter wisely describes the New Deal as a "temperament" more than anything else.[23] And it was a political temperament at that. As a politician, FDR knew he had important constituencies he had to keep in his corner. And that meant bringing along probusiness and conservative constituencies who were most likely to oppose his policies.

The first Hundred Days was as dizzying and extraordinary a period as any in the history of the presidency. To compare any successive hundred days (the artificial period of time in which all of his successors would be judged) to Roosevelt's first is patently unfair, even silly. Congress, which stayed in session for 100 days from March to June 1933, passed fifteen significant pieces of legislation without much debate, hearings, or roll calls. It was a whirlwind of measures, from legalizing 3.2 percent beer, to subsidies to farmers, to the creation of a civilian construction corps, to mortgage relief, to emergency banking legislation to stop runs on banks, to the creation of the Tennessee Valley Authority.

And the heart of FDR's approach came down to a core Roosevelt belief: government had an obligation, particularly in times of emergency, to respond to the public's wants and to provide a minimum standard of economic relief and security. Roosevelt would build on the reform legacies of both Teddy Roosevelt and Woodrow Wilson, but he took his own approach to a new level. His predecessors had used government as a steward to intercede to level the playing field in order to protect Americans against large corporate trusts and the concentration of economic power and to protect their rights. Roosevelt came to see government's role as a way to secure new rights for citizens to which they were entitled and to persuade the public that these were in effect constitutionally guaranteed. As early as 1931 in Albany, Roosevelt as governor of New York had argued that government had a "social duty" to alleviate economic dislocation by using the resources of the state.[24] He had even created at a state level a Temporary Emergency Relief Administration (TERA), perhaps the first of the alphabet soup agencies.

The 1934 midterm victories for the Democrats set the stage for the Second New Deal and for the most consequential and enduring of FDR's reforms. By 1935, pushed by Frances Perkins, his secretary of labor who had made a comprehensive social insurance program a condition of accepting her own cabinet post, and by the deteriorating conditions of the elderly caught in the throes of economic calamity, FDR had signed landmark legislation on Social Security, passing it with huge majorities in the House (372:33) and the Senate (77:6).[25] The Title II component of the 1935 Social Security Act was a new form of federal social insurance provision in which workers and their employers paid taxes into an insurance fund that would pay out worker's retirement benefits in the future. About half the nation's jobs were covered, but there were many exclusions, including farmworkers, domestics, federal employees, merchant seamen, and those employed in the nonprofit sector, among others. A system of unemployment insurance and provisions for retirees was never envisaged as a government handout or dole, but as a joint cooperative effort financed by workers and employers alike to guarantee security after retirement.

And like Lincoln before him, FDR would try to use the traditions and values of the founders to sell transformative change. Drawing from the Constitution's preamble, Roosevelt noted in a June 1934 speech that one of the purposes of government was to "promote the general welfare" and that it was "our plain duty to provide for that security upon which welfare depends."[26] Later that month in a fireside chat, FDR raised social insurance again and, in typical FDR fashion, trotted out a practical example to demonstrate that the basis of the new program was consistent with American values. Roosevelt began by noting that the White House was being renovated. He said that its "artistic lines . . . were the creation of master builders when our Republic was young." But within this "magnificent pattern," he continued, "the necessities of modern government business require constant reorganization and rebuilding. . . . Our new structure is part of a fulfillment of the old."[27]

In the 1936 election, FDR won an unprecedented 60.79 percent of the popular vote; his margin in the Electoral College was 523–8.[28] Given the challenges he had faced, by 1937 the administration had accomplished quite a bit. Payrolls were showing solid gains, unemployment had shrunk to 12 percent, and the Dow Jones Industrial Average had risen sixfold since 1933.[29] Roosevelt's activist reform philosophy was reflected in his 1936 inaugural: "Governments can err; Presidents do make mistakes . . . better the occasional faults of a government that lives in a spirit of charity than the consistent omissions of a government frozen in the ice of its own indifference."[30]

It is important to remember that FDR was a deeply polarizing figure. We have this notion of a golden age of American politics where people came together seamlessly in the face of national emergency for the benefit of the nation's well-being. Even with a crisis and a public receptive to leadership, pushing new ideas and reform has always been a struggle in American politics—hot, combustible, and at times intensely partisan and sometimes violent. From the beginning of the Republic, the debates between Federalists and Democratic Republicans over domestic and foreign policy had been bitter affairs; Jacksonian Democrats fought hard against the Bank of the United States and against South Carolina during the Nullification Crisis; and the partisan and sectional struggle over slavery eventually led to civil war. And unlike today's debates, violence and invective characterized the partisan conflict.

Most of our great and consequential presidents, Roosevelt among them, were intensely partisan figures determined to push for their ideas because they believed they were best for America. FDR understood that the key was to create a viable coalition—as broad-based as possible—for support. And he did; a coalition of liberals, white southerners, blacks, Jews, urban workers, unions, immigrants, and Catholics that would dominate Democratic and national politics for more than a generation. There were casualties. The need to preserve southern support guaranteed that not a single piece of historic civil rights legislation would be signed during FDR's twelve years; class tensions would also increase. But on balance, Roosevelt pursued partisan dominance with deep bipartisan support and without further stressing and polarizing the system.

Midway through his second term, Roosevelt, as many presidents do, began to stumble. Whether it was overconfidence, the death of trusted advisers like Louis Howe who could tell him the truth, Roosevelt's own stubbornness, or simply the long odds against a continuing streak of successes without stumbles, FDR made three serious errors that would significantly weaken his prestige and influence. His scheme to pack the Supreme Court, largely out of frustration over opposition to key pieces of his New Deal legislation; his decision to go after key Democrats who had opposed his policies; and finally cutting spending (unemployment had deceptively fallen to 12 percent), which led to recession, all left him much diminished.[31]

FDR's critics argue that World War II saved him. Perhaps instead, it created an opportunity that for a less capable leader might have become a liability. The rise of fascism in Europe and Japanese expansion in Asia afforded Roosevelt opportunities to become a great president. Rising tensions in Europe all but guaranteed that FDR would run (and win again) both in 1940 and 1944. War would save the American economy, pull it out of the Depression, generate extraordinary growth, and finally give Roosevelt and the United States the influence, power, and the incentive to play the leading role in world affairs.

Roosevelt's task was not as simple as it might have appeared. Before Pearl Harbor, part of FDR's challenge and skill was to lead effectively at a time when the country wasn't all that enthusiastic about following. During the period from 1937 to 1941, there was no direct threat to the United States or a widely shared sense among the majority of Americans that the country was in danger. FDR believed America faced that danger, particularly after Munich and Hitler's rise in Europe, but that threat was by no means clear to an isolationist Congress or a public that saw little reason for American involvement in another European war. The Japanese attack on Pearl Harbor would provide tragic clarity. But before 1941, Roosevelt was left with a tough situation: conditioning a country to the possibility of a serious threat with no compelling evidence that it was imminent.

In the years leading up to Pearl Harbor, Roosevelt served both to reflect public opinion and to push it gradually toward a greater readiness posture should war come. In a way, he would both lead and follow public opinion. In October 1937 he gave his now famous Quarantine speech in Chicago to test the public's awareness of the rising German and Japanese threats in Europe and Asia. Reaction to the notion of the need to quarantine aggressive powers was mixed. FDR later confided to adviser Samuel Rosenman that it was a terrible thing "to look over your shoulder when you're trying to lead—and find no one there."[32] Roosevelt had seen firsthand what had happened to Wilson when his predecessor had gotten out ahead of public opinion on the League of Nations; FDR, despite his admiration for his old boss, was not going to repeat Wilson's mistakes.

FDR had no doubt what American policy should be, particularly after Hitler's attack on Poland in 1939 and the beginning of the European war. Like any good politician he had gone with the isolationist flow during the 1920s, but he was an internationalist at heart, like his cousin Teddy. As assistant secretary of the navy under Wilson, he had pushed for greater resources for a navy he came to love. Well traveled, Roosevelt had as good a feel for European politics and foreign policy as any politician of his day. Roosevelt's true genius during these early years was in finding a balance among these competing pressures and continuing to condition the country toward greater readiness and support for Britain's war effort against the Nazis. In August 1941, Churchill told his cabinet that Roosevelt was prepared to "wage war but not declare it, and that he would become more and more provocative."[33] Churchill was clearly hoping for the best. During the previous year, Roosevelt had moved cautiously, agreeing to trade 50 vintage (many unusable) World War I–era destroyers to Britain in exchange for long-term authority to build and operate bases on eight British colonies in the Western Hemisphere; he had also pushed for the first peacetime draft, though it ruled out using draftees anywhere outside the Western Hemisphere or US possessions. And in May 1941, in one of the most creative if not brilliant measures of his prewar diplomacy, he came up with lend-lease—essentially creating a blank check so that the United States would be able to provide Britain with almost everything it required in the way of arms and supplies, even on the basis of a highly questionable assumption Britain would pay for all this at the war's end.

What is so remarkable about lend-lease, FDR's biographers believe, is that it was his idea, developed while he was on one of his famous cruises, this time off the coast of Antigua in December 1940.[34] We live in an era of government where aides, assistants, experts, Principals Committees and Deputies Committees (National Security Council decision-making bodies) seem to drive and define presidential decision making. Not here. There were no extensive policy debates, staff studies, no diplomatic discussions. It was scary in some respects; bold and refreshing in others. But lend-lease worked. Indeed, Roosevelt's concept

of lend-lease reflected a finely tuned sense of what he could meaning-
fully do to support Churchill in an environment in which the vast majority of Americans still opposed American entry into the war. He knew
where the country would not go but also sensed where it would. And by
the end of 1940, he knew he was on fairly firm ground. That November
Roosevelt won an unprecedented third term with 54.7 percent of the
popular vote. Fifty million Americans voted that year, 58.8 percent of
eligible voters, the highest turnout of any election during the Roosevelt
years.[35]

Much has been made of the possibility that FDR lied or deceived
the country into war. There is little doubt he feared the Axis threat and
the real possibility of British defeat. Had he been looking for a pretext,
the German submarine attacks on the USS *Greer, Kearny,* and *Reuben
James* in September and October 1941 might have provided it.[36] In the
latter two incidents, 126 Americans were killed and 22 wounded while
escorting supply convoys in the Atlantic. In any event, when war came,
it arrived not from the European but from the Pacific theater. It may
well be that FDR's policies to thwart Japanese expansion there and to
deny them access to badly needed raw materials gave the Japanese the
incentive to attack. Still, in the end, America's entry into the Second
World War came not from Roosevelt's deceptions or maneuvering, but
from the only event that could have produced and justified it—an un-
provoked attack on the US fleet at Pearl Harbor.

Within 35 minutes of his "date which will live in infamy" address
on December 8 (a mere 500-plus words), Congress had approved a
formal declaration of war against Japan.[37] Three days later, Germany
declared war on the United States; Congress countered with its own
declaration of war against Germany and Italy, and in June 1942 it also
declared war against Bulgaria, Hungary, and Romania. Remarkably,
these were America's last formal declarations of war; none would be issued for any of America's subsequent conflicts. Addressing the nation in
a fireside chat on December 9, the president set the tone of what was to

come: "We're all in it all the way. Every single man, woman, and child is a partner in the most tremendous undertaking in our American history."[38] No crisis or endeavor since the Second World War has given an American president an opportunity to utter those words, believe them, and make the country believe them too.

At least when it came to strategy and the allies, Roosevelt's wartime leadership was on balance a masterful display of strategic, big picture, hands-on leadership. He recruited and surrounded himself as he had in his New Deal years with the able, the brilliant, and the talented (Marshall, Stimson, Eisenhower); used his own personal special envoys (such as Harry Hopkins) for wartime diplomacy; and created a remarkable relationship with Churchill. Most of the big issues—unconditional surrender, opening a second front, war aims—Roosevelt got right. Much of it he did himself, including mapping out zones for the occupation of Germany on a *National Geographic* map.[39]

His wartime domestic policies were another matter. FDR all but ignored racial segregation in the military but did, through an executive order, prohibit discrimination in hiring related to federal defense contracts. But it was another executive order, no. 9066, that remains the great blot on FDR's wartime record: the forcible evacuation of 40,000 Issei (first-generation Japanese immigrants) and 80,000 Nissei (their children born in the United States) to internment camps.[40] The best that can be said about Roosevelt's motives is that he subordinated every decision to winning the war; that meant avoiding going against his military advisers when it came to security issues or creating unnecessary political complications for himself. This is also the case regarding Roosevelt's reaction to the genocide of Europe's Jews. FDR has been criticized for his unwillingness, or inability, to do more to rescue European Jewry, such as bombing the railway lines to the concentration camps. According to historians Richard Breitman and Allan Lichtman, FDR was never formally asked for a decision on the matter, though his military advisers would have argued against it as a diversion from the war effort. Breitman and Lichtman conclude in their most recent book on the subject that FDR did not do everything possible to aid the persecuted, and ultimately doomed, Jews of Europe. However, he was far better for the Jews than his isolationist and restrictionist political opposition at home, and did more for the Jews than any other world leader, including Winston Churchill.[41] In the case of the Japanese, did Roosevelt really believe that there was a real risk and danger of a fifth column by Japanese Americans? Or was he simply not prepared to risk alienating many Californians and other Americans who felt there was? Either way, his decision stands as perhaps the worst of his presidency.

FDR's approach to the postwar period was a typical blend of his basic internationalism, realism, and good political sense. Like Wilson, Roosevelt talked publicly of a different postwar world and would make an international organization (this time a United Nations rather than a League of Nations) a key theme in his 1944 election campaign. (FDR's margin of victory in the Electoral College in 1944 was 432–99. None of his four Republican opponents broke three digits in the Electoral College.)[42]

Had he lived, would FDR's postwar policies have changed the course of the Cold War? We can ask the question in much the same way with respect to Lincoln and Reconstruction. Given the impact leaders like Lincoln and FDR had on war policy and politics, there is little doubt they would have altered the situations their successors faced, and probably for the better. How much of a difference FDR would have made is another matter. By 1944, he had all but come to the conclusion that he would have to live with Soviet spheres of influence, at least in Eastern Europe. FDR, who had great confidence in the power of his own personality to win others over, probably believed that he could work with Joseph Stalin, or at least hoped he could. But it is hard to believe that Roosevelt, optimistic as he was, had any illusions that politics and geography, not to mention staggering wartime Russian losses and suffering, would not put Stalin in a position to get what he wanted, at least in Eastern Europe. Still, Roosevelt's upbeat view of a world in which nations and people would cooperate and strive for freedom, opportunity, and prosperity—even with continuing conflict, realpolitik, and sectarian ethnic strife—would shape America's policies. His inherent optimism and faith in the future would remain a salient feature of how America would continue to orient itself to the rest of the world.

However different their circumstances, each of these three undeniably great presidents read their times correctly, intuited what might be possible, met their crises, and transformed the nation too. This required a keen knowledge of the political terrain and an intuitive understanding of the public's mood and how far it might be pushed. Princeton's Cornel West stated that great presidents need to be thermostats rather than thermometers.[43] The truly great ones need to be thermometers too, capable of understanding where the public stands. But West has a point, presidents cannot just reflect the public's needs and opinions; they need to help shape, regulate, and direct them as well. As an example, West cited Lyndon Johnson on civil rights, and he was right. Great presidents see where the currents of the times are flowing, and then, within certain parameters, they work to determine if they can possibly redirect those currents when a crisis or an exceptional moment affords them the opportunity. They certainly aren't complete prisoners of their times. But neither are they total masters either. The circumstances they inherit give them the chance for greatness. These three greats sensed or perhaps knew what to do with that opportunity. And we are all stronger for it.

All three were redefiners.[44] They sold change in a manner consistent with the limitations of the system and the politics of their day. This required a strategy that merged the past, present, and future as part of the same piece. Each president used past values and a present crisis to sell change that would redefine and reshape the American future.

Washington anchored his politics in the values of the Declaration of Independence and the Revolution. Lincoln used the crisis presented by war to sell a future agenda of emancipation and the Thirteenth Amendment, rooted in the American values of the Declaration of Independence and made consistent with the principles of the Constitution. FDR had a more difficult task in selling Social Security. After all, together with other New Deal reforms, it fundamentally altered Americans' relationship with their government. But he placed it firmly within the tradition of government helping to secure and promote opportunity, even the right of all Americans to economic security.

In this respect the indispensables were all what historians Marc Landy and Sidney Milkis referred to as "conservative revolutionaries" (some might say "evolutionary revolutionaries").[45] Crisis mandated change. And if the American enterprise was to be saved and preserved, it had to be reformed. Their genius was to sell change in a way that made it seem less threatening, not revolutionary. Indeed, that change was packaged as a natural part of America's traditions and consistent with its values and practices of governance.

FOUR

Close but No Cigar

AS LONG AS THERE ARE PRESIDENTS, THERE WILL always be arguments about ranking and rating them. And for those of you who want to play this fun and profitable game, I recommend Robert Merry's wonderful book *Where They Stand*.[1] The main debate is not so much between those who rank at the top and the bottom. Those differences are clear enough. Instead, the more intriguing and difficult distinctions are between those who fall into the very top tier and those who fall just below them—what the Schlesingers, the country's most eminent father-son historical team, called the difference between great and near great. There is also the fascinating question of what to do with what I term the high/lows—those presidents who reached extraordinary accomplishment in one area but who fell stunningly low in another.

Historians in the 1948 Schlesinger Sr. poll included Jefferson, Jackson, and Wilson among the very top presidential performers along with the three presidents who rank as the greatest—Washington, Lincoln, and Roosevelt.[2] In 1962, when Schlesinger redid the poll for *New York Times Magazine*, Jefferson and Wilson were still among the top performers, with Jackson having been demoted to the "Near Great" category.[3] Finally, in 1996, when Arthur Schlesinger Jr.

reproduced the poll a third time, the top tier included only Washington, Lincoln, and FDR.[4]

What do we do with these so-called near greats? The term lacks any real precision. Indeed, it comes with the connotation that these presidents almost made it into the top rank, but not quite. Many presidential scholars rightly conclude that all of these labels are far too general. Instead, what's required is a much more detailed set of performance requirements that some even believe need to be analyzed statistically.

I understand the need for more precision. What does *near great* really mean anyway? We have enough of a challenge defining *great*. I'm not sure assigning statistical values to individual leadership skills and traits and quantifying performance advances the argument much. Indeed, this kind of analysis would still lead you to the same results—a remarkable group of leaders (Jefferson, Jackson, Teddy Roosevelt, maybe Wilson, and Truman) all deserve consideration as top performers, but they are not at the pinnacle of presidential performance.

So what separates this group from the top three? Plenty. Their times were challenging, but not nearly as dire or consequential for the country as those of the top three; their legacies were impressive, though not nearly as transformative or groundbreaking as the indispensables'; and their failures and mistakes were much more significant and noteworthy, partly because their accomplishments were not deemed as great and were unable to overshadow their mistakes. As a result, their essentiality is not quite the same. Still, all stood at critical junctures in the nation's story. And the fact that most led without the nation-encumbering calamities or crises faced by Washington, Lincoln, or FDR makes the accomplishments of this "close but no cigar" crowd, in many ways, all the more remarkable because, denied the urgency and pressure for consequential policy changes, these presidents had to do more to create their own constituencies.

At the same time, none were seen to be quite as indispensable to the American story as the three greats, and none were quite perceived and remembered that way either. The Jefferson scholar Merrill Peterson captured the essence of the distinction: "Americans venerate Washington, love Lincoln, and remember Jefferson."[5] The latter was a remarkable man and an important president. But we do not stand in awe of his challenges and triumphs as president. Neither apparently did Jefferson, who listed his key accomplishments on his gravestone without mentioning his presidency, and who seemed as eager as Washington to return home after office to his Monticello. Some, like Andrew Jackson for his policies toward Native Americans, are just too controversial. What other president (with the possible exception of Richard Nixon) would warrant a documentary with the title *Andrew Jackson: Good, Evil, & the Presidency?*[6] Another, Woodrow Wilson, seemed strangely out of touch with the tempo of his times, a tragic, stricken figure who saw his legacy renounced and repudiated by the voters.

There is a risk of course in grouping all these presidents together. They all were very different men: the enigmatic Jefferson, the Virginia Renaissance man whose reputation in America's history was secured before his presidency; Jackson, a tough backwoods lawyer, congressman, and prosecutor who fought duels, Native American tribes, and the British; Teddy Roosevelt, a Harvard man, later Navy assistant secretary, and governor of New York who had his Rough Riders' uniforms made at Brooks Brothers; Wilson, our only PhD president (and the only one buried in Washington, DC), governor of New Jersey, and president of Princeton University; Truman, a failed haberdasher and small-business man from Independence, Missouri, dubbed by his detractors as the "Second Missouri Compromise" when FDR chose him over Henry Wallace as his vice president in 1944 and then ignored him.[7]

Each of these presidents, whose collective tenure spanned a century and a half of dynamic expansion, turbulence, and profound change in the American story, left mixed legacies, but all shaped the nation and presidency in dramatic and consequential ways. And despite their differences, we can see them as part of the same piece. Above them sit our greatest presidents; below are the majority of their nineteenth- and early-twentieth-century presidential colleagues, none of whom come close to their levels of performance. These five presidents demonstrate that great acts and moments in the presidency are possible without first-order crises. Indeed, a brief overview of their accomplishments demonstrates that successful and effective presidents can do great things without necessarily going down in history and being remembered as undeniably great presidents. And this is a critically important insight to keep in mind as we grapple with our modern day hunger for greatness in the presidency without many candidates to even whet, let alone satisfy, our appetites.

Our first two "close but no cigar" presidents—Jefferson and Jackson—could not on the face of it have been more different in style, temperament, and background. Jefferson, the highly educated Renaissance man, reputed to have had one of the largest collections of fine wines in North America, hated conflict; Andrew Jackson, a rough-hewn product of a far less genteel world, was more comfortable with whiskey—and loved and sought out a good fight. Each—as proponents of individual rights, freedom, and limited government—would move to free up the political system for the benefit of the common man and to expand democratic principles and ideals. And each would have a seminal impact—Jackson even more than Jefferson as president—in transforming the relationship between the presidency and the people.

As president, Jefferson's enduring significance lay largely in the way he was able to expand both the nation's democratic character and its physical size. No sentimentalist on these matters, historian Gordon Wood goes as far as to claim that as long as there is a United States, Jefferson will remain "the supreme spokesman for America's idea of equality."[8] That he owned slaves (fathered children with one of them) fundamentally subverted this ideal. Twelve of our first eighteen presidents owned slaves, four while in office. And there is no defending Jefferson or the founders on the slavery issue by suggesting that they were men of their times and that these were the prevailing attitudes. Many in the founding generation opposed slavery; and Jefferson did too as a young man.[9] Perhaps the best that can be said is that Jefferson's fierce commitment to democratic principles and the equality of all individuals would help fashion a framework that over time would help eradicate the very prejudices and discriminatory practices that he himself practiced.

Reacting to what he believed to be a dangerous concentration of government power under the Federalists, Jefferson energized American democracy through the creation of a new Democratic Republican Party based on small government, states' rights, a strict reading of the Constitution, and a vision of a nation protecting the interests not of the aristocrats but the common men—farmers, laborers, craftsmen. He checked the growth of the expanding Federalist vision of powerful government by reducing internal taxes, eliminating the federal debt, and cutting the size of the military. And he "republicanized" the more officious trappings of the presidency—having his annual address (precursor to what would become the State of the Union) delivered in written form instead of read (a practice resumed only under Wilson); dressing plainly; wearing carpet slippers when he greeted the British ambassador; and eschewing a fancy coach and carriage.

And yet Jefferson moved quickly to reconcile his aversion to executive power with his strong use of it in acquiring the Louisiana Territory. Without a constitutional amendment and consultations with Congress, Jefferson acted decisively to purchase a block of territory from the French so remarkable that it made him the greatest expansionist president in American history. The Federalists would blast him for purchasing a "howling wilderness." But that sale resulted in the United States acquiring 828,000 square miles, a chunk of real estate as large as Britain, France, Germany, Italy, and Portugal combined. That acquisition doubled the size of the United States and would come to compose about 23 percent of its current territory.[10] Jefferson's accomplishments during his first term were followed by serious failures during his second. His embargo against France and Britain, designed to keep the United States neutral during their conflict, resulted in a severe reduction in American trade and a devastating economic downturn with no attendant diplomatic benefits. For all Jefferson's vision, his conception of an America based on small government would prove fundamentally out of step with a nation whose needs and interests at home and abroad required expansion, not contraction. Still, the purchase of Louisiana, perhaps the most consequential and transformative executive action in American history, and his effort to promote practical democracy and protect and expand the opportunities for the individual represent great acts of presidential leadership that would literally reshape the country.

Evaluating Andrew Jackson, Clinton Rossiter wrote, "His legacy is not all bright; more than one such president a century would be hard to take."[11] Yet Jackson, like Jefferson, had a profound influence on American politics and governance. Jackson was rough-hewn, self-made, violence-prone, racist, and a slave owner as president. A populist determined to fight for the small man and to combat those who wanted to use big government to further the interests of the elites, he was both easily loved and hated. When Harvard agreed to give the president an honorary degree, John Quincy Adams, a real Harvard alum (who lost the presidency to Jackson in 1828) told the college they were honoring "a barbarian who could not write a sentence of grammar and hardly could spell his own name." A nineteenth-century New England Sunday school teacher once asked a pupil who killed Abel, and the reply was "General Jackson."[12]

But Jackson, whom biographer Jon Meacham describes as "the most important American leader between Jefferson and Lincoln," profoundly reshaped democratic politics and strengthened the presidency and the Union too.[13] To justify his own actions a quarter century later, Lincoln would use Jackson's strong defense of union in the crisis over the tariff and South Carolina's threats of nullification and secession.

Jackson believed the presidency was designed to further and protect individual liberty and the interests of the common man, not the wealthy elites and banking interests. Government should be limited, but the president and government needed to act strongly in the people's name. His war against the Bank of the United States reflected that belief, as did his frequent use of the veto. (From Washington to John Quincy Adams, the veto had been used ten times. Jackson alone deployed it twelve, and was the first president to use the pocket veto.)[14] Indeed, responding to a growing political movement to end property requirements for voting and to select state electors by popular vote, Jackson presided over the decline of the elitist gentry and the rise of popular democracy. The first nominating convention held by the two major American parties took place in 1832. That year, Jackson won the presidency with 54 percent of the popular vote.[15] After Jackson, American presidents were tied to the public in a way they had never been before.

But Jackson's own personality and combustible temperament, his views on blacks, and his policies toward Native Americans would tarnish his reputation. Nowhere was this more tragically revealed than in Jackson's policies on Indian removal from Georgia, Florida, and Mississippi and relocation to areas in what is now Oklahoma.

That Jackson's own commitment to expansion of rights and liberties for the small man did not extend to Native Americans was hardly a surprise in light of the prevailing views of his time or his own battles with the tribes before he became president. At the same time, Jackson's view that the tribes had no sovereignty within the states and that they were occupying valuable land better used by whites led to tragic consequences over which Jackson presided. In the wake of Congress passing the Indian Removal Act of 1830, some tribes reluctantly agreed to exchange their land; others, like the Seminoles, would resist. The forced relocation of the Cherokees resulted in the deaths of around one quarter of the Cherokee Nation on what became known as the Trail of Tears.[16] Like Jefferson, some of Jackson's policies led to both a banking crisis and a depression. Still, Jackson's commitment to strengthening the Union, promoting the rights of the individual, and democratizing the system reflect great presidential leadership that would alter the nation's politics. And like the next president on our list, his charisma and heroic persona would help him to dominate his age in a way few other presidents have.

Our next president does not pair easily with his presidential colleagues, largely because he was in a class and category all his own. Teddy Roosevelt really is an example of the triumph of persona over circumstance. He never had a first- or even second-order crisis, and yet, as James MacGregor Burns observed, he was his own "walking crisis."[17] And he barged his way into the greatness club by sheer drive of forcefulness and conviction. "The life of TR," Dixon Wecter wrote in his classic *The Hero in America,* "was the dream of every typical American boy; he fought in a war, became president, killed lions, and quarreled with the Pope."[18] Roosevelt's presidency (and life) was very much about drama, and like Jackson he came to dominate the office and the age.

But it was also a life that reflected the contradictions and complexity of the American story too. Historian Michael McGerr reminds us that Teddy Roosevelt is admired greatly and is claimed by both liberals and conservatives. He championed governmental regulation and yet believed deeply in a rugged individualism; he loved to hunt, but also to conserve; he championed a muscular, activist foreign policy, but at the same time he was a realist and an advocate of a balance of power—in Europe where he feared, with Britain, the rise of Germany and Russia, and in Asia where his successful mediation of the 1905 Russo-Japanese War won him a Nobel Peace Prize (the first US president to receive one).[19]

TR's tenure was filled with firsts: the youngest chief executive at 42, the first to travel outside of the United States, the first to serve entirely in the twentieth century, and the first to call the president's residence the White House. Some argue that more than any of his predecessors he laid the basis of the modern presidency by making the chief executive, to use one of successor Woodrow Wilson's phrases, "the vital place of action in the system."[20]

And quite contrary to most of his predecessors, Roosevelt grasped—almost intuitively—that the president needed to be a dramatist and to orchestrate his actions in the press. Mark Twain, the master American roaster, quipped that Roosevelt "would go to Halifax for half a chance to show off" and "to hell for a whole one."[21] But beyond showmanship, he used his personal relationships with the press to draw attention to his reformist agenda. He was on a first-name basis and socialized with the key investigative journalists of his day, read their pieces before publication, and used them as part of his bully pulpit approach to educating Americans about issues relating to progressivism and social reform.

Roosevelt's accomplishments on the substantive side were all the more impressive because he held the presidency in a time of relative prosperity and during a period without a major crisis, something he very much regretted. And yet, the country continuing its transition to an industrialized, urbanized society of immigrants—with all the dislocation and anxiety those changes brought—needed a leader willful enough to promote a national agenda that would offer up a unifying vision of a strong government more responsive to societal ills. Roosevelt understood the power of capitalism and the need to regulate large corporations and business—not to undermine the capitalist enterprise but to preserve and save it. And he bought into much of the progressives' approach, and through his own force of personality and leadership gave it weight and urgency, particularly on matters related to social reform.

No Republican president since has been associated with such an activist reform agenda; and while that reform spirit would dissipate after Wilson, Roosevelt created an important precedent that government could be (really should be) employed as a kind of steward to preserve fairness and opportunity. His Square Deal, particularly actions against corporate trusts, validated the notion that the presidency should be used as a driver of action and change, and to protect the public interest against large corporations. He put teeth into the Interstate Commerce Commission and signed both the Meat Inspection Act and Pure Food and Drug Act to regulate safety standards. His tremendous legacy on conservation, the protection of 230 million acres in the form of national parks, 51 federal bird reservations, and 150 national forests, followed the same principle.[22]

Our final two presidents—Wilson and Truman—were fundamentally different in style and just about everything else. Still there are intriguing similarities. Both had little experience in foreign affairs and yet were confronted with serious foreign policy challenges that would both hurt and harm their legacies. Both ended world wars victoriously; one had great success in postwar diplomacy and the other did not; and finally, each ended his tenure with disastrous approval ratings and saw his party lose Congress and the presidency. Neither's record would allow them to be judged an uncontestably great president, and Wilson's supermoralism and idealism seems out of step with the realist view that's so much a part of presidential greatness. Still, each demonstrated great acts of presidential leadership and left the office and the country stronger for it.

Our only formally trained academic in chief, Wilson received an undergraduate degree from Princeton, a law degree from the University of Virginia, and a PhD in political science from Johns Hopkins University. He emerged as one of the leading political scientists of the day and after a successful academic career went on to become president of Princeton. His impressive speaking ability brought him to the attention of New Jersey's Democratic Party bosses, who saw him as an ideal candidate for governor, a role he served from 1911 to 1913. While there he turned against the party machine, thereby establishing himself as a leading progressive reformer. Taking advantage of a divided Republican field, he won the presidency in 1912, winning 42 percent of the popular vote to the insurgent Teddy Roosevelt's 27 percent and William Howard Taft's 23 percent.[23]

With his background in domestic affairs, Wilson would emerge, together with FDR and Lyndon Johnson, as one of America's most

consequential legislative presidents. He literally spent more time physically present on Capitol Hill than any other president, addressing the
House or Senate 27 times; indeed, the so-called President's Room in
which he worked exists there today. And it was Wilson, a brilliant orator
whose speeches were so lyrical it was said they could be danced to, who
restored the practice (after Jefferson discontinued it) of delivering the
State of the Union address in person.

Until FDR's New Deal legislation, his record was the most impressive of any American president—and perhaps even more impressive if
you consider the fact that unlike Roosevelt and Lyndon Johnson, Wilson operated without a crisis to create vital urgency. As a strong progressive, his New Freedom Agenda reduced tariffs for the first time in
40 years, and was accompanied by the first permanent income tax, the
creation of the Federal Reserve, and a new antitrust act in conjunc-
tion with the establishment of the Federal Trade Commission. And as
Wilson biographer John Milton Cooper reveals, Wilson was hands-on.
In April 1913, a month after his inauguration, Wilson called the 63rd
Congress into session, and with one brief recess it remained there for
eighteen months. Three years later Wilson would succeed in pushing
through a federal child labor law, financial aid to farmers, regulation of
maritime shipping, and an eight-hour day for railroad workers.[24]

The highs of Wilson's first term were to be met with tragic lows
during his second, emanating paradoxically from the president's own
successful wartime leadership and a war he helped Britain and France
to win.

Wilson won reelection in 1916 by promising to keep America out
of the First World War. Yet within six months, in the face of attacks
by German U-boats on US shipping and German efforts to persuade
Mexico to attack Texas, public attitudes changed, and Wilson skillfully
led the nation into what would be its first world war.

But his postwar diplomacy in the wake of the war that Wilson
hoped would end all wars undermined his reputation. Perhaps no

president was as bold, courageous, or visionary in trying to assert a postwar leadership role for the United States. Wilson attempted to do so with a League of Nations designed to promote international peace and security based on a vision that included his iconic Fourteen Points. And as fascist and Nazi powers emerged and mobilized in the 1930s, Wilson's foresight and vision would be praised and well remembered. But vision—no matter how prescient—that lacks the grounding in the political or foreign policy reality of the day can be a prescription for failure. And Wilson's own rigidity, his idealized view of what the League could accomplish, his failure to accept the reality that the British and French were determined to make Germany pay and to realize their own postwar imperial ambitions, created huge obstacles.

Several factors doomed US participation in the League: America's own reluctance and ambivalence to play a postwar role, the unraveling of Wilson's political coalition, Republican victory in the 1918 midterms, the president's personal rivalry with Senator Henry Cabot Lodge—the powerful chairman of the Senate Foreign Relations Committee—and opposition on the part of a determined minority in the Senate. In October 1919, exhausted from a national tour to sell the League, Wilson suffered a stroke from which he would never fully recover. Between November 1919 and March 1920, the Senate voted on and failed to pass the treaty three times.

Some argue that had Wilson not been stricken, he would have found a way to compromise with Lodge; others claim that his own idealism and rigidity would have made that impossible. And there is an argument that the coalition of progressive internationalists that had been so forceful in supporting Wilson's vision of US engagement had collapsed, partly in response to the nativist and xenophobic domestic policies over which Wilson had presided. Whatever the explanation, in November 1920 the public elected the Republican Warren Harding over the Democrat James Cox in a virtual landslide, with Republicans picking up 62 seats in the House and 10 in the Senate.[25] Wilson ended his presidency a tragic figure, broken by illness and failure to achieve what was then for America and the European powers an unrealistic vision for a postwar world whose time had not yet come. Wilson's travails also make a powerful statement with regard to presidential greatness. Effective presidents must always have an eye on the future, but at least one on the present too, in order to read accurately both the limits and possibilities of successful action.

The only twentieth-century president without a college degree, Harry Truman had to be one of the most underestimated of American presidents. Other than Lincoln, he was probably the American president who most exceeded expectations. Indeed, perhaps with the exception of John Adams, Truman had the toughest act to follow in American politics. He was a natural politician who understood that most Americans had benefited from FDR's reforms and wartime leadership and that he should sell himself as the dead president's successor to complete his fourth term. Like Wilson, Truman's background—as a county judge and US senator—should have prepared him to focus on domestic issues. Paradoxically, unlike Wilson, his reputation would be enhanced—and at times undermined too—from his decisions in foreign policy and national security.

As one of several post-1945 accidental presidents, Truman was thrown into the complexities of the Cold War, for which on paper he was thoroughly unprepared. As FDR's vice president, he had not been consulted about foreign policy or anything else for that matter. He had served admirably in World War I in an artillery unit and demonstrated real leadership skills, and had chaired a Senate committee on national preparedness that got him on the cover of *Time*. But could anything have prepared him to succeed a revered four-term president in a country still at war, and at the same time facing prospects of postwar challenges from a Soviet Union led by Joseph Stalin?

Truman's foreign policy record was a very mixed one. He left office with a 32 percent approval rating largely as a consequence of a very unpopular war in Korea, which he had responsibility for expanding by not opposing General Douglas MacArthur's disastrous plan to cross the 38th Parallel to destroy the Chinese-backed North Korean regime.[26] His stand-up, but politically unpopular, decision to later fire MacArthur could not save Truman from a stalemated war that would undermine his domestic initiatives and undermine a relationship with China for years to come.

At the same time, there's no denying Truman's accomplishments in foreign policy: ending the war with Japan, including the use of two atomic bombs; his initial decision to resist North Korean aggression against the South; and his historic policies in stabilizing and defending Europe through support for Greece and Turkey, the Marshall Plan on European recovery, the Berlin Airlift, and the creation of NATO. His move to desegregate the armed forces reflected a tough-minded and bold president willing and able to take big decisions. Though assisted by an all-star cast, including George Marshall, Dean Acheson, and Republican majority leader Arthur Vandenberg in the Senate, Truman deserves much of the credit. And as his successors were dragged down by Vietnam, Truman's presidential stock would rise. Aided by some favorable biographers, a good dose of nostalgia, and Truman's own no-nonsense, plain-speaking, common touch, he is remembered today as a consequential president who exhibited great leadership in foreign policy. He may well be one of the few modern presidents who exceeded expectations, and despite exceedingly low approval ratings upon leaving office, is now remembered as a president thrown into an impossible situation who made some smart, tough, and historic calls.

⚊ ⚊

All presidents fail at something, even the three indispensables, and most certainly the five other "close but no cigar" presidents discussed above. But the latter group deserves a special place partly because each managed to accomplish great things without a first-order crisis—no easy matter in the purposefully decentralized political system the founders created. Each would govern in historic times—critical junctures really—in the nation's story; each rose to meet the challenges of his time without just marking time; each was able to use the presidency—with all its constraints—to leave a legacy in domestic or foreign policy, or both, legacies not just worth remembering but that would profoundly shape a piece of America's history; and each strengthened the office without abusing its power. Indeed, none disgraced the office through a personal or policy or constitutional scandal that would have undermined the very system they were constitutionally bound and pledged to protect. None were undeniably and sustained great performers judged by the full measure of their presidencies. But all revealed greatness in at least one of their presidential endeavors. And it is not surprising that they remain high on historians' lists and—in several cases—high in the public's imagination too.

The success of these presidents would make it easier for their successors. As a result of their decisions, America not only survived the existential crises and threats, but it prospered and thrived. The policies and decisions made by this group played no small role in that success. Much work remained to be done by the middle of the twentieth century, particularly when it came to inclusion and social justice. Millions of African Americans, women, Native Americans, and minorities suffered systemic, de facto, and de jure discrimination and were denied equal opportunity. Still, in the immediate postwar period, the United States had emerged undeniably as the world's most consequential economic, military, and political power.

And yet, ironically, at the same time, the success of these presidents would also make it harder, setting the bar remarkably high for their successors. The post-FDR/Truman presidents might take some comfort in the fact that great acts of leadership in the presidency were indeed possible without first-order crises, and that human agency could, through will and skill, trump circumstances from time to time. But the record of strong presidents committed to high purpose—creating historic firsts and accomplishments during the formative years of a nation that could not or need not be replicated—would be a tough, if not impossible, act to follow. These later presidents would have power at their disposal that some of their predecessors could never even imagine. But their responsibilities at home and abroad, and the public's expectations, would grow too, as would the constraints on using that formidable power effectively and wisely. For many reasons, greatness in the presidency would prove much more elusive. And it is to this subject that we now turn.

PART II

Greatness Gone

IN ONE OF THE MOST HILARIOUS EPISODES FROM the HBO award-winning series *Curb Your Enthusiasm,* Larry David encounters his manager Jeff's brother-in-law, a staunch Republican, at a Passover Seder.

"Have you heard of the theory of the 77?" he asks Larry. "Every 77 years there's a great president. Washington, and then you go 77 years you got Lincoln, and then you go 77 years, there's FDR. And then you go another 77 years, you got W. And I think we're in historic times."

"Washington . . . Lincoln . . . FDR . . . and George W. Bush," the incredulous Larry replies.

"We're turning the whole damn world around," the brother-in-law responds.

The presidential math is a bit off, and the final link in the presidential greatness chain way off. But the vignette drives an intriguing point. Every six decades or so, in a history now stretching out 238 years, an undeniably great president has appeared—until now.

By the end of 2014, we will have gone the longest stretch in our history without one. From the final year of Washington's second term to Lincoln's inauguration is 64 years, from Lincoln's death in 1865 to

FDR's inauguration is 68, and from FDR's death to the present (in 2014) is 69 years.

This kind of presidential trivia is alternately fun, silly, and driven as much by coincidence, luck, and serendipity as by anything serious. There is no reason to believe in the so-called theory of 77 or any other theory for that matter. That we just happen to be in an extended dry patch of presidential greatness does not mean we cannot have another great president. This stretch of the presidency is no unhappier nor hapless than in previous periods where for much of the nineteenth century forgotten, faceless presidents left no legacy, footprint, or accomplishments of great consequence. It is just a matter of time before another truly great president appears, right?

If I learned anything from spending nearly a quarter century in government, it is that policy, politics, and diplomacy are driven more often by probabilities than possibilities. Getting *anything* done in government is hard, let alone great acts of leadership in the presidency. The absence of an undeniably great president in the past 60-plus years, whether or not it is tied to some clever bit of presidential math, is worth paying attention to. There are indeed new factors that have reshaped the presidential story and our politics, too. And since Franklin Roosevelt's time, new elements have emerged to make greatness in the presidency, or even what you might call sustained excellence in presidential performance, much harder. This is not a declinist trope. It is simply a realistic and sobering one.

Before we go any further it is critical to make something unmistakably clear. The dozen presidents since Franklin Roosevelt were hardly a collection of mediocrities and losers. Their stories are filled with challenges and disappointments to be sure. But it is certainly not a story of failure. A more intelligent group of presidents may never have served the Republic for as long a period of time. In fact, with the possible exception of the first five, if I had to pick the best five-president sequence in American history, I might choose FDR, Harry Truman, Dwight

Eisenhower, John Kennedy, and yes, Lyndon Johnson. Among them were competent, talented, even brilliant men, whose smarts and dedication outshone many of their predecessors. Even Richard Nixon, the next president in that sequence, had a great moment or two.

Still, the presidential story during these years tells a pretty rough and tumble tale; it's a roller coaster ride, really. Of the eleven presidents since FDR (not counting Barack Obama), three had what you might call very unhappy and unnatural ends to their presidencies: Kennedy was assassinated; Lyndon Johnson took himself out of the running for another term in 1968 because of Vietnam; and Nixon resigned the presidency to avoid impeachment. Their successors did not fare much better. Gerald Ford and Jimmy Carter, both short-timers (Ford only 30 months, Carter a one-termer), were really transitional presidents. Add it up, and you have a pretty turbulent and depressing stretch. Indeed, you might call this period—1968 to 1980—a lost decade in terms of presidential credibility. These years would seriously diminish the integrity of the office and erode the confidence Americans had in their government generally. In 1973, historian Barbara Tuchman even wondered—somewhat fantastically—whether we should not consider abolishing the presidency altogether.[1]

Finally, of the four presidents who were elected to two terms and served them out, two of them (Ronald Reagan and Bill Clinton), despite their brilliance as politicians, their popularity, and some notable accomplishments, diminished their own presidencies through self-inflicted policy and personal scandals (Iran-Contra and Lewinsky). Both would recover, but their blunders generated pretty big asterisks that would keep them out of the greatness category. That leaves Eisenhower, a very popular and much underestimated president whose stock has risen over the years, partly because of the troubled administrations of his successors, and partly because of his sound judgment and prudence. But still not a great. And finally, the two Bushes: the first a competent president with some notable foreign policy successes, and the second a president whose domestic record and foreign policy achievements will likely, with a few exceptions, suffer some of history's harshest and unkindest cuts.

But this presidential timeline tells only part of the story. The past six decades mask much deeper problems for the modern presidents and the presidency. This period contains important elements about why greatness in presidential performance of the kind we witnessed earlier in our history will be more elusive now than ever before. A president who inherits the right kind of crisis and has the combination of character and capacity to go with it—my R_x for presidential greatness—is rare under any circumstance. The last six decades have made that combination even harder to imagine.

First, dispense with the easy and the obvious. Incomparable and unsurpassed achievement in a political system as complex, constrained, and combustible as ours just does not occur very often. Fortunately, rarer still are the crisis-driven situations where the identity, sometimes the very viability and existence, of the nation is tested. In our case, those formative trials were independence, nation building, the Civil War, the Depression, two world wars, and, on rare occasion, a truly threatening postwar foreign policy challenge. The older a nation becomes, the fewer the foundational trials. For the modern president, there are fewer historic "firsts" to accomplish and fewer nation-encumbering crises to overcome. Through no fault of their own, our post–World War II presidents face a kind of "been there, done that" challenge that bears on their own performances, particularly after FDR. And that makes spectacular achievement even more elusive.

What makes it even more so is our political system and culture, which fragments political power even while it demands consensus to get things done. Change in America—true transformative change—has never been easy or all that common. How many truly transformative moments and periods have there been in our history that set the stage for nation-altering change? Four or five? Independence and the birth of the Republic; Civil War; Great Depression; Kennedy's assassination;

Vietnam and turmoil in inner cities; 9/11? And even those so-called transformative events often take years, even decades, to play out. Lincoln's 1863 Emancipation Proclamation was only the beginning of a century-plus quest for racial equality and civil rights that still is not complete.

Then there is the problem of the changing role of government in our lives. More than any other factor, the expanding role of government has created wildly exaggerated expectations for what a president can and cannot achieve. Today, we demand more, want more, and feel entitled to more from our government—and the president who heads it—than at any other time in our history. Outside of managing the nation's wars, the federal government's role was limited to providing benefits to citizen-soldiers, setting tariffs, providing land grants to settlers and aid to farmers, and limited social support to mothers and children. It's hard to imagine, but before FDR and the New Deal, the average American's most regular contact with the federal government was likely to be the postal service.

The New Deal and World War II would change all that. Government would take on new and expanded roles both regulatory and redistributive. Americans would now feel the national government in their lives, benefit from it, feel a stronger sense of obligation to and association with it, and resent it too. In a fascinating overview of government's changing role, Suzanne Mettler and Andrew Milstein show how veterans, workers, the disabled, the elderly, low-income groups, college students, and others were drawn into a federal orbit that has produced sweeping changes in the relationship between government and the public.[2] By their estimates, by the mid-twentieth century, half of all Americans observed the presence of the federal government in their lives; nearly all had family members who benefited in some way from federal programs.

FDR may have departed the scene, but at least two pieces of his legacy lived on to become the property of all his successors, regardless of their political views: first, the belief that government is largely responsible for the overall fate of the economy; and second, that it has a moral obligation to maintain a social and economic safety net for all Americans. And no president after FDR, not even Ronald Reagan (who voted for Roosevelt four times), has seriously challenged, let alone succeeded, in downsizing the size or central role of government in our lives. At a recent Tea Party rally, a movement that aspires to move America back to a simpler time of smaller government, one of the party faithful, clearly oblivious to the contradiction he was advertising, was holding a sign: "Obama don't touch my Medicare." Indeed, today, few Americans even grasp the extent of that dependence. In 2013 the Census Bureau reported that almost 50 percent of the country received at least one federal benefit: Social Security, Medicare, Medicaid, food stamps, veteran benefits, and housing subsidies.[3] If you add tax breaks and benefits, the percentage reaches almost 75 percent.

Finally, modern presidents face a world and set of responsibilities much harder to manage, let alone control. The new globalized, integrated world impinges significantly and directly, often immediately, on important domestic issues in a way their predecessors could never even imagine. 9/11 terrorists, Greek debt, Wikileaks, NSA contractor revelations roiling relations with allies, and fluctuations in oil prices as a result of political turmoil in the Middle East, all are beyond the control of a president who is even powerless to plug an oil leak in the Gulf of Mexico. As an expanding continental power, America faced troubles enough. Both Washington and Lincoln had to deal with incredible challenges (nation building and civil war, respectively) and even had to contend with the great powers of their day in North America and at sea. As monumental as these challenges were, they were still contained. They were continental problems that offered up at least the possibility of continental solutions. With largely nonpredatory neighbors to its north and south, and oceans and fish to its east and west ("our liquid assets," one historian once called them[4]), American presidents had more control and a better margin for success. Even the foreign policy challenges faced by the first three presidents who got America's feet wet in the world—William McKinley, Theodore Roosevelt, and Woodrow Wilson—paled before the complexity of those that the second Roosevelt would encounter, let alone his successors.

All of this would be complicated enough. But four additional elements in the postwar period have emerged to make presidential greatness harder to achieve in our system. Not all emerged at the same time or to the same degree. And of course, specific context always needs to be identified in trying to determine why particular presidents succeed and fail. Still, together these factors have widened the gap between presidential expectations and delivery, all but guaranteeing a wild ride for our presidents and for us. The presidency has always been an implausible job; hopefully it has not become an impossible one. As Lyndon Johnson told Nixon four decades ago: "Before you get to the presidency, you think you can do anything. You think you're the most powerful leader since God . . . the office is kind [of] like the little country boy [who] found the hoochie-koochie show at the carnival; once he'd paid his dime and got inside the tent: It ain't exactly as it was advertised."[5]

FIVE

FDR's High Bar

HARRY TRUMAN WOULD FEEL IT FIRST, BARELY A day or so after being sworn in as America's thirty-third president. It was the afternoon of Roosevelt's funeral service in the East Room of the White House. Robert Sherwood, a close Roosevelt aide, recalled three individuals that day: a terminally ill Harry Hopkins, looking like his life had ended with FDR's death; Harry Truman, who upon entering the East Room saw scores of FDR loyalists, none of whom even rose from their seats out of respect for the new president; and Eleanor Roosevelt, for whom everyone did stand.[1] Truman's indignities would not stop there. On the funeral train to Hyde Park, he heard Secretary of the Interior Harold Ickes going on and on about how the country was going to hell because there was no leadership anymore after FDR.[2]

Historian William Leuchtenburg, who wrote a wonderful book on the subject, called this FDR's shadow; I describe it as Roosevelt's high bar.[3] But however you render it, Roosevelt's legacy would continue to dominate, inspire, and haunt all of his successors. When Roosevelt collapsed and died from a cerebral hemorrhage at Warm Springs, Georgia, on April 12, 1945, the mold of America's greatest twentieth-century president was shattered. And that shattering left behind the image of a heroic presidency whose pieces would never be reassembled in quite the same way. More specifically, it left a gap between expectations and delivery on presidential performance that has never been closed or, in the minds of many, never even adequately narrowed. FDR created a new and impossible standard for what many Americans thought they needed, wanted, and expected from their presidents.

Love him or hate him. Praise him for fashioning a new relationship between Americans and their government or criticize him for that new dependency, FDR created the parameters within which all of his successors would operate. None would surpass him; all would at some point be compared unfavorably with him; and all, without exception, would invoke his name. Even Ronald Reagan, the nemesis of big government, admired Roosevelt's wartime leadership and as president did not eliminate the entitlements Roosevelt had institutionalized. Indeed, at the 1980 Republican National Convention in Detroit, Reagan enjoined the disbelieving delegates to fulfill FDR's promise, prompting the *New York Times* the next day to describe him as "Franklin D. Reagan."[4] And if Reagan—whose father had headed the Dixon, Illinois, Works Progress Administration (WPA), one of FDR's New Deal alphabet agencies—was not going to publicly walk away from Roosevelt, none of Roosevelt's other successors would either.

Truman would struggle for years with his FDR problem. Winning the 1948 election in his own right would help, as would his signature postwar initiatives such as the Truman Doctrine. But most of the policies of the Truman years had their origins in Roosevelt's, including Truman's decision to use atomic weapons against Japan. As late as Truman's second term, Washington journalists still wrote, "When Franklin Roosevelt died in 1945 and Harry Truman took his place, it was as if the star of the show had left and his role had been taken by a spear carrier from the mob scene."[5]

Indeed the Roosevelt legacy was unique in relation to his successors. Only George Washington, maybe Jefferson, had more personal contact or influence over his successors. FDR would be directly involved in advancing the careers of at least three of his successors. He had chosen Truman as vice president, appointed Eisenhower to command the Normandy invasion, and had a direct impact on advancing the political career of a young Lyndon Johnson, who would make Roosevelt not only a role model but also a rival to be bested. Indeed, on election night November 1964, Johnson seemed to be more interested in whether his share of the popular vote exceeded FDR's in the 1936 election (it did) than in trouncing Barry Goldwater.[6]

As time passed, the personal connection and influence would invariably wane. Kennedy, Nixon, Carter, and Ford all had less of a connection but could summon up FDR's name when convenient and distance themselves when it was not. And even though Bill Clinton's centrism and capacity for triangulation (much like FDR's) would create pushback from his liberal base, it was Clinton who presided at the dedication of the FDR memorial in May 1997, touting FDR as "the greatest president of this great American century."[7]

Unlike Washington and Lincoln, FDR was not a "halo" president. He was nearer to our own time and in many ways much more the triangulating, manipulative pol than a venerated, saintlike figure. The controversy over his memorial attests to it. Congress would come up $10 million short, and the money for the monument on the National Mall had to be raised from private donors.[8] But there is no denying his legacy. One journalist described him as the "Paul Bunyan" of American presidents, but in this case a larger than life figure rooted firmly in history.[9] Even with his mistakes and failures, his accomplishments were stunning and incomparable.

Roosevelt was a presidential perfect storm. He reflected a confluence of elements that produced an almost idealized conception of presidential power and image never to appear again. If you wanted to create a more compelling marriage of man, moment, and mission in a laboratory, you could not do it. His voice, persona, and capacity to surmount his own paralysis restores confidence and faith in a nation whose spirit has been crushed by the Great Depression. And he endures not through a single term or two, but almost through four, leading America through an epic world war against the forces of evil and then to the position of the world's most consequential power. Throw in some hubris (a scheme to pack the Supreme Court and purge unfriendly southern Democrats) and some human weaknesses (his adultery and arrogance) and you have a tale not even Hollywood could improve upon. Indeed, FDR dies in office, further enhancing the drama of his sacrifice. And he passes away before the complexities of conversion to a peacetime economy and Cold War could take their toll even on a president as savvy as he.

Blessing for the nation; curse for his successors. Teddy Roosevelt and Woodrow Wilson may have played formative roles in laying the groundwork for the modern presidency, but Franklin Roosevelt was the first modern president and by any standard laid the basis for a modern America at home and abroad.

The number of firsts—even 200 years plus into the nation's story—is impressive both in terms of domestic accomplishments and foreign policy. The Republicans and southern Democrats may have thought that by passing the Twenty-Second Amendment in 1947 (ratified in 1951 and limiting a president's tenure to two terms) they were getting even with Roosevelt. But in eliminating the possibility of another FDR, they actually ensured his uniqueness and greatness. No president could now rival, let alone best, him.

The problem for his successors and for anyone looking at the issue of presidential greatness is an obvious one. Roosevelt's performance risks pricing greatness out of the market. Who else among his twelve successors can compete? In almost every category—including longevity, impact, wartime leadership, media mastery, durability of coalition, ensuring party control—FDR seems to have cornered the market. Both the country and the presidency still play by the rules he set down. Even today, we continue to measure a president's performance by FDR's Hundred Days, an absurd metric. Evaluating a president's performance at a time when he likely knows less about the job than at any other point in his presidency, and when even his opponents are likely to give him the most leeway, makes little sense. As one smart journalist noted, "There are things you can do in 100 days—breed rabbits, read all of Marcel Proust, program your VCR, lose 20 pounds. Reinventing government isn't one of them."[10]

Perhaps the most dynamic aspect of FDR's legacy is the expectations he created both about our conception of the power of the presidency and the role that government now plays in our lives. Roosevelt may not have intended it this way, but the growth of the administrative state combined with America's role in the world has created a situation, to use James Q. Wilson's notion, that politics in America—once about only a few things—"today . . . is about nearly everything."[11] And for better and worse too, that began with Roosevelt.

The New Deal and its successor programs in LBJ's Great Society have expanded the reach of government in a way that would have surprised and likely disappointed even Roosevelt. And this is not just a product of the Democrats. No Republican administration has seriously challenged New Deal or Great Society entitlements; not even Ronald Reagan, who expanded the size of government and increased federal spending. Identifying the proper *role* of government may be the most critical issue separating the two main parties today; but both have broken the barrier to legitimizing big government as a vital force in our lives. Roosevelt made it possible. And in doing so he created a set of larger-than-life expectations about what most Americans want from their presidents and the presidency. In fighting the last truly good war and laying the basis for a period of prosperity during which government was actually perceived to be competent and respectable, FDR created a frame of reference for evaluating the presidency that would be impossible for his successors to match.

SIX

Not Your
Grandfather's Crisis

THERE IS REALLY NO OTHER WAY TO SAY IT. IN American politics, the greatest moments in the presidency are driven above all by crisis, and not just by your garden variety emergency. They result from calamities that are hot, combustible, and inescapable. During these moments, presidents either step up or they do not. There is no running away, hiding, or delaying action. Indeed, some of the finest hours in the post-FDR presidency flowed from leaders who acted either in the context of a Cold War crisis or, in the case of Lyndon Johnson, in response to the trauma following the assassination of John Kennedy and the turmoil and violence accompanying the civil rights movement. But as George W. Bush would discover, presidential reputations are made or broken not only by how chief executives respond immediately to national exigencies but how they handle them over time, and how presidents use them in an effort to lead the nation.

The fact that heroic greatness in the presidency has been absent since our last truly sustained nation-encumbering crisis—World War II—should not surprise us. We have already touched on why national emergencies are necessary to trigger and broaden the possibility of strong, even heroic, presidential action. The framers may not exactly have intended it this way. But they created a system that allowed a powerful presidency under certain constraints. The system—with its checks, balances, shared and separated powers—could be made to respond but not easily. Mobilizing the system, creating a consensus for action in a governing system that demanded it, let alone laying the basis for transformative change, required real urgency and threat—prospects of real pain out of which our best presidents were able to extract real long-term gain. Otherwise, the system, oriented toward incremental and evolutionary rather than revolutionary change, just could not be tamed or directed toward big change.

And so the ghost of FDR still hovers. The crises that his successors confronted were real, serious, and complex: the challenges of postwar conversion to a peacetime economy; those generated by the foreign policy challenges of Cold War, including the ever-present danger of nuclear war; others triggered by social unrest, such as the struggle for civil rights and crisis in the inner cities; still more by the various economic dislocations and downturns; and of course the crisis posed by terrorism, 9/11, and its aftermath. Still, for all the misery, suffering, angst, and dislocation these modern crises generated, they would differ from the foundational emergencies our earlier presidents confronted in three key aspects.

First, our modern-day crises were not nearly as nation-encumbering. Neustadt's notion of "in-government crises," as opposed to the out-of-government challenges that would impact the majority of Americans in some consequential way, is a good term. In 1860, the northern states had 22 million inhabitants; 10 percent served in the Union army during the Civil War, more than 360,000 died. Indeed, new studies now suggest that traditional estimates of both northern (360,222) and southern (258,000) deaths are too low by as much as 20 percent.[1] That would raise the total deaths to a staggering 750,000. In World War II, out of a population of some 130 million people, about 12 percent served. It captures a sense of the remoteness of more recent crises that leave most Americans untouched, uninvolved, and disengaged.

A fascinating Gallup poll in December 2013 measuring Americans' satisfaction with their personal lives, as opposed to their satisfaction with the direction of the country, reflected that reality. In 34 years of polling there had never been a wider margin between the first (79 percent) and the second (21 percent).[2] One way to read the results is to assume that however dire the country's condition, most people still remained positive about their personal circumstances. You might expect a different result had the country been in real turmoil—nation-encumbering economic crisis or war. The operative point is that if people are feeling that good about their personal circumstances, there is little reason for them to press their elected representatives for big solutions and thus little urgency for politicians to act. This absence of urgency—sure, things may not be all that great in the country as a whole, but I'm doing fine—partly explains why big crisis is required to move the system to act, and why, in the absence of comprehensive crisis, politicians seem loath to do so.

With some notable exceptions, the Cold War was in essence an in-government crisis. It became a way of life, routinized, with accepted rules of behavior that kept it contained and manageable. There were exceptions of course. For two weeks in October 1962, the country watched and worried as tension with the Soviet Union over missiles in Cuba threatened to go nuclear. It would be the only such moment in the US relationship with the former Soviet Union. In October 1973 an Arab-Israeli war also raised great power tensions. But both came and went quickly, albeit with important consequences for diplomacy and national security, but far less for the nation as a whole. And maybe this drives the point. The Vietnam War, on the other hand, particularly as the US role escalated between 1965 and 1969, spilled out into the streets and the university campuses. Combined with trouble in the inner cities and the civil rights movement, the war contributed heavily to the turmoil and dislocation that paradoxically produced an expectation and need for change. The war would hurt Johnson. But the times made his historic legislative achievements on civil rights and social issues possible.

September 11, of course, was different—at least initially. October 1962 carried the possibility of a nuclear exchange; but 9/11 was a real horror. No foreign enemy had ever attacked the continental United States in any serious manner since the British burned Washington in 1812. But the attacks on September 11, 2001, and the War on Terror it triggered, like the Cold War, soon became routine for the vast majority of Americans who were not part of the military or the intelligence agencies or working in homeland security. It was a kind of Cold War redux with its own rules and routine, though clearly much closer to home. Airline travel became exponentially more annoying and tedious. Coping with Transportation Security Administration guidelines, color-coded warning threats, and longer lines at airports may have been costly and inconvenient, but any real sense of sustained crisis or sense of national purpose quickly evaporated.

In terms of mobilizing the public, the president's messages were either confusing or nonexistent. On one hand, President George W. Bush described the stakes as focused on nothing less than the survival of the civilized world; on the other, when asked what Americans were expected to do against the backdrop of such a profound crisis, the president's answers seemed bizarrely disconnected: "I ask you to live your lives and hug your children . . . I ask your continued participation and confidence in the American economy . . . please continue praying for the victims of terror and their families, for those in uniform and for our great country."[3]

The desire to maintain normalcy in the face of al-Qaeda's efforts to disrupt it was understandable. And President Bush deserves enormous credit for preventing another attack on the homeland during his remaining seven years. But he gets very low marks for not even attempting to use the crisis for some broader purpose or end. Perhaps it was unrealistic and just too much to ask. In a nation this large, diverse, diffuse, and distracted, moments of real unity and focus are rare. 9/11 was one of those rare national moments. And yet there was no broader call for participation, no sustained messaging or strategy for involving the public in any national enterprise—no call to national service; no effort to educate Americans about the world from which the attacks came; and no national mobilization for energy self-sufficiency.

In fact, the wars that 9/11 produced in Afghanistan and Iraq would do the opposite and reinforce a trend that has been the norm for almost two generations. Consider the issue of military service in Congress. In the 95th Congress (1977–1978) a combined 77 percent of the House and the Senate had served in the armed forces. In 2013, only 20 percent of the Senate and 20.5 percent of the House had served.[4] Far from creating a sense of shared sacrifice, investment, and obligation, most Americans were insulated further from any immediate sense of crisis or involvement. An all-volunteer army, the public's confusion over the wars' purposes, and the wars' longevity created a bizarre situation in which most Americans had little connection to what would become the two longest wars in American history. As Defense Secretary Robert Gates only half-proudly claimed in a September 2010 speech at Duke University, at no time in American history have wars been fought with a smaller percentage of its citizens in uniform full time—2.4 million active and reserve in a country of 300-plus million people, or less than 1 percent.[5] And neither the generals nor the politicians seemed to want it any other way. The former preferred a volunteer military; the latter were spared the political risks of advocating national service. One can only surmise that was part of the reason these wars have lasted as long as they have. The army is at war, historian David Kennedy observed, "The country is not."[6]

Second, the kind of crises (and wars) America faced in the post-1945 period proved to be more pointless than purposeful. In 1933 and 1941 FDR confronted what you might call functional emergencies, the kind that generated real consensus, allowed effective national policy to emerge, and perhaps, in rare instances, actually created a basis for insti-tutional change under the right leadership.

We need to be careful here. The containment policies pursued by every president from Harry Truman to Ronald Reagan did produce an end to the Cold War on terms quite favorable to the United States. We won; the Russians lost. And more than a few of our post–World War II presidents—Truman, Eisenhower, Kennedy, Nixon, and of course Rea-gan—made their presidential foreign policy reputations in a world de-fined by the challenge of trying to achieve that ultimate victory. Nuclear war was avoided, as were direct confrontations with the Russians; and under Democratic and Republican presidents alike the basis of a longer-term, stable relationship with the Soviet Union was developed.

Still, the proxy wars that did define much of that struggle, Korea and Vietnam, were divisive, with outcomes that ranged from stalemate to outright defeat, and in the case of both the Johnson and Nixon ad-ministrations led to policies in Southeast Asia and at home that would take a frightful toll on the credibility of the presidency and on Ameri-cans' trust and confidence in their government. No twentieth-century war would be as kind to an American president as the Second World War was to Roosevelt. And none would allow a president to ask as much of the American people, nor do more to leave the United States in a stronger position at home and abroad. The war was a triple win: it pulled America out of the Depression, made its economy the stron-gest in the world, and transformed it into the world's greatest power, a liberator of people and a force for freedom and good. The war had this resonance because it was just; it was imperative, its objectives were clear, and victory total.

When I interviewed Jimmy Carter for this book, I asked him why we have not had another great president since FDR. Without hesitating, he replied, "Because we haven't had another good war."[7] He may well have been right. The last "good" one was World War II. The Asian wars have gotten many presidents, including Harry Truman and Lyndon Johnson, into varying degrees of trouble. Even George H. W. Bush's well-managed and necessary war to drive Saddam Hussein out of Kuwait could not help him win reelection.

Third, our modern crises and wars seem diffuse, harder to pin down, and systemic, without clear-cut outcomes, let alone victories. The wars in Afghanistan and Iraq are sad but true reflections of these new kinds of crises, at least on the foreign policy side. Initially, there was support. But their complexity and lack of clear goals led to frustration and lack of interest. And they drag on. After eight years, the United States is now out of Iraq. Now in its thirteenth year, the war in Afghanistan persists. Indeed, the standard for victory was not determined by how we can win, but rather how, when, and under what circumstances we can leave. And extrication is really not the only metric by which you want to measure the performance of the world's greatest power, particularly when what transpires after we depart will likely undo much of what we have accomplished while we were there and will shape matters far more after we are gone. These two post-9/11 wars, certainly Iraq, may well come to reflect negatively on the legacy of George W. Bush. And if they help the reputation of Barack Obama it will be because he ended them.

Even the war against al-Qaeda, perhaps our most productive crisis (we have not been attacked again, and Osama bin Laden and most of his lieutenants are dead), provides no real sense of finality. It is rightly a long, justifiable, and mandatory struggle; the protection of the homeland is a president's most important responsibility. But it is messy, complicated, and creates all kinds of unintended consequences: the use of drones and signature strikes results in the loss of innocent life and hatred toward the United States that only generates new terrorists; the dismantling of al-Qaeda Central has coincided with the creation or strengthening of affiliates, contractors, and spinoffs in East and North Africa, Yemen, and Iraq and Syria; and the National Security Agency's comprehensive collection dragnet of metadata for phone records designed to preempt attacks on the United States has led to vast government overreach and intrusion of privacy on millions of Americans.

Finally, continental problems that absorbed the attention of our earlier presidents have now become global and are often well beyond a president's control. To a degree, that has been true for much of the twentieth century. Now an integrated world of global markets, international financial flows, debt, and transnational oil creates a dangerous intercontinental dependency on outside events almost impossible for any president to manage. The discrete, scary threats—the ones we actually overcame, such as Hitler, the Soviet Union, Osama bin Laden—are gone. And in their place much less defined ones, like structural unemployment and loss of workforce competiveness, have emerged—scary too in the sense that they seem much harder to understand, let alone resolve. But not scary enough that they can generate the urgency and consensus required for resolution. It was no coincidence that Ronald Reagan, as our last truly Cold Warrior president, seemed to acquire a kind of mastery and authority in office for hastening the demise of the former Soviet Union. It was a clear victory we could understand and pocket. Finding and killing Osama bin Laden had finality, too. But the fight against al-Qaeda and its subsidiaries will at best always be a work in progress. Indeed, it often resembles a global game of whack-a-mole: we hit them in Afghanistan and Pakistan, they pop up somewhere else.

It is the same for our domestic challenges. Debt, deficit, decaying infrastructure, health-care costs, educational reform, alternative energy sources and dependence on hydrocarbons, and what is now a structural unemployment with many pre-2007 jobs unlikely to return—all are slower yet still deadly bleeds that over time sap the nation's strength and will. These problems took years to evolve and will require years to resolve. Still, they lack the relentlessness and unforgiving character of our earlier calamities. And perhaps that is part of the reason they guarantee division, delay, and less urgency instead of the unity, consensus, and opportunity required for decisive action.

The changing nature of America's crises and challenges presents unique problems for modern presidents. The good news is that the devastating calamities of our earlier history have passed. The bad news for presidents seeking to do great deeds is that the opportunities for heroic action in the presidency are reduced too. One can only imagine where we would have been on the presidential performance scale had there been no Cold War. That would have deprived half a dozen American presidents of legacies and credentials burnished in the foreign policy arena, often a refuge and sanctuary for presidential initiative when domestic issues, particularly economic downturns, seem beyond the capacity of presidents to resolve.

Without the Cold War, most of our postwar presidents would have been forced to turn their attention to domestic matters, where they would have had far less latitude to maneuver. A president's capacity to affect economic recovery and growth is limited. And these days the problems that confront us—call them the six deadly Ds: debt, deficit, dysfunctional politics, dependence on hydrocarbons, deteriorating infrastructure, and declining educational standards—have no immediate solutions, divide rather than unite us, and require a president to focus on close cooperation with Congress as well as pay close attention to coalition building and party politics. With the exceptions of Johnson and Reagan, none of the post-FDR presidents were that adept at party management, or even all that interested.

Crisis is critical for creating political consensus and latitude for effective presidential performance, therefore it carries serious consequences for successful governance. First, if you need a truly big crisis to move the system, you're faced with the perverse prospect that the country has to be at risk or threatened before you can save it. This calls into question the whole notion of strategic leadership and long-term planning in which a president anticipates a challenge and works to create the right environment to take it on. It's hard to identify one truly momentous legislative change that materialized in this way. Even a less threatening crisis in which a president builds on a moment—as Johnson did in the wake of Kennedy's assassination to carry on his predecessor's legacy and to promote his own on the civil rights issue—is a rarity. Obama's Affordable Care Act may well be an example of how a determined president with a focused agenda (and enough votes) used a moment (at the beginning of his presidency) to do something none of his predecessors had accomplished. But Johnson had a legitimizing partisan dominance, including large numbers of Republicans for both his major domestic achievements. Obama did not. Passed in a highly partisan environment with a public that remains deeply divided, and a troubled roll out, the future of the Obama initiative, despite some of its popular aspects, is even now very uncertain.

Second, crisis or no crisis, today there is a growing lack of confidence in government that makes the president's task all the more difficult. It is stunning to consider the paradox that at a time when we are more dependent on government than ever, we seem to have less faith in those who are charged with delivering it. A *New York Times*/CBS poll in October 2011 found that 89 percent of Americans didn't trust government to do the right thing, the highest level ever recorded.[8] Pew's October 2013 survey on popular attitudes toward trust in government revealed that only 19 percent of Americans trusted the government to do what is right "just about always" or "most of the time."[9] By comparison, in 1958, 73 percent of Americans answered in the affirmative. A decade later it was still in the mid-60th percentile. Faith in Congress, of course, is at a record low, and even if a president's personal approval rating is respectable, the loss of faith in the institutions of governance or the system itself adds to growing cynicism and despair.

And that popular cynicism applies both to government and large corporations. Between the federal government's response to Hurricane Katrina, BP's negligence in the *Deepwater Horizon* oil spill, the Wall

Street credit-derivative bubble, the 2013 government shutdown, and the NSA spying revelations, there is a broad mistrust of the entire system's institutions. Both Occupy Wall Street and the Tea Party movements drive home the point: one hammers big corporations; the other attacks big government. We do not have one crisis to focus on; instead we have a system in crisis. When you mix polarization in Congress and a frustrated, angry, and cynical public together with little consensus about how to go about addressing long-term problems, you have a very good recipe for paralysis. In the current environment without a single unifying crisis to create urgency or consensus for action, a president is trapped by too many problems to manage, too many unrealistic expectations, and a political system that is too polarized and divided. And yet we still, perhaps quite understandably, look to him to fix it. In the 1990 revision of his classic *Presidential Power and the Modern Presidents* (originally published in 1960), Richard Neustadt remained convinced that "weakness" was still the presidency's dominant theme.[10]

SEVEN

The President of America the Ungovernable?

"THE PRESIDENT NEEDS HELP." SO FAMOUSLY DE-clared the 1937 Brownlow Committee in its report on administrative management in the White House.[1]

The irony of course was that Roosevelt would need that help far less than his successors. And the help that was needed was not just more presidential assistants. Amazingly, the Brownlow Committee would recommend only six additional aides. What FDR's successors needed, though, was assistance in a different department: how to navigate the increasingly perilous waters of American politics in the decades after World War II.

One of the greatest navigational hazards confronting presidents would be the increasingly polarized nature of American politics. For the first few decades after the Second World War, America's presidents would get something of a breather. War, Cold War, and the Roosevelt legacy of productive and functional government would create a consensus and degree of bipartisanship that neither Truman nor Eisenhower would challenge. A post-Roosevelt faith in government and trust in its effectiveness and integrity was still very much the norm in American politics, and would remain so even into the late 1960s.

The 1950s had its own share of convulsions, tensions, and crises to be sure, including McCarthyism, an unpopular war in Korea, anxiety over Russia's rise—particularly the Soviet launch of Sputnik—and an economic recession at the decade's end. But on balance, after years of economic crisis and world war, those years reflected a strong desire for peacetime normalcy. Indeed, sandwiched between the 1940s with its focus on unity, sacrifice, and sense of mission and the turbulence and fractiousness of the 1960s, the 1950s seems today like a lost never-never land. And the popularity of the grandfatherly war hero, Dwight Eisenhower, reflected the popular desire that the country hark back to a simpler, less contentious time. Ike, the archives now tell us, turned out to be much more the skilled, behind-the scenes bureaucratic leader and manipulator than his amiable, uninvolved, and golf-playing image led many to believe. By comparison with his immediate successors there was not much drama. Instead there was a cool-headed realism and common sense when it came to avoiding military adventures abroad, particularly in Southeast Asia.

That sense of well-being, however, would not last long. By the late 1960s, under pressure of an unpopular war in Southeast Asia, a struggle for civil rights, and rioting in America's cities, that consensus fractured, divided American politics, stressed the public's faith in government, and undermined the credibility of both Democratic and Republican presidents. At the same time, presidents were faced with more responsibilities and challenges. But now more and more the president's agenda had to be pursued against the background of a political environment that grew ever divisive and dysfunctional. Most of FDR's successors would have a tough time of it. With some exceptions, managing their parties and politics proved increasingly difficult. After all, not until 1980, almost two decades after Eisenhower, would America elect another president who actually served out two terms.

This process of polarization evolved gradually in response to many factors, including the realignment of the South, which has become solidly Republican, and the decline of the liberal wing of the Republican Party in the Midwest and Northeast. But by the 1990s—and most certainly as America entered a new century—the divisions between the two major parties began to crystallize and become almost tribal: intense party loyalty trumped logic, subservience to the party identity dominated what was best for the national interest, and debate became intensely personal. The debate raged on as to whether the American public was so fundamentally divided or just the political elites that represented them. But there was no question that a major divide existed in Washington, reflecting at least the views of the increasingly polarized bases of the two major parties on issues ranging from the role of the government to the environment to what to do about taxes and entitlements.

A June 2012 Pew poll on trends in American values told the story. As Americans headed into the 2012 elections, the results described a stunningly stark picture of a nation in which politics divides more than race, gender, class, or age. The average partisan gap has nearly doubled since 1987. And on specific issues the divide is even wider. On the scope and performance of government that gap has grown from 6 percentage points to 33 today; on support for a social safety net, from 21 points to 41. Both parties have become smaller and more ideologically homogeneous. Republicans are dominated by self-described conservatives, while a smaller but growing number of Democrats call themselves liberals. The divisions extend to independents as well, most of who lean toward one major party or another. Not surprisingly, the party bases seem persuaded that those who represent them are not doing the job they should. A full 71 percent of Republicans and 58 percent of Democrats believe their parties are not standing up to defend their traditional beliefs.[2]

It is important to maintain perspective here. Since the nation's founding, polarized, fractious, even violent politics has been a constant.

Arguments over the Jay treaty with Great Britain in the 1790s, the Alien and Sedition Acts, and the bitter struggle between Federalists and the Democratic Republicans created a vituperative and acrimonious political environment that dwarfs our divisions today. Replete with rival newspapers sponsored by elected officials, mob violence, and dueling, America's politics were far more deadly than any noisy cable news battle between Fox News and MSNBC, or a "You lie!" outburst from a Republican representative during Barack Obama's address before Congress.

Between 1830 and 1860 the debate over slavery stressed our political system to the breaking point. Beginning in 1854, the Kansas territory witnessed terrible massacres and violence between pro- and antislavery forces. And then in 1861, the system broke down into civil war. Indeed, it is worth noting that this was the only time in our history when the political system could not contain or accommodate, let alone resolve, the fundamental divide that split the country and its political elites. And the historians tell us that partisan debate and rancor over the Gold Standard in the 1890s and political divisions during the 1930s were far more partisan and volatile than those today. Indeed, it is fascinating to consider that the most transformative moments in American history came not only from presidents with strong majorities who could draw significant bipartisan support; those moments emerged also out of intense partisan conflict and discord. How else in a political system oriented and designed for incremental change can transformations occur, except through partisan dominance? Lincoln, FDR, and Johnson were polarizers and party men. At the same time circumstances and their own capacities combined to allow these presidents to mobilize bipartisan support too, a fact that made their transformative changes sustainable and legitimate.

Today, we have created a far different political reality. Instead of functional partisan dominance, we have unproductive polarization that has proven dangerously dysfunctional and disturbingly durable. America is not ungovernable. Congress passed significant bipartisan legislation, including on tax reform and immigration (1986), welfare reform (1995), and educational reform (2001). Indeed, the 111th Congress (2008–2010) was one of the most productive since the Johnson years and produced major initiatives on the economic stimulus, health care, and financial regulations.[3] But unlike the historic 87th and 88th Congresses of the Kennedy and Johnson years, those legislative accomplishments of the 111th occurred without bipartisan support and against the backdrop of a very divided public. Despite its accomplishments, barely a quarter of the public approved of its performance. That Congress and the 112th, which has been the least productive in congressional history, were perhaps among the most ideologically polarized.[4] The most conservative Democrat was more liberal than the most liberal Republican. In her fascinating piece "Polarized We Govern?," Brookings scholar Sarah A. Binder concluded that the distance between the parties ideologically has all but returned to heights not seen since the nineteenth century. Today, 75 percent of the issues on Washington's agenda are subject to legislative gridlock, including certainly the biggest ones.[5]

The increasing divisiveness in American politics would further narrow the president's political space and create fewer opportunities for coalition building and productive, presidentially inspired legislating, let alone historic breakthroughs. In the Bush and Obama years, partisan polarization has surged. The relationships that had formerly made serious bipartisan cooperation possible on big issues have decayed and collapsed, leaving a kind of Manichaean, apocalyptic struggle between light and dark in their wake. Just being a Republican or a Democrat seems to conjure up stereotypes and prejudices, which may also serve to negatively filter information in a skewed matter. With the center shrinking, Congress pressured by their bases to toe the party line, and political activists rewarded for adopting uncompromising positions, how can any president take on the tough problems, such as deficit reduction and health care, and marshal the large majorities that are required to pass and sustain transformative change? If such legislation passes with only narrow partisan majorities, can it be sold as legitimate and broad-based? Will it be sustainable without credible support from the opposition party? And how, with an increasingly fractured political establishment and channeled electorate, can you produce real change on big issues without it?

Today, there is almost no overlap between the voting patterns of conservative Democrats in the House and the most liberal Republicans, a trend not seen since the Civil War. Is it even conceivable in today's polarized politics that a second-term president could reform the tax code and our immigration system in a single year, particularly in the run-up to midterms?

But in 1986, 28 years ago, it was. That year, seemingly light years away, in circumstances that reflected something of a reverse universe to our own, a Republican president and Senate cooperating with a Democratic majority in the House passed a fundamental revision of the tax code, and within months an overhaul of the nation's immigration laws too. What made it possible then and impossible today were strong moderate factions in each party; a president—Ronald Reagan—committed to tax reform and enough influential members of both parties willing to work with him; and what Norman Ornstein calls a "problem-solving caucus of legislators who were actually interested in the issues and in making a difference rather than just making a political point."[6] Indeed, today that kind of functional bipartisan caucus has given way to a stunning partisanship. In 1986, the number of truly competitive districts where voters selected a member of Congress from one party and a presidential candidate from the other was 45 percent; it declined to 26 percent by 1998, to 14 percent by 2006, to a mere 6 percent today, or 26 seats.[7]

The problem is not just divided government. Even during this period, legislation on welfare reform, tax reduction, trade agreements, national security reorganization after 9/11, and campaign finance reform all became law, just to list a few. Instead, the problem-solving center has vanished. Even during the 1960s and 1970s when Vietnam and civil rights roiled the political waters, the percentage of moderates was over 30 percent. A decade ago, it was less than 10 percent.[8] Now it is really anyone's guess how to construct a working center that can overcome the party faithful or the fragmenting of various groups, such as independents. Congress—the practical repository of legislative and political power in this country—has indeed gotten progressively redder and bluer, and of course more dysfunctional. Today bipartisanship does not mean creating a center against the margins; it means keeping your own party in line and stripping a few votes away from the other guys. In his 2010 health-care legislation, President Obama was not even able to do that.

Polarization has created another huge downside too. It erodes civility, and costs a president and congressional leaders the kind of personal relationships that were once critically important to getting things done in Washington. Historian Ted Widmer tells us that the founders, however much they disagreed with one another and competed over their reputations and place in history, spent a great deal of time together and also in written correspondence. The bipartisanship of the 1940s through the 1960s was grounded not just on smart politics but also on smart, tough, and accessible personalities who connected with one another.

The relationships were driven by necessity and were not touchy-feely, but they made American politics work. Truman and Arthur Vandenberg on the Marshall Plan; Johnson and Everett Dirksen on civil rights; Reagan and Tip O'Neill on Social Security; Reagan and Dan Rostenkowski on tax reform; even Clinton and Newt Gingrich on welfare reform—these did not exist in a vacuum. They came out of a context in which each side had a stake in the other's success, if only for the moment. Today, we seem to confront a zero-sum-game mentality in which the opposite is true. In Republican and Democratic parties today, it seems there can only be one winner—regardless of how destructive it is to the national interest. When bipartisanship occurs today, as it did on raising the debt ceiling or payroll tax cuts, it is usually grudging, last-minute, and narrowly drawn, resulting from the failure to cut more meaningful deals.

Today personal animus is too often a feature of our politics. In 2004 and 2005, only 15 percent of Democrats approved of George W. Bush (the figure would reach as low as 9 percent in 2006–2007), a man whom many mocked and vilified.[9] In years past, three to four times that percentage of Democrats approved of Republican presidents Eisenhower, Nixon (before Watergate), Ford, and Reagan. And George W. Bush was easy to relate to, a guy from Texas who, despite his elite background and president father, loved baseball, barbecue, and chopping wood on his ranch.

Indeed, if Bush was a polarizing figure, fast-forward to Barack Hussein Obama, whom Gallup polling in 2010 deemed the most polarizing first-year president since the organization began tracking the issue.[10] Here was a leader who was not exactly in the mold of traditional American presidents—the first black president, with a middle name Hussein, a Kenyan father, a sojourn in Indonesia, time spent as a community activist in Chicago, and an education at elite universities and law schools. For many Americans, particularly as the economy got worse, Obama became and remains Satan's finger on earth—a wild-eyed, big-spending liberal committed to socialism at home and apologizing for America's mistakes abroad. The durability of the birther issues even among some of his Republican opponents in the 2012 campaign for the presidency suggests that the anti-Obama partisan tropes continue to resonate.

Contemporary presidents also have to contend with another worrisome trend. Rising negative views of politicians and Congress inexorably lead to diminishing faith in government too. Presidents can run against Congress for a time, particularly when the legislative branch's credibility with the public is at an all-time low (9 percent), but eventually, rampant partisanship can undermine a president's credibility too.[11]

We have three distinct branches in the federal system, but the executive and legislative are, to be sure, mutually dependent on one another if government is going to be productive. A polarized Congress leads to gridlock that prevents the president from carrying out his agenda and ultimately undermines popular faith and confidence in Washington. This is particularly true during difficult economic times when people are hurting. Obama is not being blamed for what his predecessors left him, but increasingly he is held responsible for the failure of his own policies to improve the situation.

Today's new credibility gap about government is less related to scandal and conspiracy in the White House—as it was during the 1960s and 1970s, and briefly during the 1980s (Iran-Contra) and 1990s (Lewinsky); instead it is more and more about the lack of effectiveness and competency in government's overall capacity to give people what they have come to expect. People can debate and argue about how much government Americans want and need, but the government they do get ought to work and produce for them and not be hobbled or incapacitated by partisan rancor and inside-the-Washington-Beltway squabbling. On perhaps the most basic function of Congress, approving spending bills, not since 1996 have the House and Senate beat the October 1 deadline for approving all of the bills before the start of the new fiscal year.[12]

Loss of confidence in government is a very serious problem, particularly when Americans, even Tea Partiers, have become dependent on government entitlements such as Medicare, Social Security, and tax breaks—even when it is awkward or politically incorrect for them to admit it. There is a reason no American president has seriously moved against these entitlements. Forget big or small government, what Americans really want is a Washington that will work for them. Ronald Reagan was hammered in 1982 when he thought about cutting Social Security benefits for retirees. And today's Republicans face much the same problem. When US senator Marco Rubio of Florida attacks the entitlements that he believes are bankrupting America, he also has no intention of undermining a system that his own mother has paid into and benefited from. Therein lies the problem.

Here's FDR's ghost yet again. During the 1930s and 1940s, most Americans were actually convinced that government worked for them. The Democrats guided the nation through the Depression and achieved total victory in a world war. During the 1950s, under the immensely popular Dwight Eisenhower, the Republicans secured an end to the war in Korea and presided over unprecedented prosperity and opportunity. In 1964, when asked whether they trusted government to do the right thing, 75 percent of Americans said yes.[13] Contrast those numbers with the most recent *New York Times*/CBS poll indicating that 89 percent of Americans don't trust their government, or the Pew poll on trust in government conducted in October 2013, which revealed much the same thing.[14] The cause of the decline is obvious: an uncertain economy, discontent with Congress and elected officials, and a more partisan political environment. Negative reaction to government plunged even further during the health-care debate.

When numbers on trust in government plunge so does the president's credibility. In June 2013 in the wake of the NSA spying revelations, a CNN poll found that for the first time in his presidency, less than half of the respondents though Barack Obama was honest. That November, 53 percent of Americans polled did not believe the president was honest or trustworthy, findings related to the botched Affordable Care rollout and the president's misleading statements.[15] When trust falls steeply, incumbents are more likely to lose, with the president's party likely to lose the most. Following Nixon's resignation in 1974, trust in government had fallen to 36 percent from 53 percent in 1972, and Democrats made huge gains. In 1980, under Jimmy Carter, when trust levels fell to 25 percent, Republicans were the big winners; and in 1992, a collapse of confidence in government hurt both parties, especially Democrats. In 1994, Republicans gained their first majority in the House in 40 years.

Polarization and partisanship that paralyze Congress and the president and result in declining faith in government carry grave risks for the national interest. We have deep, entrenched structural problems that require cool, detached, and yet politically saleable solutions that can only be addressed over time. These slow but serious bleeds that afflict the country, from debt to dependence on hydrocarbons to decaying infrastructure, require a process to resolve them that must be owned both by Democrats and Republicans. In the past, big change in America came only with crisis and emergency, which gave presidents huge majorities; or through bipartisanship even in periods of divided government, to craft bipartisan legislation. Today neither approach is available. Indeed, we approach our challenges handicapped by a system unable and unwilling to deal with them.

Today's story is a distressing one. Our political elites have become stunningly polarized. Our politics are not just divided; they have been rent asunder by bitter, partisan, and personal attacks; on most issues the debate has been raised to a level akin to a kind of political fundamentalism. Not only do cultural issues like abortion, prayer in public schools, and gay rights carry moral overtones; now, so do economic issues, such as the role of the Federal Reserve or the size of the stimulus package. In this adversarial environment, the respective Democrat and Republican Party bases view one another not as Americans who have different points of view, but rather as nefarious agents with self-seeking agendas that can destroy the country. It's not only that in this new argue-culture making a point can be more important than making a difference; it's as if we're really not even interested in listening. Instead, the goal is to win a debate and to ready ourselves to pounce on our interlocutor's next point. Michael Gerson, Bush 43's speech writer turned *Washington Post* columnist, reminds us that civility isn't just about politeness and courtesy; it has a purpose and function.[16] If you listen and really try to understand what the other guy is saying—no matter how different the perspective—who knows, you might learn something of value that might be helpful in solving your problem. And since our problems can't be addressed through solely Democratic or Republican solutions, civility is not optional; it is imperative if we want truly good governance.

Our new polarized politics is not so new anymore. Sadly in the past twenty years it has evolved into the defining feature of our political landscape. Polarization may have some upsides. Parties are no longer Tweedledee and Tweedledum and now really do offer clear choices; the numbers of Americans voting in the past two elections are the highest since 1968 (more than 131 million in 2008 and 129 million in 2012); and the bases of the parties are clearly engaged.

But the price we pay is steep and hardly worth the benefits. Driven by a polarized Washington and a public that is also divided, particularly on the role of government, we and our presidents confront a perfect storm of genuine ideological polarization on core issues, a vanishing political center willing and able to address problems, and an increasing lack of trust in government. Together these factors have created a toxic environment that has rendered the legislative branch semidysfunctional and created huge problems for the executive too, the remaining change agent in our system.

Already constrained by checks and balances and exaggerated public expectations, the president is further hemmed in by partisanship, some of it within his own party and by the public's lack of trust in government as an active agent of effective remedy and reform. It is a cautionary tale for presidents who want to use government in this fashion or who even seek a political consensus to reduce its size. Neither Ronald Reagan nor George W. Bush got very far with Social Security reform. Barack Obama succeeded with health-care reform because he had the Democratic votes in Congress to do it. But it weakened him politically and ensured an even greater defeat for the Democrats in the 2010 midterms. The botched roll out of healthcare.gov, including his own misleading statements, further eroded his standing with the public and rescued the Republicans, who had taken the primary hit for the government shutdown in December

2013. At least temporarily, this made achieving a functional consensus almost impossible, undermined civility and partnership, and created a zero-sum mentality of winners, losers—or just plain stalemate.

The margin for the emergence of great presidents in this kind of polarized environment is really quite small. Presidents can blame their troubles on partisanship and congressional dysfunction only to a degree. They can certainly use their partisan dominance to get legislation passed. But if presidents themselves are seen as too partisan and polarizing in what they are trying to achieve, without the capacity to unite the country around some significant initiative, they take a significant hit that the opposing party is only too ready to exploit. And as we have seen, going public through compelling messaging and great speeches in an effort to bypass Congress and gain legitimacy for an agenda is severely limited. The same of course is true for acting unilaterally through executive orders; there are limits to what can be accomplished, and it usually only adds to the partisanship.

The image of a once self-described transformative and now second-term president—reelected with 51 percent of the popular vote and a more than comfortable Electoral College margin (332–206)—contrasted strongly with the Obama who laid out a strategy of governing, unilaterally if necessary, by executive order in his January 2014 State of the Union. Presidents can govern and even lead. But they will have to do so not from a sustainable center that has significant bipartisan support but from the partisan edges, a reality that will increasingly stress the system and further polarize the landscape. We have, as Stanford University's Frank Fukuyama argues, a "vetocracy" in which traditional checks and balances, interest groups, lack of trust in the state, and increasing partisanship prevent the emergence of outcomes that represent the interests of as large a part of the population as possible.[17] The president represents his party but must represent the nation too. But in this increasingly dysfunctional political climate, that is proving to be a very difficult thing to do.

EIGHT

Boxers or Briefs

MEDIA AND THE
PERSONALIZED PRESIDENCY

SITTING AT THE TOP OF THIS PRESENT-DAY pyramid of dysfunction and distrust is the modern president, fixed in the minds of the public as the go-to guy, who promised us answers and solutions to the nation's problems and said if we would be patient, there would be results. And unfairly or not (after all, the president wanted the job), we will hold him accountable for successes and failures.

The idea that we look to the president to deliver in this impossibly complex situation is a reasonable, if unrealistic, one. The president campaigns as if he is "the one," and many of us buy it every four years. Promise making, of course, is not promise keeping. But we often conflate the two. And our expectations of the president are heightened by what has become known as the personalized presidency. Presidential scholars have written extensively about this phenomenon. It is certainly not new. The framers may never have conceived of the president having a personal relationship with the people, largely out of their fear that the great man somehow might stir the masses. But there was no way an American president was going to be confined to being an administrative clerk or an appendage or subordinate to Congress. The personalized president became reality from the minute George Washington launched his two meet-the-people tours through New England and the South.

But neither Washington, with his love of hoopla and high couture (the coach he traveled in on his two tours bore a seal embossed with an ornate *GW*), nor even Kennedy, the first truly television president, could have imagined just how visible and personalized the presidency would become or how attracted Americans would become to it.[1] The elements that drive the up close and personalized presidency include the media; our own need to reduce a complex system of governance to an easily understandable narrative (one guy with a wife, kids, and a dog, stuck in a tough job); the obvious power of the president; and a more open and transparent presidential selection process that has freed candidates from closed backroom deals and controllable nominating conventions and makes them more visible (through primaries, debates, bus tours, and nonstop media coverage) and more dependent on us.

And that personal relationship starts early. To imagine that John Kennedy announced his decision to run for the presidency in January 1960, a mere eleven months before the November election, is to conjure up a political world that no longer exists in America. A full thirteen months before the November 2012 elections, we already had half a dozen Republican candidates who had been on the campaign trail for the better part of 2011. Add to this a growing trend among presidents to "go public" and make their case directly to the American people, and sprinkle in what Clinton adviser Sidney Blumenthal described as the permanent campaign (which continues from the day after a president is elected and turns governance into a nonstop effort to sell the president's image and policies and to sustain his popularity), and you have created all the ingredients for a perfect stew of unrealistic expectations that can only hype the presence, power, and promise of our man (and one day, woman) in the White House beyond any reasonable capacity to deliver.[2] By the way, this unhappy state of affairs does not result only from what the system does to the president; it is also a result of what he and his political and media advisers do to us. Selling the candidate or the president and his policies is a legitimate and inevitable aspect of democratic government. But it is not just an effort to teach, educate, or lay out tough choices. It is, when stripped to its essence, an effort to sell and to win.

For at least 40 years now we have seen our presidents up close and personal; we are now conditioned to expect nothing less than a front-row seat and to get our fair share of presidential entertainment, ritual, and drama from the White House. Within the Beltway, there is a presidential addiction. We cannot help ourselves—and may not even want to.

Anyone watching the presidential movie over the past half century can be both inspired and depressed, but never bored. Since Eisenhower retired to his farm in Pennsylvania, the presidency has been one wild and bumpy ride. It has emerged as part soap opera, part psycho drama, and part deadly serious business. The story line has been advanced by some extraordinary characters: first the drama of Kennedy and Camelot and another martyred president; next scene, the tragedy and travails of the truly larger-than-life Lyndon Johnson; next up, Richard Nixon, perhaps the most fascinating and complex character in the history of the presidency, and the Watergate scandal that did so much to damage it; followed by the short sagas of Gerald Ford, a good man whose basic goodness, decency, and resulting decision to pardon his predecessor probably made his reelection almost impossible, and of course Jimmy Carter, one of our smartest presidents, who hated politics and did not understand how to use the presidency; and then enter, stage right, a president literally from Hollywood, who did. Ronald Reagan, though not a great president like our other top performers, was great at *being* president at a time when the country needed it. The drama then winds down with the experienced and, by his own admission, visionless George H. W. Bush, and then ramps up again big-time at home and abroad for another sixteen years of roller coaster rides: eight under Bill

Clinton, compelling rascal and brilliant politician, who presided over great economic times and balanced the budget but undermined his own presidency with Monica Lewinsky; and eight under George W. Bush, who took the country into two unwinnable wars and presided over one of the worst economic crises in American history but kept America attack-free after 9/11. If you wanted to create an HBO special filled with more curious personalities, scandals and indiscretions, ups and downs, and dramatic successes and failures at home and abroad, you could not have topped the one that played out for real these many years.

All of this presidential drama points to one undeniable fact about our modern politics: our presidents have been, and will continue to be, out there on full display in a kind of presidential fishbowl that we, they, and the media swim around in together. And whether watching what goes on inside depresses or inspires, the presidential movie will play for some time to come. We may choose to tune out temporarily or change the channel. But we can always drop back in courtesy of the gargantuan 24/7 media machine that covers him.

On April 19, 1994, a young high school student from Potomac, Maryland, made pop-culture political history by posing a simple question to an American president during MTV's "Enough Is Enough" forum. "Mr. President, the world is dying to know, is it boxers or briefs?"[3] The only thing more stunning than the question itself (bold even by seventeen-year-old standards, but prompted by the show's producer), was the fact that President William Jefferson Clinton chose to answer it. "Usually briefs. I can't believe she did that," Clinton responded to a great deal of teenage laughter.

The MTV interview got a fair amount of attention, and most of the reaction played pretty positively for the hipster in chief. The *New York Times* saw Clinton's response as a way to make the presidency more understandable and approachable to a younger generation.[4] A few saw it as symbolic of everything Clinton had done to degrade and embarrass the presidency. But humor, not outrage, carried the day. A *Newsweek* piece quipped that "if a man is going to govern by the seat of his pants, as Clinton mostly does, the voters ought to know what he's sitting on."[5]

Clinton's answer about his underwear surely revealed his youthful, sharer-in-chief style as well as his political smarts in seeking to attract young voters. Another more sober president might have gently deflected the question and not risked trivializing the office of the president. Interestingly enough, candidate Barack Obama got the same question on the campaign trail and would not answer it, dismissing those kinds of questions as "humiliating."[6] But this was also a president who would prove to be no less media savvy, holding the first-ever presidential Twitter press conference in 2011.

The underwear affair was not even a minor blip in an administration that within four years would be caught up in much bigger troubles. But the episode pointed out the changing nature of the president's relationship with the media, the need to respond to and keep up with American pop culture, and the difficulty of remaining presidential in a world in which the desire to know and ask seems only eclipsed by the pressures on the man in the White House to respond. Even the more disciplined Barack Obama would fall into the pop culture trap a decade and a half later during some mindless late-night banter with *Tonight Show* host Jay Leno. The two got into a discussion of sports, first basketball then bowling. And the president offered up that he had once bowled a 129 "like the Special Olympics, or something."[7] The next day, the White House apologized and the president found himself calling Special Olympics head Tim Shriver to make amends.

The modern 24/7 nonstop media—now well into its cyber and digital phase—presents both problems and opportunities for today's presidents. Social media has created new and ever-expanding opportunities to craft and get a president's message out, though in the cluttered and noisy media world that message is often harder to hear. Quantity can edge out quality as presidents are more visible and risk overexposure, which inevitably diminishes stature and prestige. How can a president be accessible and human, yet preserve the kind of detachment and reserve that the office and effective leadership requires? Media did not create the challenge of a much diminished presidency, but it showcases it in ways a president can no longer prevent.

It was not always so complicated. The founders never envisioned such a public, personalized presidency, although the partisan press is as old as the nation itself. Indeed, in some ways, given the polarizing nature of cable and Internet news, we have come full circle. For much of the eighteenth century and a fair amount of the nineteenth, the press was affiliated with particular candidates, even presidents. Andrew Jackson set a precedent that would last until the 1860s of supporting a semi-official newspaper that represented him. It was not until the mid-1830s that a nonpartisan paper even emerged.

Not surprisingly, it was the indefatigable Teddy Roosevelt who really laid the foundations of a more public presidency and the White House's own relationship with the press. Roosevelt brought reporters directly into the White House, arranged a reporters' room, shared drafts of his speeches, critiqued their articles, used them—particularly the progressive muckrakers—as his eyes and ears on reform issues, and gave them unprecedented access to him personally at luncheons, dinners, and even during his midday shave. Woodrow Wilson would further enhance the public character of the presidency and broaden the media's exposure to the president by holding the first official press conferences.[8] He would also be the first successful presidential candidate to launch a full-blown campaign tour. Woodrow Wilson would also reintroduce the custom (which Jefferson had stopped) of delivering the State of the Union address to Congress in person rather than as a written message.[9]

For the most part, during the first two centuries or so of the nation's history, presidents were largely freed from the frenzy and intrusiveness that their modern-day successors would confront. It was not until 1860, when Abraham Lincoln was elected, that presidents would use photography for publicity purposes and to enhance their election campaigns.[10] Magazines and newspapers lacked the capacity to illustrate articles with photos until the late nineteenth century. By 1924, Americans could see their presidents in newsreels. And it was the not-so-silent Calvin Coolidge who was the first president to make use of the radio.[11] In a fascinating reflection of how fast-paced and revolutionary Americans thought even these changes were, Secretary of State Charles Evans Hughes told the *New York Times* in 1923: "We find ourselves in the age of the motor, the movie, and the radio . . . it is the day of the fleeting vision. Concentration, thoroughness, the quiet reflection that ripens the judgment are more difficult than ever."[12]

Twenty years later, Hughes's head would have been spinning still. In 1939, at the World's Fair, Franklin Roosevelt would become the first president to actually give a speech on television.[13] And his use of radio and the print media would redefine and personalize the modern presidency. No president before him, and few that followed, had so much media success. With the willing cooperation of reporters (though not the majority of their editors, who were much more critical), FDR charmed, co-opted, and controlled his own image, message, and policies.

The advent of television and the first true TV president, John F. Kennedy, altered if not revolutionized the nature of the presidency. As journalist Hedrick Smith brilliantly observed, Boss Tube replaced Boss Tweed.[14] Political parties, once responsible for the way Americans related to their politics and presidents, lost influence over the recruitment and nomination of presidential candidates and the campaign trails. By the 1970s, a new arena emerged in which media and money seemed to be the new lubricants that greased successful campaigns and elections. And money—lots of it—bought media. When Mark Hanna, President McKinley's Karl Rove, was asked what the most important things in politics were, he replied, "The first thing is money and I can't remember what the second one is."[15] Today the amount of money raised matters in the media, presidential communications scholars Kenski, Hardy, and Jamieson argue, because it provides the media with a way to measure the momentum of a candidate and it buys media time (the megaphone) at critical points in a campaign.[16]

Television would create huge opportunities for presidents who could master it (Kennedy) and liabilities for those who had a much harder time (Johnson, Nixon, Ford, Carter). Successes could be magnified, messages honed, but policy failures and personal flaws were equally microscoped and magnified. Since George Washington, presidents had always complained about biased treatment by the partisan press, fair or otherwise. Lincoln derided the "noise" and "gas" of the editorial writers of his day[17]; McKinley dubbed a convention of reporters a "Congress of inventors."[18] In his second inaugural address, Ulysses Grant actually railed against a press that heaped on him the "worse abuse and slander scarcely ever equaled in political history."[19] FDR had a "Dunce Club" to which he exiled reporters he did not like.[20]

Indeed, visibility ensured vulnerability, particularly against the backdrop of an unpopular war in Vietnam and the Watergate scandal. During the late 1960s and 1970s, an intense adversarial relationship developed between the Johnson and Nixon administrations and the media over an emerging credibility gap between what these Democratic and Republican administrations were saying and actually doing. Deception, deceit, dirty tricks, manipulation, and targeting of the press defined a level of animosity and antagonism and basic mistrust whose impact can be felt at times to this day.

By the 1980s, the golden age of television, which for some presidents had been a boon, now morphed into the not-so-golden age of cable, in which it was harder to keep up with the breathlessness and urgency of breaking news, a 24/7 news cycle, and the demand for immediate reaction. Had Charles Evans Hughes been able to look at fast-paced America at the turn of the twenty-first century, he would have believed he was visiting another planet. FDR may have mastered radio; Jack Kennedy and Ronald Reagan ruled on television; but after Reagan there would be no masters of the modern globalized media world that increasingly defined the public dynamic of American politics. By September 2012, 46 percent of Americans were getting their news online at least three times per week, with all of the up- and downsides that an increasingly hard to check, hard to verify, opinionated information world brought with it.[21]

The media did not create the basic dilemma or predicament of the modern presidency. Expectations are simply too high, the president's challenges and responsibilities too great, and the system too constraining—all aspects rooted in the politics of the American polity well before Boss Tube and the Internet made their appearance. To blame the travails of the presidency, as every White House does, on the bad media coverage it receives is as unfair as it is understandable. A mediocre president will still be a mediocre one regardless of White House spin and media coverage; the same applies to a great one. In the end it is success or failure, what gets done and what does not, that creates or undermines presidents' reputations.

Still, the media is an awesome and powerful enabler and a fierce facilitator that makes almost all the challenges a president confronts much harder. The media helps widen the gap between expectations and delivery; pumps up presidents while also dragging them down; both reflects and drives the divided and polarized politics that constrain successful public policy; and makes the presidential image more visible, valuable, and vulnerable. Indeed, there is no doubt that the promiscuity and lack of discipline on the web allows instant proliferation and immediate access to every kind of unsubstantiated rumor, innuendo, and ad hominem attack.

The old adage that Washington is really Hollywood without attractive people seems unfair, but there has always been a certain artificial quality about the two towns—one focused on image and celebrity, the other on politics and power. Both can be described in their own way as tinsel towns. Indeed, for many the real convergence of Hollywood east and west occurred during Ronald Reagan's presidency, which many unfairly saw as the complete triumph of style over substance, illusion over reality, and celebrity over serious policy making.

The Reagan presidency was more complex than that. But there was no question that his media successes highlighted the value of image, and particularly of physical appearance. If there is one issue in which media has driven rather than reflected trends in the post-FDR presidency, it has to be on the value of the presidential physical appearance. Who was our last bald, short, or obese president? Answers, respectively: Eisenhower, Truman, and Taft. In short, it's been quite awhile.

Focus on the president's physical image and appearance is not new. Nineteenth-century presidents, sitting and former, including Andrew Jackson, James Polk, and even John Quincy Adams, posed for American daguerreotypers. (Adams thought his image was "hideous"; Walt Whitman disagreed, describing Adams's eyes as "individual but still quenchless fire.")[22] And then there was Lincoln, whose images are perhaps the most enduring. Lincoln wanted it this way and posed frequently for portraits, photographs, and sculpture.[23]

Both Roosevelts courted the media. In FDR's case, that relationship and control was critical to the president's leadership. Great pains were taken to ensure that he was photographed largely from the waist up and not in his wheelchair. On the contrary, what Americans heard and saw was that lustrous voice, which actually carried his message further into their hearts and minds than any pair of working legs ever could, and that radiant smile and cocked jaw exuding self-confidence, optimism, and strength. With television came Jack Kennedy, whose voice, smile, physical persona, and good looks created a standard that none of his successors could match. Kennedy, of course, never had an opportunity to grow old and infirm (a host of undisclosed ailments, including Addison's disease and anxiety, and meds to deal with them notwithstanding), and his image would be fixed forever in time. Lyndon Johnson, on the other hand, revealed the limitations of image management. With practice, staging, and media coaching, LBJ would try to find his way.

But he never could, neither in the way he spoke nor appeared. His best photo and image was taken on his ranch after he left the presidency. It is an extraordinary image of a relaxed Johnson in western shirt and cowboy hat, with a ruggedly handsome face—depicting a cowboy, a mix of John Wayne and the Marlboro Man.[24]

These days we seem to demand and accept nothing less than robust, tall, physically attractive men (with plenty of hair). It is no coincidence that after LBJ, the next half-dozen presidents—successful or not—had height and hair, but not heft. Indeed, since Reagan our presidents have been a pretty good-looking bunch of white and black alpha males, any of whom could have modeled clothes at an earlier age in a J.Crew catalog.

It is intriguing to ponder the fact that today 35 percent of American adults are obese, and 40 to 70 percent of American men over the age of 35 are bald or balding, and yet there does not seem to be much interest in expanding the presidential candidate search to capture these demographics.[25] Pundits actually speculated how his receding hairline would affect Mitch Daniels's presidential prospects.[26] Indeed, as noted, we haven't had an elected bald president since Eisenhower (Gerald Ford doesn't count); before that, in a well-follicled nineteenth century full of beards, goatees, and mustaches, you would have to go back to Martin Van Buren in 1836.[27]

Our own expectations of what is presidential in appearance follows a certain look—strong, confident men (and women, in the case of candidates such as Hillary Clinton, Sarah Palin, and Michelle Bachmann), well follicled, who are attractive and very easy on the eyes given their nonstop appearances.

Presidents also want to present the right character as well as physical image. Where a president vacations, how the first family comports itself, which venues are selected for speeches and announcements, all are part of the same piece when it comes to creating the image of a president's character. Ronald Reagan's media team was masterful at creating what Hedrick Smith called a storybook presidency. He had a big advantage following Jimmy Carter, who did his best to deritualize many aspects of the presidency. The Reagan team brought back "Hail to the Chief," which Carter had not used, and ensured the return of symbols, plenty of flapping flags, anthems, and other patriotic accoutrements. Reagan used foreign travel as well to Versailles, Normandy, the Korean DMZ, and China's Great Wall to act presidential on the world stage and to show an American president standing tall in the world. On the Normandy trip to mark the fortieth anniversary of D-Day, the White House rejected French president François Mitterrand's insistence that all foreign leaders convene at a common gathering point in France, since that would have pushed the timing of the event too late for the morning news cycle in America. Instead, the White House pushed the French to allow Reagan to proceed directly to Pointe du Hoc, a dramatic cliff overlooking the beaches and the sea. Reagan's appearance was perfectly timed for the TV audience back home.[28]

The Bush 43 White House, this time against the backdrop of the war against terror and campaigns in Afghanistan and Iraq, went to great lengths to burnish the president's image as a wartime leader, most famously in May 2003 with its orchestration of the president's arrival in flight suit on a US carrier that had just returned from the Persian Gulf; the carrier deck was flanked by a banner that read "Mission Accomplished." The scene was a brilliant piece of presidential theater, but would later prove somewhat embarrassing as an intensified insurgency in Iraq created huge problems for the American military. Managing the president's image also means marshaling the president's strengths while understanding and avoiding his weaknesses. George W. Bush, never terribly skilled at solo press conferences, gave fewer of them than any other recent president.

Back in the day, presidents and their staffs had more control over image, more opportunity to mask flaws, keep secrets, and a great deal more cooperation from a press corps that accepted certain rules of the road on what was appropriate to disclose and what wasn't. Presidential scholar Larry Sabato calls this phase of American press coverage "lap dog journalism."[29] Infidelities—from FDR's to Ike's, to Kennedy's, to Johnson's—were never revealed, even if they were generally known at the time. In June 1959, the FBI had a letter and photographs containing allegations of "personal immorality" on the part of Kennedy, which had been sent to 35 reporters, not one of whom used the information in their stories.[30] The unwritten rules of the day—Kennedy was actually quite confident that his womanizing would not create a problem—made these kinds of personal revelations off limits, including credible reports of sex parties with call girls at the White House. Had Kennedy not been assassinated and had his serial philandering been revealed, however, he would likely not have won reelection in 1964. The same applied to issues relating to health concerns and medical issues. Given the extent of Kennedy's maladies, including his Addison's disease, back pain, and the amount of medication and drugs he took to deal with his illnesses, he might have been precluded from running for the White House had his condition been known at the time. It is also likely that FDR's leadership style would have been badly compromised had the full extent of his paralysis been known to the public and his daily movements covered by the press—and unlikely that he could have been elected president in the first place.

Today's investigative and supersensationalized media offer no such breaks and discretion. The media intrudes into privacy, scrutinizes and hypes to be sure, and forces reactions in real time that make thoughtful and deliberate response harder. But it also has the opposite effect: coverage doesn't sensationalize only; it can make a president seem ordinary. When presidents are as visible as they are today, it is increasingly hard to maintain the reserve, detachment, and authenticity required to maintain the mystique so important to leadership. Charles de Gaulle said: "There can be no prestige without mystery."[31] And Walter Bagehot, the nineteenth-century journalist, essayist, and editor of the *Economist,* was even more poetic: "Royalty is to be reverenced . . . its mystery is its life. We must not let in daylight upon magic."[32] All of this may seem antiquated in our sharing, Oprah-style, reveal-all culture. But there is a serious point here. Our greatest presidents—regardless of their public personas—were our most private ones too, particularly Lincoln and FDR. They kept—and were able to keep—their distance.

Today that just isn't possible. And the problem builds on itself. Eager to stay ahead of the media and not lose opportunities to promote presidents in high-profile public opportunities, White House staffers facilitate the saturation exposure; by doing so, they cannot help but trivialize what they want to make special. After ten minutes of late-night bantering with either Jon Stewart or Jay Leno, it is hard to imagine, Fox News' Howard Kurtz told me, how any president can remain presidential.[33] The whole point of the interview is to humanize the president, but in doing so, the access also brings the president down a notch or two. He can't help but seem more ordinary. It may be smart politics, but it still diminishes.

In some fascinating observations centered around the notion of lowering the political hero to our level, scholar Joshua Meyrowitz argues that we see too much of our politicians.[34] Clearly part of the aura of the greats, from our modern-day perspective, is that we never saw or heard them in real time. Had Lincoln been president today with his high, thin voice and ungainly manner, the media would have had a field day. Today we see and hear a great deal more. We see Nixon sweating, Ford stumbling, Reagan dozing, Clinton misbehaving, and George W. Bush fumbling with words and inventing new ones.

Meyrowitz's analysis may push the envelope too far. Nineteenth- and twentieth-century presidents operated in a different world that allowed a greater detachment and less exposure. But he is on to an important point. Too much profile does devalue, expose, and make presidents seem as if they are expected to have views (and solutions) to everything. This kind of overexposure raises a president's profile and diminishes it at the same time. Lincoln gave four major speeches during the course of his presidency; FDR gave only four fireside chats his first year, and only a total of eight during his first term, thirty during the course of his entire presidency. According to political scientist Martha Kumar, Barack Obama gave 515 speeches his first year; that includes major addresses—many on radio—speeches, and remarks.[35] Times have changed, to be sure. When the Berlin Wall was erected in 1961, Kennedy was on vacation, historian Michael Beschloss reminds us, and no one pressed him for a substantive reaction for six days.[36] No president would get away with that today. Indeed, some would argue that the president is in a no-win situation. If he comments too much, he is overexposed; if he does not address the issue quickly, he is criticized. Finding just the right balance in dealing with this new media challenge is likely not possible, certainly not in a world where in 2010 an American president, largely in response to media frenzy, felt compelled to denounce the actions of one loony pastor from Florida who threatened to and then later did burn a Quran.[37]

Indeed, in a revolutionized media world where Americans are drowning in choices, the president's voice may not be just another. But it simply does not carry the same weight. Obama's weekly web addresses, the modern-day counterpart to the fireside chat, are largely ignored. During the golden age of television, close to half of American household's would watch a primetime presidential address. With expanding cable access, the numbers began to decline as viewers had more choices and presidents more competition. President Obama's January 2014 State of the Union was seen by 33 million Americans, the second-lowest viewership since Nielsen began counting in 1993.[38]

The other aspect of the media's impact on the presidency is the way it has interposed itself between the president and the public. The president alone among American politicians can command a national audience, particularly during times of crisis. But the intriguing fact is that in recent years, he is not by himself when he gives a major speech, press conference, or makes an appearance. Media commentary now sets the stage for any major address, like the State of the Union (including very often a digitalized countdown display ticking off minutes to the address) and, of course, provides postmortem analysis, using tiered rows of journalists and analysts, all of whom have their own laptops. Immediately after the president speaks, the analysts begin interpreting the president's words, sometimes with focus groups, to gauge what Americans think and how they reacted.

In short, he may be the president, but his voice is no longer as authoritative or dominant. We are told even before we have time to make sense of the president's words ourselves what he meant and even how we should react.

Compare this to an earlier day when a president related to the public without media commentary. After Kennedy addressed the nation the evening of October 22, 1962, during the height of the Cuban Missile Crisis, all three networks (as was their custom) went back to normal programming.[39] Even the next day, there was no real analysis of the president's speech in either the *New York Times* or the *Washington Post*, which did run an editorial largely supporting the steps Kennedy had outlined. They were different times; a Cold War consensus prevailed, Americans gave their presidents the benefit of the doubt, and the argue-culture that is the defining characteristic of the modern media age had not yet set in. That night, Americans who watched President Kennedy had to come to terms with his message, his character under pressure, and his policies pretty much on their own. In one respect, it is certainly better, even in the breathless 24/7 media world in which we live, to analyze and critique the policies of our leaders, particularly when the stakes are high. Good analysis, tough questions, and views that incorporate a variety of perspectives are critical to producing an informed and engaged citizenry. At the same time, today's media commentary often does our thinking for us or, in our opinion-driven debate culture, our arguing for us; the facts matter less than the opinions. The good news is that there is a great deal more perspective and analysis out there to be sampled; the bad news is that we may not be sampling it. Instead, we are going to one or another of the media outlets to have our views and prejudgments validated and vindicated. In any event, the media, as the president's not-so-silent partner, is here to stay. Still, the thought of Rachel Maddow, or Bill O'Reilly, or even the experienced David Gergen analyzing one of FDR's fireside chats is truly disheartening.

NINE

Traces of Greatness?

OF THE TWELVE MEN WHO HELD THE PRESIDENCY after Franklin Roosevelt, none could make a claim to undeniable greatness. The alignment of crisis, character, and capacity that might have made that possible has not appeared again. At the same time, the troubles the greats managed to avoid were nearly as important as what they accomplished. Their successors would not be as fortunate in steering clear of scandal and nation-wounding policy failures. Before 1960, only once in American history had there been an effort to impeach a president. Of the nine presidents since, there have been serious discussions and or impeachment proceedings directed against five (Johnson; Nixon; Reagan; Clinton; and Bush 43). That may tell us far more about our fractious politics than it does about the severity of transgressions that warranted these proceedings. And admittedly, my standard is a tough one and produces a very small club of great presidents. Admission has become much more difficult for reasons we have discussed. Even Truman, whom most historians and much of the public have placed near the top, stumbled badly on Korea and left office with one of the lowest approval ratings in history. Nor can Dwight Eisenhower, a much underestimated president whose prudence and experience kept America out of foreign wars, make the greatness cut because he did not achieve any single, incomparable, and enduring achievements in the White House.

And yet, significant challenges, even missteps, in the presidency do not necessarily mean a failed or an unproductive one. With the exception of Richard Nixon, there are no truly failed presidencies during this period. And even in Nixon's case, his domestic policies, including creating the Environmental Protection Agency, Clean Air and Clean Water Acts, not to mention some notable foreign policy achievements, such as the opening to China, make it imperative that we look at the full context of his presidency, even with Watergate's long, dark shadow. Still, the founders put the inaugural oath in the Constitution for a reason (the only time "I" and "my" occur in the document). Nixon might have read the Constitution, Harry Truman once quipped, but he did not understand it.

So what do we make of the post-FDR presidency, and what does it say about great presidents? It is, to be sure, an uneven record of remarkable accomplishment: deep failure, and competent, but at times subpar, performance. Is there nothing more we can say about greatness in the presidency during these years, other than to comment and dwell on the fact that it was missing?

I think there is. Three presidents stand out from all the others; each in his own way was the beneficiary of a unique mix of personal circumstances, the times, and his own talent and accomplishments. Their own stumbles, policy failures, and particular circumstances prevent them from getting presidential halos or being candidates for another Mount Rushmore. Two left the presidency early, one in terribly tragic circumstances, the other was a tragic figure too; and a third rode off into the sunset, certainly much as he had hoped. Still, in their own right (and in relationship to most of their modern-day successors), each distinguished himself in a very special way that set him apart from the others. What I call traces of greatness, both real and perceived, either in the way they governed or have come to be remembered, were evident in all three. I readily concede to a certain bias here, and there is great subjectivity in my choices. But if you asked me to pick three presidents who made the greatest impression on policy and politics in America since the FDR/Truman years, these would be my picks. So let's argue about them. All were larger than life figures. Indeed, John F. Kennedy and Ronald Reagan continue to capture the affection and imagination of the successors and much of the public, less for what they actually accomplished and more for what they represented—a bold optimism and faith in the future of America. Lyndon Johnson, on the other hand, actually accomplished far more and is remembered far less positively, a casualty of his own demons and a disastrous war in Southeast Asia.

Jack Kennedy served for 1,037 days, hardly long enough for proper evaluation, let alone a label of greatness. And yet his own persona, his words (the last president to give a truly great presidential inaugural address, and along with FDR's 1933 inaugural, one of the two best of the twentieth century), and his tragic assassination make his impact far greater than the sum of his days. There are presidents who come to represent and reflect the times, such as Teddy Roosevelt, Andrew Jackson; larger than life personalities whose very character (as if playing a role on a stage) comes to embody and dominate their days. Kennedy's youth, his family, his wife, and his heroic wartime service created a role for him that, when married to the power of the televised visual image, made an extraordinary impression that will never be forgotten.

Kennedy was also the last president before the proverbial fall, a decade of disillusionment and disenchantment with the presidency that remains with us to this day. Despite all the knocks (his serial philandering, which could have doomed his presidency had it been revealed, the Bay of Pigs fiasco, meager legislative accomplishments, particularly his delay and prevarication on the civil rights issue), he is fixed in the public's mind forever, if only for his capacity to inspire and for a life cut short. It is fascinating to consider how much of the post-FDR presidency is bereft of the words and ideas that motivate and capture the national mood. The New Frontier and the "Ask Not" inaugural were the last, best tropes of national mission and sacrifice in America. The power of the Kennedy legacy remains compelling still. His image in high school textbooks has taken a beating and now reflects his flaws and mistakes. But the popular appeal lives on. In a Hart and Garin poll, commissioned for Larry Sabato's book *The Kennedy Half Century,* Americans rated JFK the best of any president from Eisenhower to George W. Bush, a result quite consistent with past polling.[1]

But Kennedy's short presidency was not just about style and image. His defusing a potential nuclear confrontation with Nikita Khrushchev over Soviet missiles in Cuba is a legitimate claim to a great achievement. Mythology surrounding those twelve days abounds, helped by the Kennedys themselves, who would portray the crisis diplomacy in the most heroic of terms—though there is little doubt that by authorizing the Bay of Pigs invasion of Cuba a year earlier, Kennedy himself contributed to the crisis he would have to resolve. There is also the legitimate question of how much of a threat the missiles really were. The Soviets already had ICBMs on submarines that could hit the continental United States at will.

Still, once in the crisis, Kennedy demonstrated the right mix of toughness and restraint, both with Khrushchev and Kennedy's own generals, who were pushing for military action almost from the beginning. The pragmatism and flexibility (as well as Kennedy's willingness to learn from his earlier mistakes), married to a conviction that nuclear war was an unacceptable outcome (what he deemed the final failure), led to a quarantine/naval blockade of Cuba, which bought time and allowed for a negotiated solution. If indispensability is a feature of greatness then Jack Kennedy had his great moment. Myth or not, Kennedy was the right man in the right place at the right time, if only because he was patient and determined enough to resist his generals' preference for a tough military response. Indeed, Kennedy's contribution proved an enduring one on perhaps the most basic question of all. Sobered by the reality of just how close they had come to nuclear war, either by design or accident, the Russians and Americans would develop procedures to ensure they would never reach that point again.

Jack Kennedy brilliantly reflected and embodied his times. Lyndon Baines Johnson (along with Truman and later Gerald Ford, one of three accidental presidents in the postwar period) would quickly grow terribly at odds with his. Within three years of LBJ's landslide victory over Barry Goldwater in 1964—an achievement that would partly bring Johnson out of Kennedy's shadow—the president would become a detested symbol of a polarizing war in Southeast Asia, deep distrust in government, and a divided Democratic Party. And in 1968 Johnson would become one of a handful of presidents in America's history to voluntarily choose not to run for a second term.

Still, those three years would also give him a trace of greatness too. Johnson's commitment to civil rights, and to his Great Society social and economic programs, made him the only truly transformative president since Roosevelt. If Kennedy's brush with greatness was more about image and the embodiment of an age and two weeks of crisis diplomacy over Cuba, Johnson is an example of a president whose extraordinary political instincts and talents as a legislator enabled him to rise to great heights in one area, even while falling tragically low in another. Historian Robert Dallek's notion of Johnson as a flawed giant captures the essence of both the tragedy and triumph that made him worthy and worth remembering as one of our most consequential presidents.[2]

If crisis, character, and capacity were the required elements of presidential greatness, Johnson had enough of the first and third to try to accomplish great things. LBJ's crisis was not a civil war, an economic depression, or world war. But it was a crisis nonetheless. The tragic assassination of a young president stunned the country. Unlike with William McKinley in 1901, Kennedy's image, his youth, and the power of television made the impact of his assassination much greater. And unlike Lincoln's assassination, Kennedy's death occurred not at the end of a bloody civil war in which Americans had become conditioned to violence and death, but during a period of relative peace and prosperity.

Kennedy's death also coincided with a remarkable decade of uncertainty and turmoil and generational divide in American society. Indeed, there has never been another quite like it since. And yet a confluence of factors, a kind of perfect storm of energy, idealism, turmoil, fear, and anxiety, made the public open to change under the leadership of a strong president and unified government. And Johnson rose to the challenge. In this regard, he too was an indispensable man at that moment. A southerner with a long-held commitment to civil rights, a master legislator, and a president with extraordinary drive and vision, Johnson was also the right man at the right time—at least on domestic issues.

Five days after Dallas, Johnson addressed Congress and urged Americans to show that "from the brutal loss of our leader we will derive not weakness, but strength."[3] Summoning the martyred president's phrase "let us begin," LBJ intoned "let us continue." In the first year of his presidency, he pledged to continue the fallen president's policies and reassured the nation with strength and confidence that he would get America through a tough transition.

Unlike his four predecessors, which includes FDR, Johnson really did have a long-time, deep commitment to civil rights and to social and economic reform. His own family experience in Texas, where they often had no food and constantly feared losing the family home to foreclosure, had given Johnson a deep familiarity with poverty and affinity with the poor. And Johnson had the *capacity*—the drive, experience, and legislative skills and the votes—to do something about it. Against the backdrop of Kennedy's murder, a divided Republican Party, and huge Democratic majorities in the House and Senate as a result of the 1964 elections, Johnson pushed ahead on his civil rights and Great

Society agendas. Using his vast experience and knowledge of Congress and his personal relationships, Johnson relentlessly pursued these initiatives. FDR had described a young LBJ in their first meeting as "coming on like a freight train."[4] Hubert Humphrey, Johnson's vice president in 1964, saw him as a "tidal wave"; he would "come through a door and he'd take the whole room over."[5] By 1966, Johnson's legislative successes encompassed two historic civil rights acts ("we gave the South to the Republican Party for your lifetime and mine," he quipped to aide Bill Moyers), federal education funding, and environmental and antipoverty programs, just to cite a few.[6]

Without trivializing Johnson's role in the historic civil rights legislation, particularly the 1964 Civil Rights Act, which author Clay Risen rightly describes as perhaps the "single most important piece of legislation passed in twentieth century America," it is critical to see the context of the times and the politics that created the urgency and consensus to make the effort possible to begin with.[7] The civil rights movement—the thousands of activists, lobbyists, and religious groups who pressed, marched, lobbied, and organized, and the violence of the segregationists—brought the issue to the nation's attention, as did the bipartisan cooperation of Democrats and Great Plains and Midwestern Republicans, who banded together to overcome conservative southern Democrat opposition. The point is that it was urgency and crisis that first set the stage and that opened the door so that LBJ could bring the force of his character and his legislative capacity to bear in facilitating the bill's passage. We've not seen another marriage of crisis and bipartisanship quite like it since.

Johnson reveled in his success, which became a numbers game to see how many bills he could pass. By October 1966, Congress had passed 181 of the 200 pieces of legislation he had requested.[8] As a result, many of his Great Society programs were ill-conceived, not suited to the problems they sought to address, and, according to some economists, actually increased rather than reduced economic hardship. Moreover, while Americans may have been ready to support the moral imperative of civil rights and equality of opportunity, they were much less receptive to Johnson's broader conception of equality of condition and result, particularly when it came to housing and employment for minorities. Here there was no consensus. The outbreak of violence in the inner cities, militancy in the black community, and of course the escalation of the war in Vietnam would doom much of Johnson's later domestic agenda. And there was another, more mundane reality that cuts to the core of presidential and legislative success and the myths surrounding them. Simply put, in 1964, Johnson had the votes to make his success tangible; in 1966, in the midterm Congress, he did not.

Historian Dallek writes that LBJ was a "man possessed by demons."[9] If LBJ had crisis and capacity on his side, the character deficit was huge. A combination of a compulsion to win at all costs and to best his heroes and his rivals, combined with a deep sense of weakness, self-doubt, and a grandiose self-image, made Johnson (along with Richard Nixon) perhaps one of our most emotionally scarred and least psychologically secure presidents. Johnson could be funny and charming, with a biting, yet also ingratiating, Texas wit. Visiting German chancellor Ludwig Erhard once asked Johnson if it were true that he was born in a log cabin. "No, no," LBJ replied. "You're confusing me with Abe Lincoln. I was born in a manger."[10] At the same time, Johnson could be crude, abusive, and relentlessly aggressive. The famous Johnson treatment in which LBJ would press his interlocutor psychologically and physically (literally pushing his nose up to yours) was described by a childhood friend. "If he'd differ with you, he'd hover right up against you, breathing right in your face . . . I got disgusted with him."[11]

Johnson's grandiosity and his obsession with winning and his own Cold War mentality led to a disastrous policy on Vietnam. It is not that Johnson lacked experience in foreign policy—as Kennedy's vice president he had traveled widely—nor was he unaware of the risks of escalating a land war in Asia. But his drive to succeed, to avoid being the first American president to lose a war, and not to give his opponents a political advantage, along with his own anti-appeasement ideology, so in step with the currents of his time, locked him into a course of action based on escalation. Johnson may have known better. But under the circumstances he simply couldn't do any better. His own self-image wouldn't allow it. Beginning in 1965 Johnson intensified the bombing campaign in Vietnam, and that summer saw the introduction of the first 100,000 ground forces (The total would rise to 535,000 by the end of his presidency.)[12] Johnson knew the war could doom his Great Society program but could not bring himself to any decision other than to escalate it. It is unlikely that any revisionism will rescue his reputation when it comes to Vietnam.

In passing the Civil Rights Act of 1964, the Voting Rights Act of 1965, the 1968 Fair Housing Act, the Medicare Bill, Medicaid, federal aid to education, and by creating Head Start and the Departments of Housing and Urban Development and Transportation, Johnson set about to transform American society in a way no other president had done since Franklin Roosevelt. It is tempting to conclude that if it were not for Vietnam, LBJ would have been a great president. But as John Kenneth Galbraith quipped, that is like saying Switzerland would be a flat country if it were not for the Alps.[13] The war resulted in the deaths of 58,000 Americans, created deep rifts within American society, and undermined Americans' faith in their government. Had Kennedy lived, there's no certainty that he might not have chosen escalation too. We will never know. But Johnson did and it wrecked his presidency. Despite his leadership skills in the wake of Kennedy's death and his domestic achievements, LBJ's legacy remains a tarnished one because of Vietnam. And for most Americans, he remains, unfairly or not, neither a well remembered nor well regarded president.

The third and final president on my list who has staked a claim to a trace of greatness is Ronald Reagan. Twenty-five years after the end of his second term, wrestling with the Reagan presidency is a struggle;

I suspect it is not going to get any easier. What is so fascinating about that challenge is the certainty with which his detractors and supporters make their cases. To some, such as Reagan speechwriter Peggy Noonan, Reagan was an undeniably great president, a uniquely principled and transformative politician with clear objectives, all of which he accomplished. To his detractors he was alternately the amiable dunce and the empty suit, an illusionist who used skillful Hollywood production techniques to create the triumph of style over substance; his legacy, they would argue, is driven by a determined bunch of acolytes who praised far-fetched theories of trickle-down economics and Reagan's central role in bringing about the end of the former Soviet Union.

Having weighed these extremes, particularly against the history of the post-FDR presidency, there is an argument for a middle ground that recognizes Reagan's deficits but also his strengths, both on their merits and measured against those who preceded and followed him. Unlike many presidents, Reagan does not suffer from a before-and-after problem. His political time actually benefits him. John Adams had a huge expectations problem simply by following Washington. So did Andrew Johnson after Lincoln, and Harry Truman after Roosevelt. Reagan does not. He was preceded by a weak president and a decade of disappointment in the presidency and followed by a very competent one-termer but a man who could never match Republican expectations. And remember, Reagan was only the second president since Roosevelt to serve two full terms, and only the second in the twentieth century to have done so and left his own party in charge. The fact is, if you take the shorter Johnson, Nixon, Ford, Carter, and Bush 41 presidencies out of the running, Reagan is left in the company of the three other two-termers—Eisenhower, Clinton, and Bush 43. And in terms of consequential achievements he can hold his own with any of them.

There is no doubt that Reagan has had great postpresidency PR. He has his name on the capital's airport and on the largest federal office building in Washington. Efforts to bump Grant off the 50-dollar bill have stalled. Whether he will have an actual monument on the National Mall is doubtful; he comes nowhere close to the three indispensables. What nation-threatening crises did he resolve? What nation-transforming, revolutionary accomplishments define his legacy? Still, he may well be among the most successful and consequential American presidents since FDR. And here is why.

Reagan was certainly not an undeniably great president. His accomplishments weren't large enough and his flaws too big for that. Nor would he have claimed membership in that club. But he understood how to use the office in style and symbols. That is important. He followed a president who did not. And whatever Hollywood tactics his communications team used to sell his presidency, it drove a worthwhile objective: the restoration of the status and prestige of the presidency after a decade in which the office had lost its credibility, moral value, and dignity. In this sense, Reagan was the right man at the right time.

Sadly, as close observers of the Reagan presidency have pointed out, while the Reagan restoration was in progress, so was its partial destruction. Greatness eludes Reagan for many reasons, but one stands above the others: whether by omission or commission, he crossed a line into illegality and extraconstitutional actions during Iran-Contra that places him beyond consideration. It is worth repeating that the founders put the president's inaugural oath in the Constitution for a reason. Roosevelt's court-packing scheme was viewed as a threat to the Constitution, though it wasn't pursued in secret and no laws were broken. It matters little that the Iran-Contra affair wasn't the gravest scandal in American history, or that Reagan's motives (freeing hostages) were well intentioned. Reagan presided over a set of policies that subverted congressional authority and violated the law. It was, as presidential scholar Hugh Heclo points out, about "big lies in high places."[14] The presidency is about moral leadership anchored in constitutional process and in the people's will. Those lines cannot be crossed; if they are, do not expect greatness in return.

That Reagan (whether he knew the details of his advisers' illegalities or not) was forgiven, remembered so fondly, and reappraised favorably (even as a potentially great president by well-credentialed historians) also tells us something else about him. Ronald Reagan was popular, likeable, and despite a very closed, private side, an accessible president. But more than that, he came to be viewed as an authentic reflection of the American spirit and character and an embodiment of values most Americans hold dear. Not only did Reagan really believe what he said (and it showed, actor or not), but what he believed—at least when it came to an America that had faith in the future, one that could win a Cold War and overcome its challenges—was shared by most Americans. Reagan survived an assassination attempt as well as cancer, and did both with humor, dignity, and an "aw shucks" humility, making him memorable, human, and capturing the spirit of a nation that needed a leader with optimism and confidence. More than anything else, it was that quality that people remember. And understanding, capturing, and reflecting the tone and temper of the times is part of the greatness portfolio.

His record was decidedly mixed. On the domestic side, Reagan demonstrated a mix of pragmatism, status quo politics, and revolution-ary thinking, which together left things pretty much unchanged as they related to any serious assault on the notion of big government. Richard Neustadt was probably right; Reagan was the last Roosevelt Democrat. His early effort to cut Social Security benefits to early retirees backfired politically and led to a 1983 commission that pretty much preserved the status quo. There was no Reagan Revolution, not in the sense that Reagan succeeded in overturning the real revolution (FDR's) and the entitlement and administrative state it created.

What there was—a serious introduction and legitimization of the idea that government had gotten too big, that taxes were too high, that

Washington should be encouraging individual initiative as much as government as remedy—did have a lasting impact on all of Reagan's successors, including Bill Clinton and Barack Obama. Both would refer to him in laudatory terms. Reagan succeeded in changing the debate and its parameters regarding the role of government in American society. Indeed, after Reagan no serious president could or would talk about the virtues of big government as remedy, or talk about tax cuts, in quite the same way.

Reagan did preside over one of the longest periods of continuous economic growth in America's peacetime history.[15] But his policies also added to the crushing deficits that tripled the national debt. Federal government and spending actually grew significantly; the number of federal employees increased. Reagan abandoned a campaign pledge to eliminate two cabinet agencies (Energy and Education) and added a new one, Veterans Affairs. His 1981 tax cut was dramatic. But with the exceptions of his first and last years, Reagan raised taxes every other year. The 1982 Tax Equity and Fiscal Responsibility Act was the largest peacetime tax in American history.[16]

Some of our greatest presidents were liberators, the argument goes. Lincoln freed the slaves; FDR freed Europe from Nazism; and Reagan, his most enthusiastic supporters argue, was a liberator too, bringing down the Soviet Union and ending its oppressive grip on Eastern Europe. Reagan was certainly a tough anti-Communist, committed to ending the evil empire, but he was also a smart and pragmatic one too. In the end, it was less bluster or the actual projection of military power but compromise, negotiations, and restraint that enabled Reagan (who feared nuclear war and was determined to end its possibility) and Mikhail Gorbachev (who deserves the real credit for the reforms that brought down an oppressive empire already in an advanced state of decay) to find common ground. Both Chief of Staff James Baker and Secretary of State George Shultz encouraged Reagan's pragmatic trend in negotiating on arms control. All of this represented pretty deft management of a complex relationship with the Soviet Union, for which Reagan deserves credit. Far from the myth spun out about Reagan as a hawkish, committed, do-or-die anti-Communist, Reagan's policies were in the best tradition of the other Cold War presidents—Eisenhower, a post–Bay of Pigs Kennedy, Nixon, and Bush 41. Like so many of his predecessors, Reagan saw Moscow's nefarious hand everywhere. But he was also quite cautious in the way he used American military power. Indeed, it is restraint and pragmatism, not recklessness, that made Reagan a successful foreign policy president.

None of Reagan's successors could claim the greatness mantle, let alone traces of greatness, real or perceived. And there were good reasons why. A new presidential generation, exemplified by two younger southern governors, would inherit a more complex post–Cold War world. Both Bill Clinton (who lamented he lacked a good war to fight) and George W. Bush (who ended up involved in two costly wars, one of which drags on to this day) never measured up to either Reagan's legislative or foreign policy record. Despite the Lewinsky scandal, Clinton presided over a robust economy, balanced the budget, and left a surplus. For that and his political charm, some Americans lamented they could not elect him a third time. Indeed, he left office with one of the highest approval ratings of any president.

George W. Bush didn't fare nearly as well. By 2008, there was not much pro–Bush 43 sentiment left in America. Wars without end, let alone victory, in Iraq and Afghanistan and a hurricane in New Orleans and the Gulf Coast revealed both the limitations of a president's reach, and the administration's lack of preparedness and strategy to cope with a natural disaster. In the fall of 2008, a decade-in-the-making man-made economic disaster—driven by a giant housing and credit bubble—wiped out billions in accumulated wealth, devastated IRA accounts, unleashed waves of home foreclosures, and deepened an already weak job market and a recession described as the worst economic disaster since the Great Depression.

That November in a presidential election that reflected difficult but historic times, 53 percent of those who voted (voting in numbers not seen since the mid-1960s) elected a young senator from Illinois, the first black president in American history.[17] Americans wanted a change; perhaps some even wanted a transformation and rescue. Once again expectations were unrealistically high. And once again, in the face of a terribly partisan environment and an array of impossible problems without easy solutions, Americans looked for a president who could deliver an end to their economic travails and ease the uncertainty and anxiety about the future. If crisis bred greatness then maybe another extraordinary moment had come. Was America on the cusp of producing another great president?

PART III

What's So Great about Being Great, Anyway?

THE MORNING AFTER BARACK OBAMA'S ELECTION as America's forty-fourth president, I could not find a newspaper in downtown Washington. I had lived in the nation's capital for almost 40 years. Yet this was a first, at least for me. There had been a great deal of buzz about Bill Clinton's election (only natural after a dozen years of Republican rule). But not since Jack Kennedy and Camelot had there been so much excitement and anticipation.

Bill Clinton's sexual shenanigans with a White House intern led to a good deal of head shaking and hand wringing about the sad state of the presidency. Frustration and disappointment with George W. Bush's handling of Hurricane Katrina, a severe economic meltdown, and two costly foreign wars made Americans wonder even more: Could they ever have another great president? But Obama's election—driven by millions who wanted to believe in him and the change he embodied—seemed to herald a different moment. Maybe, just maybe, America could.

For its part, the Obama campaign did little to dampen those expectations or even downplay the president-elect's association with the great presidents of the past. Indeed, Obama and his team seemed to be doing precisely the opposite.

Obama had chosen the steps of the old statehouse in Springfield, Illinois, to launch his campaign, as Abraham Lincoln had done. In the days ahead, we would learn that the president-elect had been reading Doris Kearns Goodwin's *Team of Rivals* about Lincoln's cabinet, a concept that pundits and analysts of the presidency beat to death in an effort to speculate on Obama's own cabinet strategy, particularly with regard to rival in chief and soon to be secretary of state Hillary Clinton. The president-elect would go on to re-create a small part of Lincoln's nearly two-week, 2,000-mile journey to Washington (in Obama's case, about 130 miles from Philadelphia to Washington). Obama would also hold the Lincoln bible at his swearing in and dine afterward on a meal modeled after Lincoln's—pheasant with sour cherry chutney, seafood stew, and sweet potatoes all served on replicas of Mary Todd Lincoln's china.[1] All presidents invoke Lincoln. Still, Obama's Lincoln connection seemed truly special. After all, the new president was the direct beneficiary of Lincoln's extraordinary freedom agenda in ways that could not be said about any of his predecessors.

Circumstances, as they often do, contributed to the hope that Obama himself could be another great. As the 2008 economic crisis deepened, it carried with it analogies, images, and tropes of the Great Depression and FDR's Hundred Days. And the media, academics, and economists made the most of it. *Time* ran a cover of Obama as FDR replete with Roosevelt's trademark smile, fedora, and cigarette holder.[2] The *New Yorker* followed suit with a cover of its own depicting the president to be as George Washington in a white-powdered wig.[3]

With all the hype, Americans, certainly Obama's supporters, could be forgiven for thinking they had just elected another great president. As America's first African American president, Obama was already assured a place in the history books. His charisma, youth, powerful speaking style, and "yes we can" message of change seemed to elevate him from a symbol to a prospective great leader.

Within a year of his election and without any real justification, the Nobel committee nominated him for its prestigious peace prize, the third sitting president (Theodore Roosevelt, Woodrow Wilson) to receive one. *Life* would include the new president in its glossy magazine *100 People Who Changed the World*.[4] Indeed, there was a palpable sense that Obama was the man of the hour. After all, the United States had three undeniably great presidents, one each in the eighteenth, nineteenth, and twentieth centuries. Perhaps it was time for another in the twenty-first.

Sadly, the Obama presidency would prove to be a very cautionary tale. But no one should have been surprised by Obama mania and its historical associations with great presidents. Every time a president is elected, journalists, academics, and presidential scholars play the presidents' rating game and trot out a variety of presidential exemplars. Indeed, our fascination with American presidents and our search and hope for great ones has been an enduring part of the American story. In the *Atlantic's* December 2006 list of the 100 most influential Americans, presidents grabbed the top four spots, with Richard Nixon bringing up the rear in second-to-last place.[5]

No single aspect of our government evokes as much fascination, interest, and, at times, frustration. Presidents have been drawing crowds ever since George Washington's 1789 tour of New England, where village and town residents turned out to see the famous man ride his great white parade horse into town. In 1903, the *New York Times* informed Americans in an article entitled "Odd Facts about Our Presidents" that James Buchanan was their only bachelor president and that of their first 25 presidents, 15 had no middle names.[6] Almost 90 years later, the *New York Times* reported on a study of longevity in the presidency that revealed the nation's top executives actually lived longer than average American men of the same period.[7] In fact, the first eight presidents lived on average 79.8 years when life expectancy for men in America was likely to have been under 40. It was true then and it is true today. Americans just cannot seem to get enough of their presidents.

As head of state, the president represents the nation, commands its military, often conducts its head of state diplomatic summitry, and, as the only nationally elected leader, reflects its values. Listen to President Calvin Coolidge speaking in August 1927 at the groundbreaking of Mount Rushmore, that stunning presidential rock cameo immortalized in Alfred Hitchcock's film *North by Northwest:* "The fundamental principles which they [the Rushmore presidents: Washington, Jefferson, Lincoln, Theodore Roosevelt] represented have been wrought into the very being of our country. They are as steadfast as these ancient hills."[8] That the South Dakota site had been seized from the Lakota Indians, or that sculptor Gutzon Borglum, who selected the four presidents to represent the first century and a half of American history, was reputed to be a member of the Klan, were illuminating reminders of the America that was. Still, venerating past presidents was safe, compelling, and inspiring. Fast forward 70 years to Bill Clinton's 1997 dedication of the FDR memorial on the National Mall: "Now we are surrounded by the monuments of the leaders who built our democracy. . . . Today, before the pantheon of our democracy, let us resolve to honor them all by shepherding their legacy into a new century, into a new millennium."[9]

But the centrality of the presidency derives not just from high-minded principles. It reflects practical realities in our system. In moments of crisis—war, diplomacy, natural and man-made disasters—the other branches—Congress and the judiciary, particularly the Supreme Court—can neither lead nor motivate, let alone speak for the nation as a whole. The Supreme Court is too opaque and inscrutable—nine legal geniuses in black robes handing down complex legal decisions that even lawyers sometimes have trouble following, forget about the rest of us. Congress, on the other hand, is too big, unwieldy, and held in too much disdain these days to inspire much confidence or interest beyond

Washington pundits, journalists, talking heads, and of course late-night comedians.

Other branches can have a huge impact. Consider the Supreme Court's 2000 *Bush v. Gore* decision, the congressionally driven stimulus legislation of 2009, or the Affordable Care Act of 2010. But how many senators, representatives, and justices are on our currency, have monuments on the National Mall, have their names on towns, cities, counties, states, or figure prominently in Hollywood movies, television, or cable series? Congress and the Supreme Court can be in or out of session. The president is the Energizer Bunny™ of the American government. He keeps going, going, going. That the press and the punditocracy have turned the presidents' vacations (where, when, and for how long) into a national conversation that lends itself to both fascination and controversy proves the point.

We see the special character of this bond when a president dies in or even out of office. Warren Harding may have been one of our worst presidents. But when he died of an apparent heart attack in San Francisco (the shortest-tenured of our twentieth-century presidents), millions turned out to pay their respects as the train carrying his body made its way back to Washington. Kennedy's assassination resonates profoundly still, even among those who never experienced the trauma of those terrible days.

And only the president as mourner and consoler in chief can inspire, try to ease the nation's sorrow, and impart meaning to national tragedy. Ronald Reagan's speech after the space shuttle *Challenger* tragedy and Bill Clinton's eulogy following the Oklahoma City terrorist bombing are two of the finest examples of these presidential moments. Two American presidents, who could not have been more different when it came to policy, used their impressive rhetorical power to help the nation grieve when it needed them. A third, President George W. Bush, was not as rhetorically gifted; still, he seized his own moment to rally the country as he stood at Ground Zero shortly after one of the bloodiest and most tragic days in American history. The presidency is indeed central to our politics and our lives. It becomes an irresistible repository of our hopes and aspirations as a people. There are even serious scholarly studies purporting to show the existence of a "presidential death dip," fewer suicides correlating to periods in the run-up to presidential elections.[10]

What makes all of this so remarkable is that the presidency—battered and bruised these many years, written off by scholars, journalists, and at times by the rest of us as imperiled, imperial, impossible, implausible, and overly personalized—has remained so vibrant an institution.

At the same time, our fascination with the presidency and particularly our desire for great presidents comes at a price. If the supply of great or even consistently top performers in the presidency were equal to the demand, we would not be in the presidential pickle in which we now find ourselves. Acts of greatness in the presidency are still possible. Great presidents who defuse great crises and transform the nation in the process are probably not. There is a strong case to be made that America seldom needs those kinds of leaders anymore; that we were truly fortunate to have them at critical crisis points in our history or at turning points where their political skills and legislative or foreign policy accomplishments profoundly guided the nation in the right direction. We have survived and prospered as a nation these many years without the giants of old. That we cannot have another giant seems self-evident. That we seldom need one, now that the country has moved beyond the kind of profoundly nation-threatening and encumbering crises that confronted it in the past, seems clear too.

But is it possible, even beneficial, that we would not want another great? The very notion seems to offend. At best it is counterintuitive; at worst it appears illogical, even irrational. Of course we want another great president. What possible reason could there be for not desiring an extraordinary leader to guide us out of current travails and re-instill a sense of national identity, purpose, and bipartisanship into our angry and dysfunctional political discourse? If we could have one, who would not wish to see the likes of another Washington, Lincoln, or Roosevelt, albeit in a more contemporary guise? A great for our times, so to speak.

But that is precisely the point. For the reasons we have identified, the return of great presidents may not be possible, or at least the prospect is highly unlikely. And while wanting and aspiring to something you cannot have may not appear to be all that harmful, and may even, under certain circumstances, be ennobling, it does carry serious downsides. The search for extraordinary leaders creates unrealistic and unreasonable expectations, skews the standards by which we judge our presidents, leads to presidential overreach, and creates a distorted understanding of the office and the way in which leaders more often than not actually lead. This is not a recommendation for giving up or giving in to what has become an all too fashionable defeatist or declinist trope. It is simply a recognition of history and political reality. With rare exception, the presidency has been far more a story of the limits of power and of promise unfulfilled than a tale of heroic accomplishment. And it is time we accepted it. In short, we need to stop expecting and demanding our presidents to be great so that we can at least give them an opportunity to be good, both as moral and effective leaders. And here is why.

TEN

Too Ambivalent
about Greatness

STRANGE AS IT MAY SEEM, EVEN AS WE ASPIRE TO have great leaders in the presidency, Americans have not been completely comfortable with the idea of greatness in their politics. The uneasiness is driven by several elements, including a suspicion and mistrust of power and authority and an irreverence, indeed at times a contempt for the pomp and prestige of the trappings of power.

In short, we may be too ambivalent about greatness to appreciate it, but certainly we are ambivalent enough to love and blast our presidents at the same time. Writing in the early 1960s, John Steinbeck captured the contradiction: "We give the President more work than a man can do, more responsibility than a man should take, more pressure than man can bear. We abuse him often and rarely praise him. We wear him out, use him up, eat him up. And with all this, Americans have a love for the President that goes beyond loyalty or party nationality [sic]; he is ours and we exercise the right to destroy him."[1] In a way, this ambivalence should make it easier for us to let go of greatness in our politics. The greatness thing has never been a natural for us anyway.

It is tempting to conclude that our uneasiness and ambivalence with strong leaders began in the late 1960s and early 1970s with Vietnam and

Watergate. And the presidency did take a real hit during these years. The lying, cover-ups, and policy failures opened up the famous credibility gap, a term popularized by Senator William Fulbright largely in response to his frustration with and opposition to Lyndon Johnson's policies in Vietnam. The questioning of authority, generational divide, and breaking of cultural norms further eroded the respect and authority of the office. Trust in government remained paradoxically high. But the image of the presidency as a largely benevolent institution would be tarnished.

But America's problem with "the greatness thing" is hardly a new story. It has been alive and well since the founding of the Republic. Driven by a fierce individualism, freedom, and suspicion of concentrated power, the American creed is antithetical to the idea of great leaders except under extreme circumstances, and even then it is with a wary and suspicious eye. The founders were highly attentive to their own reputations and image (and their own place in history), but they were acutely sensitive to charges of self-promotion and aggrandizement. With the possible exception of the mob and anarchy, they feared nothing more than the concentration of power in the hands of kings, royal governors, and great men. To Benjamin Rush, a signer of the Declaration of Independence, "great men are a lie," a "superstition," no better than a belief in "witches and conjurors."[2] For Benjamin Franklin, they ranked only behind famine and plague as the greatest threat to mankind.[3]

In a constitutional democracy like ours, talk of great leaders seemed to be somehow misplaced, almost un-American. European and world history chronicled great leaders—Alexander, Charlemagne, Frederick, Peter, Catherine (all greats with a capital G). We may have been tempted at times, at least with the symbols and trappings of greatness. Washington was presented with several titles, including "His High Mightiness, the President of the United States and Protector of Their Liberties" (John Adams's favorite). He was likely rescued by his own good sense and by a more grounded James Madison, who favored a simple "Mr. President." Still, our first president, ever the clothes horse (he designed his own uniforms), did wear silk stockings, pumps with silver buckles, and a ceremonial sword at his inauguration.[4] Sensitive to the public's fears of strong military men, Washington shunned his uniforms once president.

But pomp and circumstance in the presidency did not last long. Always the democrat, Jefferson was eager to distinguish himself from his Federalist predecessors. He revised the dress code dramatically, dressing plainly and walking to his 1801 swearing in rather than riding in a carriage.[5] By 1824, the first election in which the popular vote was actually recorded, presidential candidates were wearing pants, shirts, and ties. There were no wigs, breeches, or swords in sight.[6]

The greatness thing just did not seem to fit the American story. Americans, Alexis de Tocqueville observed, do not "recognize any signs of incontestable greatness or superiority in any of their fellows."[7] Fifty years later James Bryce, the Scottish politician, author, and later British ambassador to Washington, would publish his *American Commonwealth*, a kind of de Tocqueville follow-on that included the wonderfully titled essay "Why Great Men Are Not Chosen President."[8] Bryce argued that because political parties and their bosses controlled nominations, mediocrity was inevitably the result. You could hardly take issue with his observation. On two of Bryce's three visits, Chester A. Arthur and Rutherford B. Hayes were the presidents. But Henry Adams (a grandson of one president and a great-grandson of another) topped them all for his cutting-edge wit. In his *Education*, Adams observed that had Darwin considered the arc of the presidency from Washington to Grant, he would have to reconsider his theory of evolution.[9] Adams was not being fair to Grant. At the time of his death, the Civil War general was one of the most revered men in America and a president who accomplished quite a bit, including the creation of the first national park (Yellowstone) and serious efforts to protect the rights of freed slaves during Reconstruction.

The informality and common-touch quality of our presidents was also tough on the greatness image. Grant's drinking, while hard on his reputation, also made him human and accessible. Americans wanted their heroes cast with a kind of extraordinary ordinariness. Homespun Davy Crockett was one of the most popular men in nineteenth-century America. Jefferson may have lived at Monticello and had the largest collection of fine wine in North America, but he sometimes opened the door of the White House himself, often in stocking feet. Lincoln was the rough-hewn archetype: rail splitter, wrestler, and country lawyer. President Grover Cleveland answered his own phone. And while it is still hard to imagine from today's vantage point, in 1953, the summer after he left the White House, Harry Truman and wife Bess got in the president's new Chrysler New Yorker (it was a gift) and drove 2,500 miles through the Midwest and East Coast without Secret Service or media handlers.[10] Truman pumped his own gas, ate in diners, stayed in motels, and got pulled over by the police on the Pennsylvania Turnpike.

Kennedy's assassination, the attempts on both Ford and Reagan, an increasingly dangerous threat environment (and a greater techno-logical capacity to be aware of them), and 9/11 have long precluded any presidential outings like Truman's "excellent adventure."[11] But the commonness of the uncommon presidency—he is just like us—con-tinued. Whether it is a presidential passion for the burger (Bill Clinton at McDonald's), for sports (George W. Bush's passion for baseball), or for their pets (most presidents), it is all part of the same common-touch trope. Indeed, no president has been more identified with pop culture than Barack Obama. Whether it is burgers at Ray's Hell Burger, pick-up basketball games, following *Star Trek* as a kid and later admitting to a crush on Nichelle Nichols (who played Lieutenant Uhura on the show), or watching SportsCenter, the forty-fourth president can pop culture with the best of them.[12] We admire our leaders, historian Daniel Boorstin wrote in *The Image,* because they possess the "common touch": "American democracy is embarrassed in the charismatic presence."[13]

Verbal attacks on presidents did not do much for the greatness image either. The personal attacks on President Obama—accusations that he is a Muslim, that he is not a US citizen, and the not-so-subtle racial undertones—do separate him out from most of the recent presidents. But a "you lie" comment by a Republican representative is still mild in comparison with some of the rhetoric that was thrown at his predecessors. Andrew Jackson was accused of bigamy, alcoholism, and serial murders. Lincoln was attacked as a "half-witted usurper," the "original gorilla," and a "ridiculous joke."[14] Nor was our most saintly president, George Washington, immune. In the public outcry following the announcement of the Jay treaty with Great Britain, his detractors blasted him as a "tyrannical monster," a "usurper with dark schemes of ambition," and a man who treated public opinion with "all the insolence of an Emperor of Rome."[15] And fast-forward to FDR, branded by one critic a "megalomaniac cripple."[16]

Presidents were also targets of more than just words. Four were assassinated in office (Lincoln, James A. Garfield, William McKinley, Kennedy); six were targets of assassination, either as candidates or in office (Jackson, Theodore Roosevelt, FDR, Truman, Ford twice, and Reagan). In the 1835 attempt on Jackson's life, the attacker's gun misfired, giving Old Hickory a chance to beat his assailant with the presidential cane.[17] Teddy Roosevelt, who occasionally carried a revolver, was unarmed at the time he was attacked, probably much to his dismay and regret; otherwise he probably would have been the first presidential candidate (while he was running his Bull Moose campaign in 1912) to kill somebody. The bullet penetrated his chest wall but was apparently blunted by his eyeglass case and the text of the thick speech he was about to give (both in his breast pocket). Ever the Rough Rider, Roosevelt delivered his address anyway with blood oozing out of his shirt.[18]

The assassinations of Lincoln and Kennedy, and the attempt on Reagan, would enhance all of their images and reputations; in Lincoln's case it elevated him from mortal to mythlike status, and in Kennedy's it created a more modern tragedy that enthralled an entire generation. But the killing of three underprotected presidents in the nineteenth and early twentieth centuries (Lincoln, Garfield, and McKinley) tells you something about the way the office was regarded. That we lost three presidents in a 37-year period also tells you something about the quality of the protection. Presidential protection was the oldest specific protective assignment in public law. But it was not until 1906 that Congress was willing to grant statutory authorization for it. Until then, presidents were protected by the army, local police, private body guards, and after 1865 by the Secret Service.

And we certainly do not make that big of a deal about our presidents once they leave office, at least from the standpoint of benefits. Congress did not even authorize a presidential pension until 1958.[19] Once presidents leave office they do get lifetime protection. Pensions are taxable and paid out at $199,700 (in 2013), a sum equal to the annual rate of the base pay of cabinet secretaries. Presidents and their families are eligible for medical treatment in military hospitals, but on their own dime. Presidents do get help with transitions to private life, including an allowance for an office and staff as well as travel expenses. Each president is also entitled to a state funeral. It is the least we can do.

We have also been very withholding when it comes to according official commemorative space for our departed presidents. Only five major monuments to presidents adorn the National Mall—Washington, Jefferson, Lincoln, Grant, and Franklin Roosevelt. And each was the product of a long struggle defined by politics, space, and arguments over architectural design. (Interestingly, from death to dedication, FDR got his in record time, 52 years; it took Washington 86 years, most likely because the Civil War got in the way; Lincoln 57, and Jefferson a whopping 117.) An Eisenhower memorial is now in the planning stages. His memorial will almost certainly add to growing pressure for a Reagan site. At the moment, Reagan's name is on Washington's national airport and on the largest federal office building in the city. The last truly great American political figure we honored with a monument on the Mall was Martin Luther King Jr. We should be careful and deliberate in whom we choose to honor and how. Crowding the National Mall with presidents who fall below the greatness bar will only further dilute the significance of those who have crossed it.

Nor have we been all that forthcoming in honoring our presidents in other ways. Consider the strange and confusing tale of Presidents' Day—perhaps the best snapshot of the state of our historical sensibilities and our attitudes toward our chief executives. We lived for most of our history without a generic Presidents' Day. Instead we had Washington's Birthday, a federal holiday mandated by Congress in 1879 during the Hayes administration.[20] Washington may have lost some buzz in recent years, but back then, he was a real star, the only American (until Martin Luther King Jr.) whose birthday was made into a federal holiday. Right through the end of World War II, and then even beyond, civic organizations and state and local governments marked Washington's Birthday. Newspapers put his image on their front pages. Federal offices, banks, and most businesses were closed. Actual events, including movie features and basketball games, were held in his honor.

Today, Presidents' Day ranks somewhere between Groundhog Day and Opening Day of Major League Baseball on the list of Americans' priorities. The occasion has been emptied of any meaning beyond the commercial and is celebrated vigorously at the mall, and I am not referring to the National one. It is part of a transition, sociologists tell us, from "commitment holidays" (more about remembering) to "tension management holidays" (more about forgetting and recreating) like Halloween, Valentine's Day, and the Fourth of July. Psychologist Barry Schwartz argues that Presidents' Day is "an abortive holiday."[21] Abortive holidays are occasions that refer to the past without instructing, inspiring, or indicating what or whom is being commemorated.

It was not the first, nor last, time presidents would be used for commercial purposes. In his wonderful book *Inventing George Washington,* Edward Lengel tells the story of how our first president, in particular, would be used not only to adorn money but to make it. In 1835, P. T. Barnum, the great American showman and scammer, always looking for angles, bought the marketing rights to one Joice Heth, a freed slave whom he advertised as a 161-year-old African princess and once nursing mother to tiny George.[22] That people paid Barnum for this nonsense, at least until Heth started babbling that she was "Washington's lady," reveals how fascinated Americans were with the first president, and how susceptible always to the showman's touch. Collectors still knowingly pay thousands for bogus Lincoln letters if they can be traced back to the most accomplished of the early-twentieth-century forgers.[23] And in 2012, believe it or not, a three-year-old frozen chicken nugget bearing an uncanny resemblance to George Washington's profile sold on eBay for $8,100.[24]

The ambivalence toward our presidents, great and not so great, reflects our ambivalent interest in our own history. On one level, we seem more interested in presidents now than ever. An estimated 16,000 books and article titles exist on Lincoln alone, not to mention the national obsession with the Civil War.[25] Presidential biographies are hugely popular; the History Channel is a dead president's dream; and cable miniseries are always in demand, whether they are building up presidential reputations (John Adams) or occasionally tearing them down (Jack Kennedy). I recall visiting the renovated Museum of American History on the National Mall after it opened. The most crowded and busy exhibit was the Hall of Presidents. Even more impressive is the Disney World Hall of Presidents in Orlando.[26] Set in a 700-person theater, each of the 43 different presidents (we've had 44, but Grover Cleveland was president twice in nonconsecutive terms) are featured on stage both audibly and animatronically. As their names are called, each president gestures or nods. The program concludes with speeches by

Barack Obama and Abraham Lincoln, who rises from his chair to give the Gettysburg Address.

At the same time, we seem remarkably detached from our history and have a remarkably shallow attachment to our presidents too. Indeed, our connection to presidents seems to occur on an individual level without broader resonance in the national debate and discussion about what we value as a society and what we do not. That is really not all that surprising. Collective memory, including how we relate to great presidents, according to Schwartz, is about the distribution of beliefs, feelings, and moral judgments relating to the historical past. And it is disseminated through our understanding of history and commemoration. In order to appreciate past presidents, we would have to value historical continuity and the importance of history itself. And while that should be easier now than ever with an extraordinary amount of information available at a click of a mouse, we seem to know less history than ever. In justifying the Presidential $1 Coin Act of 2005 (a program designed to put presidents on attractive dollar coins), the authorizing legislation noted that "many people cannot name all of the presidents, and fewer can name the spouses nor can many people accurately place each President in the proper time period of American history." The program was canceled in 2011; at the time, 1.4 billion coins (more than 40 percent of the total) had been returned to the Federal Reserve.[27] Naming the spouses is a stretch even for the most accomplished. But our ignorance of history is not. *Newsweek* asked 1,000 US citizens to take America's citizenship test and found that 29 percent could not name the vice president, and 73 percent could not say why we fought the Cold War. Forty-four percent could not define the Bill of Rights, and 6 percent could not even circle Independence Day on the calendar.[28]

We do have moments of collective identity and memory, but they usually come in response to trauma and tragedy: gun violence at a high school, a terrorist attack, or the shooting of a member of Congress. Memorializing our past, remembering the positive as well as the negative aspects of our own history, and creating a national narrative that seems to be legitimate and widely understood is an uphill battle. There just may not be enough common ground or interest these days to build such a national narrative—let alone a historically legitimate one. History in America is used more as a means to validate specific group identity, highlight group grievances, or to sell as entertainment. And if there are few, if any, politicians that seem to warrant our respect, what is the point of paying homage to the ones who are now seen like distant historical artifacts? After all, as Hendrick Hertzberg wrote on Presidents' Day 2007, "Isn't the United States a little too president ridden" already?[29] The capital "groans under the weight of obelisks, equestrian statues, and grandiose temples fit for the gods but devoted to the winners of presidential elections." Maybe it's time, he wrote, "to throttle down."

It is a fair point. But if we are down on presidents and politicians (partly because they have disappointed us) we have intensified our fascination with celebrity and entertainment. We have long celebrated our actors, entertainers, and athletes. Valentine's Day is now more important than Presidents' Day. If politicians disappoint (and they do) we can easily transfer our loyalties, affections, and regard elsewhere, even to fictional characters. (In a recent survey of the heroes of 450 individuals, 34 percent identified their heroes as fictional characters, 32 percent were family members, and only 3 percent were heads of state.)[30] We are still enamored of genuine heroes—the 9/11 first responders; or the US Airways pilot, Captain Chesley Sullenberger, who made the dramatic emergency water landing on the Hudson in 2009. And we do honor the service of Americans in the military, especially those deployed in Iraq and Afghanistan.

Still, it is far easier and a good deal more fun to confer greatness on our athletes, actors, musicians, and what you might call our entertainment/celebrity complex. (He is a great hitter; she is a great musician or a great actor.) They can disappoint us too (Tiger Woods, Roger Clemens, Barry Bonds, and Lance Armstrong). But event tickets, no matter how expensive, are a good deal cheaper than having to invest our time and energy in politicians who disappoint or in causes that seem too complex and time consuming. Besides, why do we need to do that? Why participate in politics when we have stand-ins, substitutes, and surrogates—Democrat and Republican activists, talk show hosts, dueling political analysts, comedian/politicians (Jon Stewart and Stephen Colbert), and even volunteer militaries—to do our political and national service for us? Who needs greatness in the presidency when we already have it on cable? Our surrogate presidency—depicted in Aaron Sorkin's brilliant Emmy-winning series *The West Wing*—is without a doubt a more compelling portrayal of the presidency than the real thing. If we get bored with the real presidency, we can always watch our presidential fantasies play out on cable.

ELEVEN

Too Rare to Be
Relevant and Too
Dangerous to
Be Desirable

WHEN I BEGAN THIS BOOK, DAVID GREENBERG, then a colleague at the Wilson Center and one terrific presidential historian on leave from Rutgers, asked me why I was so focused, hung-up really, on the idea and notion of greatness. It all seemed, well, so nineteenth century. And greatness was an elusive, perhaps illusory notion, very hard to define. I have previously defined greatness in the presidency as the mastery of a nation-encumbering crisis or challenge and using the results to produce a transformative change that leaves America fundamentally changed in some aspect of its political governance or social and economic structure. In America today, greatness, and its adjectival partner *great,* have either been exaggerated or trivialized to the point that they have lost any real meaning and significance. In fact, the word can mean next to nothing, a kind of all-purpose boilerplate.

Great can be fairly prosaic and connote something simply very large in size or character, as in "the book reviewers caused me a great deal of trouble"; or it can mean distinguished or preeminent. But even here, the word lacks any real precision. America is indeed a great country. But what precisely does that mean? If you are a great tennis player, that means skilled at some level, but how skilled? If you had a great time, that means you really enjoyed yourself, but how much and in what way? How many times during the course of a 24-hour period have I said to someone, "Have a great day"? And what does being a great guy really mean? *Great,* like the word *nice,* has become a kind of verbal lubricant, a mindless way of facilitating the scores of innocuous and routine social interactions that occur in our daily lives. Sometimes the way the word *great* is deployed reminds me of a younger generation's annoying use of the word *like,* which seems to be a way of avoiding real words in an effort to compare or explain something.

Maybe in an odd way, the use of the term today is really well suited, perfect for our postmodern world. *Great* can mean anything you want it to mean. It is self-defining, shaped primarily in the eye of the beholder. And today, greatness means very little, particularly in our politics. Incomparable, unsurpassed achievement of a heroic caliber really does not seem to be terribly relevant anymore in our political arena. We really do not know how to judge its worth. And perhaps that is why we can no longer define or recognize it, particularly in our political leaders. After all, how do you describe something of presumed value, let alone understand it, when you can no longer see or experience it?

The absence of greatness in our political life would not be much of a problem if we could get over the fact that it is gone. We know at one point it was real. And even though there has always been an anti-greatness trope in our history, we still aspire to it. There may well be something ennobling about wanting something that is almost impossible to have. But there is also an illogical and irrational side to such a contradiction that is bound to create problems. In this case our unrequited search for what we want but cannot seem to have leads to frustration and inevitable disappointment. And one of the principal reasons is the most basic: greatness in the presidency is just too rare to be relevant.

By definition, incomparable and unsurpassed achievement in any field of the human enterprise is rare. But there are a number of aspects of greatness in presidential politics that make it even more elusive still.

First, there is contingency. Unlike individual creative acts in music, art, literature, or athletics, extraordinary achievement in politics is more contingent and dependent on others and presents a universe of complexity that goes well beyond more individualized creative endeavors. In 2004, shortly before his break-out speech at the National Democratic Convention, then Senator Barack Obama quipped to *Chicago Tribune* reporter David Mendell, "I'm LeBron, baby, I can play on this level. I got some game."[1] The future president's playful yet stunning self-confidence aside, Obama's comparison of politics to James's superstar NBA exploits was hardly apt. Without taking anything away from James's extraordinary skills, the variables involved in succeeding in the two fields are stunningly different. Those that define James's success on the court, his conditioning, the opposing team's level of play, his own team's ability, the quality of the coaching, refereeing, etc., pale by comparison with the complexities of seeking the White House and governing, let alone becoming a great president.

The point cannot be emphasized enough. But there are so many variables beyond an individual's control that can determine success and failure in the presidency. And that only adds to both the difficulty and the singularity of great achievement. The sheer magnitude of presidential responsibilities introduces such a degree of complexity into success that it makes succeeding almost impossible. *Vanity Fair*'s Todd Purdum followed President Obama around for a day, which in the White House seems like a week. And here was a typical Wednesday: Obama had to deal with a Supreme Court vacancy, a controversial new law in Arizona dealing with law enforcement officials and illegal immigrants, the aftermath of the West Virginia coal mine tragedy, a FEMA funding shortage, plans for trying Khalid Sheikh Mohammed, decisions on thirteen federal appointees (judges and federal marshals), and a special award to Garth Brooks.[2] The presidency is essentially managing chaos, or creating the perception that a president can. Most cannot, a fact that only adds to the odds against having a great one. Lincoln's famous comment in 1864 to Albert Hodges makes the point: "I claim not to have controlled events, but confess plainly that events controlled me."[3]

Second, there are the uncertainties and unknowns of what is required for extraordinary performance in the White House. What does it take to be president? We do not have a school for great presidents. And that fact, together with the uncertainty involved in trying to figure out who might be a great one, increases the odds against having one. It would be nice to have a ready-made formula and not have our elections turn into presidential roulette. But all presidents, as Jonathan Alter noted, are blind dates.[4] Of our 43 different chief executives, more than 30 were either lawyers or military men (or both), reflecting, quite appropriately, the nation-building requirements of the first 150 years of the American story. The others pursued a variety of different career paths—among them an engineer, a newspaper editor, a PhD in political science, and a movie actor. Do you need a long, impressive resume and deep experience in politics and government? Not necessarily. Diplomacy, war, and politics may be a natural training ground for presidents.

But none of it guarantees effective performance, let alone great accomplishment. James Buchanan, who probably had the best resume in the business until Teddy and Franklin Roosevelt came along—a senator for eleven years, secretary of state, minister to Russia and Britain—was one of our worst presidents. The same was true for Herbert Hoover, a brilliant mining engineer and first-class administrator who won international acclaim for coordinating humanitarian assistance in Europe during World War I; yet he lacked the temperament and leadership skills to cope with the crisis he faced in 1929. And then, of course, there is Lincoln, probably our greatest president, a politician who literally came in from the hinterlands and who had only one term in the Illinois statehouse and another in Congress. Clearly, intellect and experience are necessary, but not sufficient, to guarantee top presidential performance. Jimmy Carter—Annapolis grad, submariner, and nuclear engineer—was not a great president. Harry Truman, our only twentieth-century president without a college degree, proved much more consequential.

Third, there is the matter of timing, another rareness enhancer. Consider the vagaries of the before-and-after problem. The great presidents were preceded by much weaker leaders: Buchanan and Lincoln are one pair; Hoover and Roosevelt another. Generally, those that followed the greats were rarely as strong or accomplished. Part of Ronald Reagan's consequential standing in the presidency is driven by the one-term presidents Carter and George H. W. Bush, who preceded and followed him. Succeeding Washington, John Adams had one of the hardest acts to follow in the history of the presidency. However accomplished as a president, his one-term act never really had a chance to make the greatness cut. On the other hand, look at the issue of the accidental presidents, created by unforeseen circumstances including death, assassination, and scandal. Some, like Truman and Lyndon Johnson, would emerge to become quite consequential. Others, like Andrew Johnson and Gerald Ford, would be much less so. All validate how rare and difficult it is to actually foresee or anticipate great presidents or identify when and under what circumstances great presidents appear.

Fourth, there is the times. Beyond who came before and after, there is the closely related issue of the circumstances a president inherits. Woody Allen was both right and wrong. Ninety percent of life may well be just showing up. But clearly success in life is showing up at the right time. And greatness in the presidency is, more often than not, showing up in times of enormous stress, crisis, and emergency: the door openers to great performances in the presidency. And the fact is, no matter how talented the individual, unless the times offer up the opportunity, the margin for heroic action diminishes, particularly in a political system that constrains the accretion of power and the desire for significant change in ordinary times. This kind of serendipity with regard to circumstances makes greatness even more elusive and frustratingly rare. Not only do you need the right times (and they come along rarely) and the right character, but also a leader who possesses the right set of skills.

Just consider, as an example of rare and singular, the paucity of great presidential speeches. Presidents give many speeches; they have talented speech writers and generally plenty of time to prepare, to perfect, and to rehearse. And they can choose from among the most dramatic of venues: the Oval Office, a joint session of Congress, or an aircraft carrier. And yet in the entire history of the presidency, you might identify perhaps only a half dozen or so truly great and memorable presidential speeches. Washington's Farewell Address; Lincoln's first and second inaugurals and the Gettysburg Address; Roosevelt's first inaugural and his "Rendezvous with Destiny" speech. Even the very good speeches and remarks—Reagan's 1981 inaugural, his *Challenger* eulogy, his "tear down this wall" remarks; and Clinton's remarks after the Oklahoma City bombing—do not compare with those.

More intriguing is the issue of inaugural addresses, the venue where you might expect great rhetoric. Still, in the past 60 years there has been only one that has made the greatness cut. And that is Kennedy's January 1961 "Ask Not" speech. A dozen presidents since Roosevelt, and we have had only one truly great inaugural speech. And those words and that message were given powerful durability and meaning by Kennedy's unique persona and speaking style; the graceful phrasing and artful juxtaposition of the words and the simplicity and elegance of its language; the special character of his times and the sense of possibility; and the tragedy of his assassination. That is rarity quadrupled.

Finally, there is the "over time" problem. As if we needed anything else to price ourselves out of the greatness market, there is the matter of greatness being appreciated and assessed over time. Kennedy is a historic figure, partly because he was a barrier buster—America's first Catholic president. As the nation's first black president, Barack Obama is a historic figure too. And our first female president will be historic as well. But there is a marked difference between being a historic president and a great one. And that is partly driven by separating out who they are, what they accomplished, and whether what was achieved stands up over time.

Indeed, the greatest presidents were great because what they accomplished stands up to the vagaries of history and to time, the ultimate arbiter of what creates value in life. As historian J. H. Plumb reminds us, history is a potentially destructive force that can, through revision and reassessment, undermine an appreciation of what has been accomplished.[5] What the greats achieved held up over time in the evaluations of historians, the public, and political elites, and became enshrined in the nation's story. Their handiwork was redefined and amended, to be sure. But the changes they introduced took root and transformed the American story in profound ways. And as a consequence the presidents who shepherded and presided over them entered a kind of zone of immunity, their reputations largely protected from serious debunking. In short there is no real margin for running them down. In the case of our contemporary presidents, more time and perspective are required. But until now no president since FDR has entered that zone. And more than likely, none of those that followed him so far ever will.

Lucky for us, greatness in the presidency is rare. And we should be in no hurry to see it return. The reason should be painfully obvious. Simply put, greatness is too dangerous and risky to be desirable. Greatness in the presidency is almost always driven by some kind of crisis, trauma, or calamity that exposes the nation to risk, peril, and sometimes mortal vulnerability. At the same time, it offers certain presidents a national stage to become stars. Indeed, in our peculiar political system, only crisis creates the opportunity, margin, and latitude for heroic action in the presidency and for broadly accepted transformative change in the country. And so a perverse yet intriguing question arises: If threat, danger, and calamity are required for greatness in the presidency, why would we ever want another great president?

Before continuing, it is critical to repeat again one point that will help guide us to the answer. Discrete acts of successful, even great and wise leadership in the presidency are possible without first-order crisis. Had this not been the case, the presidency would have largely been an empty shell, a story of mediocrity these many years rather than a cata- lyst frequently for bold, even imaginative remedy. Executive actions and decisions, such as the Louisiana Purchase, the Marshall Plan, desegre- gating the US military, the creation of the federal highway system, the Moon landing, brokering an Egyptian-Israeli peace treaty, and other consequential achievements throughout the nation's history did not re- quire first-order crisis nor undeniably great presidential decision makers. Both Jefferson and Jackson lacked Lincoln's and Roosevelt's first-order crises. Yet they are considered top performers because they helped re- define, reshape, and reinvent the nation's politics. Theodore Roosevelt openly regretted the absence of a true calamity during his administra- tion, and yet his strong public voice and energy as a progressive reformer allowed him to dominate his times in a way few presidents have. Suc- cessful presidents do not require nation-encumbering crises, but truly great presidents do.

And that is why our three greatest presidents governed in periods in which either the fate of the nation, its well-being, its social and eco- nomic stability, or political viability was at stake. And some of the others we remember as consequential too have made their reputations—mixed though they remain—against the backdrop of some discrete domestic or foreign policy challenge that presented both risk and opportunity: Wilson in leading America to victory in a world war, though not in the postwar peace diplomacy; Truman for strong policies in post–Cold War Europe, but not in Asia; Kennedy in the Cuban Missile Crisis; and John- son for historic civil rights legislation in the wake of the traumatic as- sassination of his predecessor. And like an Olympic diver who is judged by degree of difficulty of the dive, the more calamitous the crisis, the greater a president's prospective legacy. Keeping the Union whole and ending slavery made Lincoln our greatest president. Conversely so, the presidents we deem the worst are either those personally caught up in constitutional scandals or those who could not or would not rise to the challenge when the nation was in its greatest jeopardy. Both Buchanan and Hoover were accomplished men with some of the best resumes in the business. But neither had the temperament nor the capacity to deal effectively with the political and economic crises of their days.

It is only natural that we have been conditioned to think of the presidency in heroic, crisis-oriented terms and to favor those presidents who meet and overcome their challenges. After all, the presidents we remember well are generally connected and associated with a historic event or two. And those are usually related to some kind of crisis or emergency, assuming of course it is handled well. It is fascinating to observe that war, traditionally regarded as the wellspring of boldness, even greatness, in the presidency, has lost some of its luster as an enhancer of presidential reputations since World War II, the last conflict that was kind to a president's legacy. Indeed, war aggrandizes a president's power but not necessarily his ratings, let alone a prestigious place in history. Truman, Lyndon Johnson, and George W. Bush are notable examples. Even Wilson and George H. W. Bush, who won their wars, found victory a much more complicated matter. In Wilson's case, it led to overreach and failure in the postwar period. In Bush 41's, an impressive military campaign to push Saddam out of Kuwait was not enough to ensure his reelection.

With only 43 different presidents, we are bound to focus on the boldest and most heroic, particularly the ones who, to paraphrase Barack Obama's former chief of staff and current mayor of Chicago, Rahm Emanuel, did not waste their crisis, but who instead converted the exigency into some lasting accomplishment that transformed the nation in the process.[6] Indeed, throughout the nineteenth century most of our presidents *presided* as the Latin root *praesidens* suggests. But today we want them to act and to lead. As Arthur Schlesinger Sr. wrote years ago, our best presidents took "timely action" and achieved "timeless re-sults."[7] But these presidents did not just mark time; we expected them to make the most of it, and they did.

The problem of crisis and greatness in the presidency highlights a closely related problem that is critical to understanding the presidency and why our views of presidential performance are so skewed and our expectations so high. Indeed, if we are to free ourselves from those un-realistic expectations, we must come to terms with this structural and permanent reality. The media and the high-profiled personalized presi-dency drive it.

Part of the reason we have such high expectations for our presidents is our tendency to separate the office holder from the office itself, to see the president as a separate personality apart from the presidency and the broader system in which it is situated. The media attention the presi-dents receive, their own efforts to personalize their presidencies, and our need to relate personally make it quite natural and understandable. But it is still misplaced. This personalized conception of the presidency places too much focus on the individual and not enough on the limita-tions of the office itself and the way it is constrained within our political system.

If we focus more on the presidency's institutional dimension, it might sober us up quite a bit and downsize our expectations, and our desire for bold and decisive action from our presidents. Perhaps that is why we choose not to. It is probably not that much an exaggeration to suggest that one of the greatest challenges to greatness in the presidency is the presidency itself. The founders never imagined the president as an unhinged and unmoored free agent or actor, but as a strong executive, accountable and constrained. And so with an eye always on George Washington, whom the founders trusted and assumed would be that strong but accountable first president, they created what turned out to be both a balance to check unrestrained power and a "president friendly" system. The shared and separated powers that the Constitution created for the three branches did give the president power, but it constrained that power too. The president might suggest legislation, but Congress passes it; the president would wage war, but Congress declares it; the president appoints department heads, but Congress creates the departments in the first place; the president negotiates treaties, but Congress ratifies them. By separating and sharing powers among the executive, legislative, and judiciary, the new republic could prevent domination by any single branch.

But what the founders could never anticipate completely was that over time an expanding, industrializing, burgeoning nation would require a stronger presidency to deal with the realities of governing at home and protecting the national interest abroad. Even then, it was apparent that the new nation faced threats that required decisive leadership that a collective body like a legislature could not provide. The War of Independence had quickly revealed the dysfunctions of the Continental Congress in matters of war and peace. In 1787, at least three foreign powers threatened the young nation in North America. Indeed, the British had five military forts in New York State alone.[8] It is no coincidence that a general became America's first president, nor that six of the next seven presidents were either diplomats or generals. As constitutional scholar Akhil Reed Amar points out, not until the 1840s, when America was somewhat more secure than in 1787, did Americans elect a president who had no diplomatic or military experience.[9]

The power of the presidency and its centrality in the American system flows much less from the scant powers enumerated in the Constitution than from two other factors. First, there was the Constitution's own ambiguities, silences, and vagueness when it came to defining those powers. After all, these were difficult issues; the document would have to face a tough and lengthy ratification process, and allowing the uncertainties to be worked out over time in practice probably seemed the wiser course of action. And the fact that the trusted Washington would be the first president provided reassurance that presidential powers would not be abused. Writing to a relative in England, Pierce Butler observed: "Entre nous, I do [not] believe they [the powers of the executive] would have been so great, had not many of the members cast their eyes toward General Washington as President; and shaped their ideas of the Powers to be given a President, by their opinions of his virtue."[10]

Second, expanding presidential powers would also be driven by the simple reality that none of the other branches could possibly play that role or had the capacity, resources, or flexibility to respond to challenges or to initiate policies. The ambiguities regarding presidential powers suggested that there would be a constant struggle between the president and Congress and all but guaranteed that the president would try to assume power where the Constitution was silent or ambiguous. And the realities of governing would give the president the reason, justification, and the legitimacy to do so. And as long as presidents were seen to be playing by the rules and acting within the broad parameters of what the public and political elites perceived to be the national interest and the common good, there was a strong inclination to acquiesce.

The problem of the modern presidency is not that the president had trouble acquiring power. Instead the challenge was how to use power effectively in an environment in which presidents' responsibilities and constraints make that exceeding difficult. The capacity to use and direct presidential power effectively would have to contend not just with what James Madison called the parchment barriers in the Constitution, but with a second set too—the broader environment that imposed not paper constraints but real world ones, making success so hard.[11] In addition to Congress and the courts, the president had to contend with public opinion, interest groups, political opponents, reelection constraints, the bureaucracy, international crises, foreign actors, a political system where change was more likely incremental and evolutionary, and a death-defying job description that would terrify even the most intrepid of souls. And the grinding realities of what it takes to govern in this environment hemmed in even the most talented and proactive of presidents.

More often than not, and certainly in the case of our greatest presidents, what enabled certain presidents to break free from some of these constraints and to have an opportunity—under the right circumstances—to act boldly, wisely, and effectively was crisis. And that is the reason to focus not just on the personality, even the skills of a president, but to understand the critical importance of circumstance in shaping effective and successful action in the presidency. Those circumstances are in so many cases serendipitous. But crisis carries the urgency, immediacy, and at times relentlessness to generate the imperative that there is no escape or refuge and that action, not delay, is the only course available.

Lincoln's election prompted the secession of eight southern states; the Union was collapsing; and among other exigencies, Fort Sumter had to be resupplied. And that reality allowed him to adopt forceful steps, including mobilizing more men, spending unappropriated funds, blockading southern ports without congressional authorization, and other measures as well, including censoring the press, intercepting mail, and suspending habeas corpus, which many saw as unconstitutional. And crisis would also set the stage not just for successful crisis management in overcoming civil war, but for transformational change too—ending slavery and creating a framework to expand individual freedoms and rights.

Similarly, crisis (unemployment had reached 25.2 percent in the winter of 1933) would give Roosevelt the margin for action to transact and transform too.[12] In a first term to act, experiment, and to try to generate confidence with New Deal legislation; in a second, to transform with historic legislation on Social Security that would create a new role for government to improve the lives of the American public. The trauma of Kennedy's death was not a first-order crisis of the same magnitude as civil war or economic depression, but the turbulence of the times (turmoil on the university campuses, in the inner cities, and the violence unleashed by a repressive South against civil rights marches and activists), and the public's receptivity to change in the wake of a martyred president allowed Johnson, the skilled legislator, to pass civil rights and antipoverty legislation that had not been possible before.

And it is the pain and urgency of crisis that widens the margin for bold and imaginative action that simply is not possible in ordinary times. Consider how much leeway and discretion Congress and the public were prepared to give George W. Bush—and Barack Obama still, for that matter—on national security issues and counterterrorism in the wake of 9/11. Indeed, the public expects and is willing to some degree to acquiesce if the president has the skills to lead forcefully and imaginatively. Crisis and trauma shake the system and in doing so overcome inertia, the fear of change, and the narrow, partisan political interest of a normally unruly and oppositional political system. Make no mistake: without crisis and a president who recognizes the inherent opportunity of the moment, the seeds of transformative change in American society do not get planted and cannot grow.

The downsides to the crisis-equals-greatness equation are all too clear and offer more cautionary tales as to why we should be wary about wishing for strong presidents who ride crisis into greatness. First, crisis by no means guarantees greatness in the presidency any more than the possession of great presidential power guarantees great presidents. Indeed, crisis and the opportunities it can generate can lead to wrong-headed tactics, aims, and strategies, as well as abuse of power and the Constitution. Crisis—like power—needs to be pursued with good judgment, humility, and the right ends in mind. And this requires a special set of skills that not every president as crisis manager possesses. Even the three greats were accused of abuse of power and bumping up against, if not violating, constitutional limits, usually during crisis situations. Washington provoked objections from Congress when he sought to censure citizens from gathering to criticize federal policy during the Whiskey Rebellion. Lincoln admitted he was acting beyond his constitutional powers in adopting certain wartime measures.

Crises can be managed well or lead to policy disasters and constitutional abuses. On balance our greatest presidents—Washington, Lincoln, and Roosevelt—fared remarkably well in avoiding both. When it came to the respective crises of others, Woodrow Wilson's realism would help win a world war, but his unrealism and overreach for a chance for America to play a role in a postwar peace would contribute to losing it; Harry Truman would stumble badly in Korea; Lyndon Johnson would overreach disastrously in Vietnam; and George W. Bush would end up pursuing a discretionary war in Iraq whose results could not possibly justify the terrible sacrifices America made, and in the process he crossed constitutional and privacy red lines that alarmed many constitutional scholars and jurists. Barack Obama's aggressive counter-terrorism policies, particularly revelations of the giant NSA metadata dragnet, would do the same. Crisis, particularly war, may generate great moments or low moments and actions in the presidency. But it almost always comes with the difficult challenge of maintaining a balance between security and individual rights too.

The short answer to the question posed above—if greatness means crisis, do we want another great president?—should have been evident from the start. No, we do not. It is an absurd proposition to even consider the notion that we might want to willingly expose the nation to risk and danger because of the hope that a great leader could emerge to rescue us. We should not push our luck and assume that such a leader can emerge again. After all, more than a few presidents since FDR have stumbled in handling the less-than-first-order crises and wars we have faced. Indeed, we want to elect presidents that we hope can rise to the challenge of handling the big crisis should it arise. But even more important, we should want to select those whom we sense have the judgment and prudence to avoid getting the nation into the unnecessary crisis to begin with.

TWELVE

Distorts History and
Our Politics Too

IN HIS HILARIOUS *ATLANTIC* PIECE ABOUT THE
NBC series *The West Wing,* Yair Rosenberg recounts how, in the sixth
season, the charismatic and lovable President Josiah Bartlet locks himself in a room with the Chinese president and through sheer force of
personality—despite suffering from an attack of multiple sclerosis—
persuades his counterpart to agree to a summit with North Korea on the
nuclear issue.[1] Earlier that season, Bartlet singlehandedly brings peace
to the Middle East at a Camp David summit, commits US forces to
police the agreement, and if that were not enough, persuades a tough Israeli prime minister to agree to a division of Jerusalem all in a couple of
episodes. The Israeli and Palestinian leaders are portrayed as cardboard
figures, the president and his staff as dynamic diplomats who do all the
heavy lifting off camera. Middle East peace is somehow immaculately
conceived. Having been at the last Camp David summit in July 2000, I
can only say I really wish life worked that way.

Aaron Sorkin's sensationally entertaining series is, well . . . only
entertainment. And despite a confession from European Union foreign
minister Catherine Ashton that she learned a great deal about life in
Washington from the series, it is hardly the kind of primer to prepare

anyone for anything remotely resembling the real presidency. But it is a perfect reflection of the power of the office in our imagination and of a need to create great presidents even when they do not exist in real life. It also validates how unrealistic and unrealizable our expectations for our presidents have become.

Not all of Hollywood's renditions of presidents are so uplifting of course. There are any number of portrayals of presidents who are far less heroic and admirable than Josiah Bartlet: Andrew Shepherd (Michael Douglas) in *The American President,* or James Marshall (Harrison Ford) in *Air Force One.* Turn on the newly minted hit series *Scandal* and observe the adulterous and backhanded escapades of President Fitzgerald Thomas Grant III. Or watch Harrison Ford in Tom Clancy's book-turned-Hollywood-thriller *Clear and Present Danger,* in which President Bennett (Donald Moffat) is a venal and "I don't want to know about it" president who willingly agrees to the schemes of his equally slimy national security adviser (Harris Yulin). Or worse, watch another Hollywood thriller, *Absolute Power,* in which the sex-crazed President Allen Richmond (Gene Hackman) accidentally murders the beautiful wife of a close friend in one of the steamier scenes for a PG-13 movie. These kinds of roles reflect the darker view of presidents as unscrupulous men with too much power, precisely what the founders feared. Still, we do not willfully send these kinds of characters to the White House.

With their focus on personality, character, and big acts and deeds, Hollywood's president heroes may not be what the actual presidency has produced of late. But they are still what we would like to see if it were possible. We want presidents who can inspire, lead, and be practical and principled at the same time. And we want transformers too— presidents who can change things in big ways, who do not mark time, and who are prepared to lead with big visions and grand plans. Indeed, other than character, what George H. W. Bush referred to as the "vision thing" has been treated, analyzed, and interpreted as perhaps the most important aspect in gaining the White House, governing, and being remembered as a successful president.[2] The only thing that seems to be worse for a president than reaching for an unrealizable vision and failing is not having any vision at all. Henry Adams famously compared the president to a captain of a ship at sea. He needs a "helm to grasp, a course to steer, a port to seek."[3]

Clearly, for those great presidents who were able to guide America to that destination, and to change the nation in some irreversibly positive or profound way, the vision thing becomes the ticket into the presidential pantheon. Today, the vision thing represents a serious challenge, if not a trap or presidential bind, for our contemporary presidents. Our leaders are expected to have it. Those that do not cannot claim a significant piece of transformational change and are stuck in the shallow end of the greatness pool—Bush 41 or Bill Clinton. And yet those who try face a serious challenge because the bar on vision has been set so high and the chances of success in realizing it are so low, particularly in our dysfunctional politics where bipartisan consensus has proven too difficult on the really big issues.

First, their performances are measured against a historical standard of achievement of great presidents they cannot possibly meet. Historians have created these high standards. "We honor the great presidents of the past," Clinton Rossiter wrote, "not for their strength, but for the fact that they used it to build a better America."[4] And building a better America means adding some critically important dimension to the house, not just basic home improvements. Neither George H. W. Bush, Bill Clinton, or George W. Bush can claim an addition that would fall into that category. The Schlesingers identified the greats as strong, progressive presidents, reformers all who saw the office as an agent of change and governed at turning points in the nation's history. James MacGregor Burns coined the term *transformational leader* and set the bar even higher by describing great leaders as those who use crisis and conflict to raise their followers' consciousness by appealing to their higher ideals and moral values.[5] David Gergen, who advised half a dozen presidents of both parties, argued that successful presidents need a compelling purpose rooted in the nation's core values. And historian Robert Merry calls the handful of transformational visionary presidents the "leaders of destiny." What recent president can meet that standard? Indeed, among recent presidents, Gergen argues that only Ronald Reagan was clear about his central goals.[6] But even in Reagan's case it was not so much enduring a revolution but more what historians Landy and Miklis described as a coup d'état.[7]

Second, you might think that after so much disappointment with our politics and politicians, the country would just abandon the "hope and change" thing entirely. And certainly not every election, incumbent, or challenger creates a frenzy of excitement and passion around the possibilities of somehow transforming the nation's politics. That the 2008 election did, however, validates the reality that Americans do still believe and indeed are prepared to rally around such a potentially powerful change agent. Ken Auletta, the savvy media critic for the *New Yorker,* observed a year after Obama's election that the candidate "was the object of near veneration, possessed of a persona and a campaign that was irresistibly compelling to all but his rivals and the right wing press."[8] That sense of hope and optimism is deeply ingrained in American politics too, particularly during times of real uncertainty. And the search for the hero and savior is an ancient but still powerful need, even in irreverent America. Given the powerful place the president still occupies in the imagination and mind of America, the temptation to succumb was overwhelming, though a fantasy to be sure. But *New York Times* columnist Ross Douthat was right when he wrote that Obama supporters hoped that a one-term senator with an appealing biography and silver tongue "would turn out to be Franklin Delano Roosevelt, Robert F. Kennedy and Mahatma Gandhi all rolled into one."[9] Americans love to begin anew, to re-create. And as wrongheaded as it now appears, the 2008 election was deemed to be such an act of renewal. It was not the first time that a young Democrat with powerful rhetorical skills promising to overcome challenges would generate such excitement. In the minds of many Obama supporters, and the media too, a Kennedy connection seemed natural and only made the dream seem more attainable.

Third, presidents play to these instincts both because they believe in their own sense of mission and, frankly, in the competitive world of American politics because they do not have much of a choice. From the beginning of the Republic, Americans have been captivated by what is innovative and new. And presidents and their advisers have led the way by trying to reinvent their campaigns and their agendas as fresh and aspirational and to brand themselves in the process. Think about the consistency of the slogans: Theodore Roosevelt's New Nationalism; Wilson's New Freedom; FDR's New Deal; JFK's New Frontier; Reagan's New Beginning; George H. W. Bush's New World Order; Clinton's New Covenant; and how can we forget Obama's New Foundation, a slogan the president used in his inaugural address, repeated throughout 2009, and wisely dropped thereafter because it lacked punch and clarity.[10]

All of this "new" or "renew" is designed not only to separate the incoming president from his predecessor but also to look forward and create a prospect and expectation of change. The problem, of course, is that the very system in which presidential candidates compete forces them to make promises and commitments in the most aspirational and idealized of terms in order to win. And then, the very system in which they govern requires the kind of compromise and negotiating that makes it almost impossible for them to realize those aspirational goals. Even though studies show that there is a high degree of correlation between commitments made and kept, the gap between expectations and delivery that is actually felt by the public is a large one, particularly when the voters' expectations are not fulfilled on a big issue, such as improving the economy.[11] Of the eleven postwar presidents, only three left office with higher approval ratings than when they entered (Reagan, from

51 percent to 63 percent; Bush 41, from 51 percent to 56 percent; and Clinton, from 58 percent to 66 percent).[12]

The bind that we and our presidents share is made all the tighter, and the expectations gap all the greater, by the images the presidents have of themselves and those predecessors that they choose to reference and admire publicly. Similarly, the comparisons and contrasts that journalists, historians, and columnists use to describe a president also create a public frame of reference that can both add to and detract from how presidents are viewed.

And presidents do have their role models and frequently reference their exemplars. How could they not? They join an elite and historic club of only 43 men; they live in a house, actually a museum, once inhabited by some of the country's greatest leaders, and surrounded by extraordinary artifacts, in some cases desks and chairs their predecessors actually used, or paintings and other art they had admired. The overwhelming presence of the past and of their connection to history and links in the presidential chain cannot but help sway even the most grounded of presidents. LBJ adviser George Reedy observed that the atmosphere in the White House is "calculated to instill in any man a sense of destiny." How could it not, Reedy continues, "after he has become enshrined in a pantheon of semi-divine mortals who have shaken the world, and that he has taken from their hands the heritage of American dreams and aspirations."[13] Listen to then senator-elect Barack Obama describe his visit to the White House in January 2004: "It was impossible to forget the history that had been made there—John and Bobby Kennedy huddling over the Cuban Missile Crisis; FDR making last-minute changes to a radio address; Lincoln alone, pacing the halls and shouldering the weight of a nation."[14]

Clearly Washington had no presidential exemplars. But many of the nineteenth- and twentieth-century presidents would wrap themselves in Washington and the other founding presidents. Lincoln's hero was Washington, whom he invoked in his first speech at Cooper Union to kick off his presidential campaign.[15] And of course most of our presidents would invoke Lincoln, not always to great effect. When Harry Truman offered his aged mother, an unreconstructed Confederate, the opportunity to sleep in the Lincoln bedroom, she told Harry she would rather sleep on the floor. Dwight Eisenhower kept an edition of Lincoln's collected works in his office, sat in Lincoln's pew in New York at the Presbyterian Church, and quoted him repeatedly.[16] FDR would turn to Jefferson as the reverential democrat and founder of the Democratic Party. That was somewhat ironic. The New Deal's broad accretion of government power seemed to owe a much greater debt to Alexander Hamilton than Jefferson. It was during FDR's second term that Jefferson and Monticello replaced the Indian brave and buffalo on the front and back sides of the nickel.[17]

More recent presidents would reach back to the earlier presidents too. And all could not help but fall short. We have already seen how long a shadow Franklin Roosevelt cast. As Historian William Leuchtenburg demonstrates, every president from Truman to George W. Bush has invoked FDR, either because they were generally in awe of what he had accomplished or out of political necessity.[18] Indeed, through no fault of their own, none could possibly measure up. Theodore White's observation that "all contemporary national politics descend from Franklin Roosevelt" retains much relevance, and FDR's high bar continues to offer a reference point by which presidents are judged.[19] That was certainly the case for Barack Obama as he confronted the most severe economic crisis since the Great Depression.

The second presidential exemplar should not come as a surprise either. John Kennedy's successors saw tremendous merit in wrapping themselves in the presidency of a young, martyred leader whose vitality, energy, and rhetorical skills had such a powerful impact on how the office could be used as a focal point for national leadership. Indeed, Democrats and Republicans alike, notably Ronald Reagan, sought to wrap themselves in the Kennedy image. Indeed, Reagan's public references to Kennedy exceeded all of JFK's successors except, of course, Lyndon Johnson and Bill Clinton.[20] Reagan no doubt identified with Kennedy's optimism, his powerful speaking style, and his tax cuts.

But, it was Bill Clinton who drew on and reached for Kennedy in a way no other president had.[21] Clinton drew on any number of great presidents, including Jefferson, Lincoln, both Roosevelts, and Truman.[22] But it was Kennedy to whom he felt the closest connection.[23] From the sixteen-year-old's Rose Garden handshake with Kennedy in 1963, to visiting the Kennedy family and the president's gravesite on the eve of his own inauguration, and to the Camelot tropes of the early Clinton years, Bill Clinton steeped himself in Kennedy comparisons and even exceeded Johnson's references to JFK. Some, of course, were not entirely favorable. Clinton's inaugural address was compared unfavorably to his hero's, and his reported womanizing brought back Kennedy associations that were better left unremembered. And like Kennedy, Clinton too had difficulties dealing with a Democratic Congress in which conservatives and Republicans frustrated his initiatives.[24] How much one president can derive from associating himself with the positive images of another is unclear. But in Clinton's case, he did seek to emulate JFK's youthful style. Given Clinton's approval ratings as he left office, some of Kennedy's charm and charisma clearly rubbed off.

A third president has emerged as a frequent exemplar too: Ronald Reagan. Clearly his two Republican successors and a Republican Party for whom he had become a kind of patron saint and a role model all sought refuge in the Reagan mystique. At the same time, none could match or recapture it. That Reagan's appeal crossed party lines, and that both Clinton and Obama, the only two Democratic presidents to hold office after him, would speak so positively of him—policy differences notwithstanding—was no surprise either. Like Kennedy, Reagan impressed through his persona and his powerful and simple style. Like Kennedy and FDR, Reagan projected confidence, optimism, and a natural-born faith in America. And like those two Democratic predecessors, he knew how to use the power of the presidency as a platform to project a clear message, sense of mission, and even transformational goals. Obama would say during the 2008 campaign that unlike Clinton or Nixon, Reagan "changed the trajectory of America . . . and put us on a fundamentally different path because the country was ready for it."[25] And there is little doubt that sentiment reflected Obama's aspirations too.

Obama had apparently been thinking about Reagan for quite some time. In his autobiography, *The Audacity of Hope,* Obama praised Reagan's ability to speak to America's "need to believe that we are not simply subject to blind, impersonal forces but that we can shape our individual and collective destinies, so long as we rediscover the traditional virtues of hard work, patriotism, personal responsibility, optimism and faith."[26] Obama would go on to re-create that message in his own first inaugural. Indeed, he would also borrow part of Reagan's most famous line from his 1981 inaugural, about government not being the solution to our problems. Obama said that we should not want to abolish government but "to make it work, work with us not over us."[27] The question, Obama said in his own 2009 inaugural address, is not whether government is too big or small, "but whether it works." For Obama, it was not Reagan's policies that he sought to emulate. He looked to see what he might borrow from Reagan's style to implement his own.[28]

Historic moments set the stage for thinking about historic presidents. And it was hardly surprising that the historic 2008 election would conjure up all sorts of associations with past presidents. There were no direct precedents of course. As America's first African American president, Obama was a new chapter in the nation's story. At the same time, Obama's style, his aspirational rhetoric and objectives, the urgency of the times, and the new president's own exemplars summoned up any number of presidential spirits. Obama saw Kennedy, Reagan, and, as we will see, Franklin Roosevelt too as presidents for whom their times offered up the possibility of change. But it was Lincoln whom Obama had long admired most, and with whom he sought to identify. "In Lincoln's rise from poverty, his ultimate mastery of language and law, his capacity to overcome personal loss and remain determined in the face of repeated defeat—in all this, he reminded me not just of my own struggles," Obama wrote in *Time* in 2005.[29] For years, Obama had been drawing on Lincoln's better lines—America and Americans must think anew and act anew, strive to become the "better angels of our nature." Lincoln's second inaugural—the "with malice toward none" speech—was one of Obama's favorites. Indeed, Obama admired Lincoln's humanity, his empathy, his capacity to weigh both sides of an issue and ferret out the balance. And in his speech announcing his first run for president, Obama referred to the fact that like Lincoln, he too had served in the state legislature. And like Lincoln, Obama's career and rise seemed to erupt rather suddenly from the margins to the mainstream of American politics.

It was certainly no coincidence that the president would draw on Lincoln for inspiration for his presidency. "Everyone wants Lincoln," historian Harold Holzer observed.[30] And every twentieth-century president has invoked some aspect of the legacy of America's greatest and most beloved leader and found refuge there. Indeed, in his final press conference as president, George W. Bush (who had dedicated the new Lincoln library and museum in Springfield, in 2005) compared his harshest critics to those of Lincoln.[31]

Yet perhaps more than any other American president, Obama had reason to invoke, admire, and situate his presidency directly in Lincoln's line. Arguably, without Lincoln there might not have been an Obama presidency, and it is no coincidence that Obama's Oval Office sports busts of his two heroes—Lincoln and Martin Luther King Jr. Obama's election was in essence a culmination, or at least a historic milestone, in the journey that Lincoln had begun with the Emancipation Proclamation.

At the same time, rarely has a president wrapped himself and his inauguration in the tropes, images, and symbols of a predecessor. Inaugurals send messages, generate aspirations and expectations. And Barack Obama was aiming high. The Joint Congressional Committee on Inaugural Ceremonies had made the decision that the official inaugural theme would be "A New Birth of Freedom," a phrase drawn directly from Lincoln's Gettysburg Address, and they would also plan the postinaugural lunch in Statuary Hall.[32] Obama's lunch, modeled after Lincoln's; the new president holding the 1853 printed Bible bound in burgundy and velvet purchased for Lincoln's own inauguration; and the concert at the Lincoln Memorial, all could only have been designed to convey the historic character of Obama's moment and its connection to the nation's greatest president.[33]

Obama certainly had enough humility, common sense, and perspective to know he was not a latter day Lincoln. Still, Lincoln associations were designed to send a clear message: like Lincoln's, Obama's election raised a real opportunity for transformation and required a leader of vision and courage. "Only a handful of times in our history has a generation been confronted with challenges so vast," Obama intoned in Philadelphia.[34] Indeed, wrapping himself not only in Lincoln but in the symbols of the founders, Obama promised to bring the nation a new Declaration of Independence—"free from small thinking, prejudice, and bigotry." This was more than an ordinary train ride, vice president elect Joe Biden told those on board: "This is a new beginning."

In all the excitement and sense of anticipation, few begrudged the new president his moment. Historian Sean Wilentz thought some of Obama's supporters had gone a bit too far but dismissed most of it as "twaddle . . . harmless twaddle."[35] Brookings presidential scholar Stephen Hess thought Obama "should draw back a bit."[36] Still, inaugurations and new beginnings send messages, set directions, and create expectations. And in summoning up the ghosts of presidents past, including Kennedy, Reagan, and Lincoln, Obama likely was creating his own high bar and aspiring to much more than his own capacities, his opposition, and the times would ever allow him to accomplish. Indeed, as he sought to confront a severe economic emergency, he would also reach for inspiration from FDR, yet another transformer. New presidents always create new expectations. But in this case, those expectations were running dangerously high. And Barack Obama and those around him did their fair share in helping to create and sustain them.

Our hopes and aspirations for great and transformative presidents lead us to ignore the realities of our own history and our contemporary politics too. We have an idealized view of how presidents get things done that not only is out of sync with current realities, it is also out of step with the way even the transformative presidents we admire most managed to succeed in the first place.

Part of the problem is that it is simpler this way, much easier to relate to individuals who change things rather than to have to contend with the complexities of broader historical forces that provide the context within which that change occurs. And so too, we may not like the lessons that the past or history offer up. Change is rare; great and principled leaders rarer still. Any sober and grounded look at the past half century of the presidential tale would validate Neustadt's chilling observation that weakness is still the dominant characteristic of the modern presidency.[37] We do not want to accept this and neither do our presidents. We all envision the presidency in more heroic roles: Jackson and Lincoln preserving the Union; Wilson and FDR winning world wars; Kennedy and Reagan confronting the Soviets; George W. Bush and Barack Obama settling scores with al-Qaeda for 9/11.

In any event, every four or eight years, the world seems to begin anew, created de novo with a new candidate, a new slogan, and new hope for a better future. And more often than not, even though we are tired of politicians' promises, cynical about our politics, and more mistrustful of government than ever, we have no choice but to play the game, hope for the best, and wait for the once-in-a-lifetime leader who may come round to rescue us.

For a whole host of reasons, the media gets excited too and often, with little knowledge of history, decides to confer unmerited titles and impossible roles upon new presidents who are only too ready to receive them. In some cases this kind of transference never occurs. Nobody thought George H. W. Bush would be another Ronald Reagan, nor Harry Truman another Franklin Roosevelt. But paradoxically, those reduced expectations worked to these presidents' advantage. They were not oversold from the beginning, and they did manage to achieve significant things in their presidencies. In Barack Obama's case, comparisons to Lincoln and FDR were not helpful. First, he bore little resemblance to either of these greats. And yet there he was on the cover of *Time* as the black Franklin Roosevelt with serious analysts comparing his opportunity and crisis to FDR's. Silly to be sure. But far worse, it was misleading and bound to create expectations that could never be fulfilled.

Still, like moths to a flame, we are drawn to an idealized and distorted conception of leadership that we seem unwilling or unable to abandon. We are right to draw inspiration from great and consequential presidents who used their singular skills and power to good ends. But we have bought into a wrongheaded notion of how they did it. The fable of the transformative president goes something like this: a strong president claiming a mandate sets an ambitious policy agenda, acts through the force of personality and high moral purpose by using the vast powers of the presidency as a bully pulpit; and the people and Congress follow. And almost always when that conception of leadership fails, the lesson is that the president was unable or unwilling to lead boldly, create a compelling story, and lobby Congress in a way that sways political elites and the nation too. "This is a big country," Obama mused to Steve Kroft on *60 Minutes* in late 2010. "I'm never gonna persuade on some issues." But the president still insisted that leadership was a matter of "persuading people."[38]

Presidents have acted unilaterally many times and quite success-fully: Washington put down the Whiskey Rebellion; Jefferson bought Louisiana; Jackson backed down South Carolina in the Nullification Crisis; Lincoln freed the slaves as a wartime expedient; Teddy Roos-evelt busted trusts; Truman resupplied Berlin; Kennedy put a man on the moon. But when it came to transformative changes at home on big social, political, and economic issues—situations in which a presi-dent needs to work the system rather than try to either hammer it into submission or persuade it to follow—our heroic, highly stylized, and personalized conception of leadership misses the context within which the presidential effort is taking place. It fails to situate the critical ingre-dients of personality, message, and mission in the even more important issue of what the times make possible. Yes, America's most successful presidents were partly persuaders. Presidential scholar Stephen Hess told me our best presidents were teachers; they essentially took the na-tion to school in an effort to highlight an opportunity, define a choice, raise moral consciousness.[39] But to have maximum impact, those teach-able moments must be driven by some sense of urgency that makes the students not only pay attention but also be willing to listen and then be predisposed to absorb and accept the lesson.

Consider the travails of the two best persuaders in the contempo-rary presidency—Ronald Reagan and Bill Clinton. One was formally anointed as the Great Communicator; the other might just as well have been. Both had major difficulties moving the public on key issues about which they cared—Reagan on Nicaragua and defense spending, particu-larly by the end of his administration, and Clinton on health care. Neither president introduced lasting changes in America's policy preferences. Rea-gan would go out on the stump, "draw huge throngs," his press secretary Martin Fitzwater remembered, "and convert no one at all."[40]

Today, no president has the capacity to command that kind of persuasive power, particularly in an environment in which the presi-dent's voice is only one among many and the congressional math—the support presidents need to push legislation—is just not there. Even in the wake of a compelling national tragedy—for example, the killing of 26 children and teachers at a Connecticut elementary school—a presidentially sanctioned campaign to secure meaningful gun control legislation could not succeed. And yet presidents continue to believe they do have that capacity. As Barack Obama told Ron Suskind: "I think I was so consumed with the problems in front of me that I didn't step back and remember . . . what the president can do, that nobody else can do, is to tell a story to the American people about where we are and where we are going."[41]

Our idealized conception of how presidents lead is driven by at least two historical and political realities that we seem unwilling to accept, or perhaps willfully ignore. Maybe the problem is we just simply do not want to bust our idealized presidential bubble.

First is the simple and cruel reality that disappointing constituencies is part of the president's job description. Indeed, it is a built-in structural reality that comes along with Air Force One and Secret Service protection. Whatever politicians promise during their campaigns, the grinding realities of governing in our system serves to constrain, limit, and often block what a president wants to accomplish. "Every presidential candidate, whether running the first time or for reelection, is a person of aspiration," Senator Richard Durbin of Illinois observed in early 2012. "Then they are going to face reality and the desperation of achieving what is possible."[42] Even in cases where presidents can claim success, the achievement may stress the system, undermine a president's support rather than enhance it, disappoint constituents, and create opportunities for political opponents. The Affordable Care Act is one example of such a success generating potential downsides and failures largely from the absence of broad public consensus to support the effort, a botched rollout, and uncertainties over whether the legislation will actually improve coverage and reduce costs—and the opportunities all of that generates for Republicans eager to exploit the vulnerabilities.

Barack Obama is only the latest in a series of presidents who confronted the aspiration-to-disappointment cycle. The fall was particularly hard in his case because expectations were running so high. Take the issue of Obama's view on the balance between preserving American security and freedoms. In his 2009 inaugural, the president decried what he termed "the false choice between our safety and our ideals."[43] And yet five years later, even in the wake of the revelations of the NSA's metadata dragnet, the president has been forced to walk back lofty rhetoric in favor of imperfect choices that reflect his appreciation of security threats to the nation. Failure to close the detention center at Guantanamo was another casualty of the very real challenge of reconciling campaign rhetoric with governing realities. Promising a much more accelerated economic recovery and a quicker return to lower unemployment numbers was yet another. Portraying himself as a postpartisan president determined to fix Washington's broken political system yet another. Obama was not the first president and will not be the last to experience this disconnect. During his run for president against Richard Nixon, Kennedy sought to burnish his Cold Warrior credentials by committing to close a nonexistent missile gap with the Russians and then had little choice but to walk away from it. Ronald Reagan promised to cut taxes and reduce deficits—a promise that came undone amid ballooning deficits. And Bill Clinton and George W. Bush promised major legislation on health care and Social Security reform without delivering either.[44]

Not paying attention to why presidents continue to disappoint is one thing. Failing to understand why and under what circumstances the best ones manage to succeed is another. This question cuts to the core of how leaders actually lead, particularly when it comes to the issue of producing big change. The issue is central because most presidents want to do big things; they campaign on these aspirations and want us to believe in them too. At the same time, how and why these kinds of large-scale changes come about and endure has a great deal more to do with the opportunities presidents inherit than the ones they themselves can create.

No factor is more misleading and damaging to the way we relate to and evaluate our presidents than the notion of the transforming president who, by sheer force of personality and will, motivates followers and manages to introduce sweeping change in a system that somehow bends to his will. First, change in America is evolutionary and incremental even in its most dramatic manifestations. It would take a century or more after Lincoln's Emancipation Proclamation to begin to really deliver on meaningful civil rights and equality for African Americans. And Reconstruction in the South would make a mockery of the freed slaves newfound paper emancipation. In 1937, despite Roosevelt's New Deal reforms, he could say without exaggerating that he still saw a nation of which a third were "ill-housed, ill-clad, and ill-nourished."[45]

Second, the transforming leader who ends up inducing sweeping and systemic change is also transactional too, one who can bargain, broker, negotiate, and compromise in an effort to defuse crisis. The lion and the fox—James MacGregor Burns's famous description (drawn from Machiavelli) of Roosevelt's caution and boldness—describes two elements of the same leadership package.[46] Transaction is required for transformation. How can you transform without negotiating the crisis at hand, without looking for opportunities to make use of the crisis to push for and justify broader changer? FDR was both bold and conservative in his first term and pushed for bolder action in his second. Lincoln too, whose views on slavery would evolve, pursued a careful course toward the transformational change he sought.

Third, great presidents are principled but very opportunistic too. But—and this is the key component—they cannot create the opportunities so necessary for systemic change. In essence, as paradoxical as it may seem, leading is partly about following, about specifically understanding the conditions on the ground, intuiting that political and popular temper of the times that make change possible, and then exploiting that change. The notion that the president's job is to create a story or a compelling narrative in order to teach and inspire is absolutely on target. But to be compelling, meaningful, and productive, the story must have authenticity, and that means grounded in an urgent reality of the day.

In his book *Overreach,* George Edwards demonstrates that presidential leadership is much more about what he terms facilitation than it is about dramatic efforts to create opportunities through persuasion or moral force.[47] The predilection, even the hunger, for change already exists, usually as a consequence of some emergency or crisis. The president then sees the opportunities inherent in favorable circumstances and has the right skills and persona to exploit them. Roosevelt knew that he must try something and experimented with a flurry of legislative efforts during the first 100 days. But could he have succeeded without the urgency and exigency of the moment, and in the absence of a political coalition that was prepared to sustain those efforts? The first piece of New Deal legislation, on keeping the banks open, passed in 38 minutes without a roll call in the House and with only a single copy of the actual legislation available to read; in the Senate the vote was 73–7. From beginning to end, including FDR's signing, the entire effort took less than six hours.[48]

Lyndon Johnson was indeed the master legislator, with a knowledge of Congress without parallel. And he was relentless in his effort to press both civil rights and Great Society legislation. But it was Johnson's persuasion married to the circumstances and the times—Kennedy's assassination, Johnson's landslide victory in 1964, Democratic majorities, the sense of urgency created by violence in the South and the 1963 March on Washington, and the general receptivity to change—that gave him a moment to exploit. After the disastrous 1966 midterms, in which Democrats lost 42 seats in the House, LBJ's legislative juggernaut stalled. And in the words of Norman Ornstein, his mastery of Congress "meant squat."[49]

The idea that presidents alone, by virtue of their own personal or persuasive skills, can lead with real effect seems detached from historical experience. Calls for President Obama to work more closely with Congress on big issues when the times, divisions between Republicans and Democrats, and intraparty disputes makes meaningful bipartisanship impossible, is a willful misreading of the political terrain and a prescription for failure, or at best endless process. On a key issue, such as a grand bargain on tax increases and entitlement reform, the reality—or to use the concept making the rounds on Capitol Hill, the "dirty secret"—is that neither Democrats nor Republicans are ready to do such a deal. In the 1980s, Reagan had Democrats that were willing to work with him. Today, at least on a big budget deal, Obama has neither Republicans nor Democrats.[50]

It may not seem like a heroic notion that presidents exploit conditions that already exist for change rather than create them out of whole cloth. But that, more often than not, is precisely what the best ones do. It's not a Hollywood presidency. But it carries its own share of drama all the same. And that is not to trivialize how hard it is to do even that. The great presidents read the real estate correctly; they knew what they could and could not do with what they inherited; and above all they had the skills, the personas to dominate the change process to make it work. It is no coincidence that these kinds of transformative moments in our history are rare. And the reason is that they are simply not just products of strong-conviction presidents elected to carry out the popular will. Instead they require rare alignments of the right times and the right personalities. Reading the past—and history—soberly leads to the inescapable conclusion that our presidents are highly constrained servants. It is only the circumstances they inherit and their own ability to know what to do with them that has the potential to set them free.

THIRTEEN

Disappointer in Chief?

ALL PRESIDENTS DISAPPOINT. IT COMES WITH THE job, the unreasonable expectations Americans have for the presidency and the inherent conflict and disconnect between campaigning (promising people what they can have) and governing (explaining to them why they may not get it, partly or even at all).

But for our forty-fourth president the downward spiral from hope to disappointment somehow seemed more severe and precipitous. It was partly the times and burning desire on the part of millions of Americans to be relieved—even rescued—from the uncertainties and pain of economic dislocation and the frustrations of two long wars.

There was no escaping the fact too that the candidate himself— coolly self-confident and at times hotly determined—created a set of expectations that would have been hard for any mortal to meet even in more propitious times. Real or not, his acolytes saw a bit of the savior and redeemer in Barack Obama. Indeed, during the campaign, his closest staff had reportedly taken to referring to him as "Black Jesus."[1]

And the candidate and then president elect didn't do much to discourage them. If campaigning is about moments of poetry and governing about the hard slog of prose, Barack Obama was surely in his moment. Having just won the Iowa primary in 2008 (a state that was 95 percent white), his aspirations and hopes knew few bounds.

> Hope is what led a band of colonists to rise up against an empire. What led the greatest of generations to free a continent and heal a nation. What led young women and young men to sit at lunch counters and brave fire hoses and march through Selma and Montgomery for freedom's cause. . . . Hope is what led me here today. With a father from Kenya, a mother from Kansas, and a story that could only happen in the United States of America. . . . We are the United States of America. And at this moment, in this election, we are ready to believe again.[2]

In the fall of 2008, there is no question that millions of Americans were prepared to do precisely that. It really was a unique moment in the country's history, particularly in American politics.

Perhaps no Republican candidate, with the possible exception of a resurrected Ronald Reagan, could have won the White House that year. The worst economic crisis since the Great Depression, two lengthy and unpopular wars, a dysfunctional political system, and a deep dissatisfaction with the administration of George W. Bush had persuaded enough Americans that the country needed a real change and a different kind of leader to preside over it. With powerful rhetorical skills and a message that mixed vision and pragmatism, Barack Obama seemed to offer up a new look and promise in American politics and a "yes we can" bipartisanship in a "no you won't" partisan Washington.

Voting in numbers not seen since the mid-1960s Americans were willing to give Obama a chance to make good on those promises.[3] It had been a good win too. A young, charismatic, historic president had just been elected with 53 percent of the popular vote, a greater percentage than any Democratic candidate since Johnson (including Jimmy Carter, who barely crossed the 50 percent mark). And Obama, the first president since Jack Kennedy to win the White House directly from the

Senate, had a Democratic Congress to back him up. Democrats doubled their majority in the House and eventually gained a 60-seat majority in the Senate. At 68 percent, the new president's personal approval rating held its own with some of America's most popular presidents.[4] Of his nine immediate predecessors, only Eisenhower and Kennedy began their presidencies with higher numbers.

Expectations had risen through the ozone layer. And the media, in thrall of the new president, certainly played its role. In 2008 alone, *Time* magazine featured Obama on its cover fifteen times.[5] Obama and his team also did their fair share in hyping matters too. "Now there are some who question the scale of our ambitions, who suggest that our system cannot tolerate too many big plans," the new president declared in his inaugural address to a crowd estimated at 1.8 million on the National Mall. "What the cynics fail to understand is that the ground has shifted beneath them, that the stale political arguments that have consumed us for so long, no longer apply."[6]

Because for so many the ascent to the mountaintop of promise and expectation had been so heady and fast, the disappointment seemed all the greater when the realities of politics and governance set in. By the summer of 2010, the economy was again weakening and shedding more jobs. On the eve of the November 2010 midterm elections, Obama's approval numbers stood at 45 percent.[7] The next day, the country woke up (yet again) to a dramatically changed political landscape. Democrats lost six seats in the Senate and 60 in the House, the most in a midterm election since 1938. The midterm results shouldn't have come as much of a surprise. Two months earlier Gallup recorded strong opposition to all of the president's signature initiatives: 52 percent against the stimulus; 56 percent against the auto bailout and health care; and 61 percent disapproval of the bank bailouts.[8] To be sure, this was a congressional midterm, an event rarely kind to incumbent presidents. Only twice in the twentieth century have parties of the incumbent actually picked up seats. But the wave that washed over Washington was more than just dissatisfaction with Congress; it seemed to be a serious indictment of the direction of the president's own policies.

The next two years would have their presidential highs. But the transformative promise of groundbreaking change—always idealized and overdone—collided with the realities of Republican opposition and obstructionism, divisions within the president's own party, and the sheer complexity of the issues the administration wanted to address. In the fall of 2012, a visibly older, grayer, and perhaps wiser Barack Obama took the stage at his party's convention in Charlotte, North Carolina, hoping to regain some of the "yes we can" spirit of the earlier days. In 2008, the president's convention speech had used the word *promise* 32 times. That night, Obama mentioned it 7. Indeed, the speech seemed long on encouraging patience and looking toward the future. It was just as well. With unemployment still over 8 percent and the president's personal approval rating below 50 percent, it was not smart politics to dwell on the present.

Still, despite an uncertain and fitful economic recovery and a very unpopular health-care law, the president won reelection with a mandate that confounded his Republican opponents and delighted his support- ers, who saw legitimacy in the voters' verdict and validation too of the Affordable Care Act. Older white males had deserted Obama in droves. But the president was now in a more elite club with only sixteen of his predecessors who had been elected to a second term. It was even pos- sible to imagine that during a second term, the president might be able to fulfill many of the objectives that eluded him in his first, including gun control legislation, immigration reform, and maybe something sig- nificant on debt and spending. The horrific shootings at Sandy Hook Elementary School even offered up a rare national moment in which he might begin to lead the country forward out of its partisan morass.

It is a stunning testament to the challenges of the presidency, and this president's in particular, that 2013 would prove to be the tough- est and most frustrating year—even the worst year—of Obama's presidency. Obama should not have been all that surprised. The sixth year of a two-term president, otherwise known as the sixth-year curse, is indeed a tough one. Scandal, attrition to a political coalition, fatigue, bad midterms for the incumbent's party, all have to varying degrees plagued every president in his sixth year since Grant.[9]

It started hopefully enough, with a successful bipartisan deal to manage the fiscal cliff. But there would be no soft landings for the president and his administration. A series of self-inflicted wounds—scandals involving the IRS and then the NSA's Eric Snowden revelations, as well as hearings on the terror attack on the Benghazi consulate—created a sense that the administration was not only filled with bunglers and incompetents, but also that the president was not in charge and that government could not be trusted. The immense failure of the rollout of his signature health-care initiative only seemed to highlight the marriage of mistrust and incompetence. And it was hardly surprising early in 2014 that the president's general approval ratings fell to 42 percent, only two points higher than George W. Bush's in the fifth year of his presidency.[10] More seriously, the trust in Obama personally plummeted, particularly after the "you can keep your doctor" controversy. According to a CNN/ORC poll in November 2013, 53 percent of Americans found Obama to be not honest and trustworthy.[11] Indeed, the president seemed buoyant and relaxed as he delivered his 2014 State of the Union address, but the substance of the speech reflected a much-diminished presidency. From the pinnacle of wanting to transform in 2008, Barack Obama was reduced in 2014 to not even transacting with uncooperative Republicans and to using unilateral executive orders to maintain the forward momentum of his presidency. "At the end of the day, we're part of a long running story," he told the *New Yorker*'s David Remnick, in a phrase stunning in its scale of reduced expectations. "We just try to get our paragraph right."[12]

What happened? How could a president who four years earlier had been compared to Lincoln, Roosevelt, and Kennedy all rolled into one have fallen so low that journalists now wondered whether Jimmy Carter would not be a more appropriate presidential comparison? Among recent presidents, only George W. Bush's (40 percent) and Richard Nixon's (27 percent) approval ratings were lower than Obama's at year five of his presidency. There was certainly plenty of time left on Obama's presidential clock, and more than one presidency has been prematurely written off. As Obama told Peter Baker of the *New York Times* early in 2010, "I start slow and finish strong."[13] But still the doubts persisted. Could it be that Obama was done and that the president would spend his entire second term trying to preserve—if he could—the accomplishments of his first? How did it come to this?

Obama's critics and defenders have their own answers about why matters turned out as they did. Republicans were simply unwilling to work with him on any of the big issues; the president wouldn't reach out to them. The stimulus was too small or it had been too big; health care was a great historic achievement or it had been a terrible overreach; Obama had been too exposed in the media on one hand, or had not used the bully pulpit enough to explain his policies on the other. The president had tried to be too bipartisan, even postpartisan, or he had not been partisan and fiercely passionate enough.

The polarity of much of the criticism was validated by a 2009 Gallup poll revealing that Barack Obama was the most polarizing first-year president in more than half a century.[14] For some, Obama was nothing short of an alien president and could have arrived from another planet. To others, he was not a real Christian, maybe even a Muslim; for the birthers, he had won the presidency illegitimately because they believed he had not even been born in America. Independents were worried and confused about the growing costs of his health-care initiative. Even his supporters began to wonder who he was and whether he was up to the job. *Harper's* had already featured Obama on its cover as Herbert Hoover with the caption "the best and the brightest blow it again."[15] Like Hoover, Kevin Baker wrote, Obama wanted to realize a new vision for society without cutting himself free from the dogmas of the past. Andrew Sullivan, on the other hand, who never expected a messiah, argues that Obama has been playing the long game and under trying circumstances has accomplished much.[16]

Assessing the significance of a presidency in the middle of a second term is a perilous enterprise. Obama's harshest critics believe he was a disaster; his erstwhile supporters judge him an extraordinary president who accomplished at least one great thing, health-care reform, and they believe he could have done more had it not been for willfully obstructionist Republicans. Time will be required to see the Obama presidency for what it was on its own merits and in comparison with those that came before and will come after. Indeed, who succeeds Obama will matter. Should it be a Democrat, the chances of a more sustainable legacy not undone will be greater: Obama will enter an even more elite group of two-term presidents (he will be the first to serve two full terms in the new century, together with only two in the last, to have maintained party control). Though how much of that achievement will be Obama's or his Democrat successor's appeal will be arguable to say the least. But what can we say about Obama's presidency almost six years in?

First, as with any president, performance is judged by the confluence of man and moment, and that moment includes all the other actors that both help and hinder a president. Barack Obama inherited, as all presidents do, a unique set of circumstances—his scarier than most, to be sure. But neither the political system in which he operated nor the crises he faced were created de novo, wholly untethered from his predecessors' problems and experiences. The challenges of the post-FDR presidency plagued Obama too: high expectations, an intractable crisis, intensifying political polarization, and an intrusive and ubiquitous media. However unique his circumstances, Barack Obama was still—like many of his predecessors—part poster child for the travails of the modern presidency. As such, he is also exhibit A in validating the central premise of this book. To put it simply, the job is just too big and expectations too high. Convinced he was living in historic times, he raised expectations further by seeking to transform both American politics and policies without fully understanding that neither the times nor the political environment would support dramatic change. He has certainly not been a failed president. But neither will he be a great one. Unlike FDR, JFK, or even LBJ, there will not be a BHO.

Second, Barack Obama is a poster child for something else too: disappointer in chief. Whatever your judgment of his policies or whether they prove to have harmed or benefited the nation, there is a deep dissatisfaction across the board. He disappointed many of those who voted for him and would vote for him again; disappointed those who thought he would end partisanship and change Washington; disappointed those who believed he could transform the country and America's foreign policy too; and disappointed those who believed he would be different than any other president since Kennedy. Simply put, the president has failed to live up to the expectations his supporters had for him and the ones he set for himself—stunningly so.

I'll say it again, because its important: all presidents disappoint, partly because campaigning demands the articulation of promises that governing simply cannot deliver. It is in the nature of the job description, the challenges presidents face, and the system within which they operate. But Obama was different. By virtue of who he was and what he said, he took America to the Mount Everest of the possible; he promised transformation, an end to business as usual politics in Washington, pledged himself to a new postpartisan politics and to a remaking of America at home and abroad. "I am running for president of the United States because the dreams of the American people must not be endangered anymore," candidate Obama proclaimed in 2008.[17]

We can soften the edges of the critique all we want: he averted another Great Depression; delivered a historic if deeply polarizing health-care bill; saved the auto industry; withdrew from Iraq; killed Osama bin Laden; ended "don't ask, don't tell"; improved America's image abroad. According to Politifact's "Obameter," the president made over 500 separate promises during his campaigns; of these he's made good on 241

(45 percent), and broken about 22 percent of his commitments.[18] And we can come up with a slew of explanations as to why he couldn't do more: he inherited a deep economic crisis, the Republicans were out to get him, etc.

But in the end, there is still a vast sense of emptiness in the space between what he pledged to deliver and what he actually produced. Maybe part of it is driven by Obama's sense of grandiosity and self-confidence. "It took time to free the slaves; it took time for women to get the vote; it took time for workers to get the right to organize," he told a fundraiser in the fall of 2010.[19] Maybe it is his high-sounding rhetoric, the lyrical uplift that started many Americans believing again only to have expectations fall flat when reality intruded again and again; or the gap between his promise to break with the past and the reality that much of his economic and foreign policy was mired in it; or maybe it is his professorial conviction that he has all the answers to what ails America and his students, in this case the American people, should listen. "We're hardwired," the president told a room full of physicians at a fundraiser, "not to always think clearly when we're scared."[20] *I know you're worried,* the president seemed to be saying, *but follow me, I know exactly what to do.*

Barack Obama wanted to do great things; behind his cool, detached demeanor was the hot, combustible drive of a man who wanted greatness. That is certainly no transgression, certainly not in a man Americans elect and empower to lead them out of a crisis toward a better future. He saw a nation in great peril and moved to seek transformation on a variety of social issues while he was battling the nastiest economic crisis since the 1930s and fighting three wars—in Iraq, Afghanistan, and against terror. But that kind of reach also requires another kind of responsibility—to see the world clearly as it is before you seek to fashion it the way you want it to be. Not reading the terrain accurately, failing to assess whether his administration had the political muscle to negotiate it, and missing what the public expected and wanted from a president can lead to unhappy consequences. Barack Obama found himself trapped in a classic no-win situation and wandering in a political no-man's-land. He had raised expectations for economic recovery he could never meet, spoke of a postpartisan America he could not produce, and on other issues, such as health care, he stressed an already broken political system. By doing so, he disappointed his liberal base; confused and alienated independents, swing voters, and moderates who elected him; energized Republicans; and even helped midwife a new phenomenon called the Tea Party.

Third, that Barack Obama managed to accomplish as much as he did, given the circumstances he inherited—disappointer in chief or not—is impressive. But while Obama will be judged a historic president for who he is—America's first black president—he will not be judged to be a great one for what he has done. The ingredients for presidential greatness did not blend together in a way to make that judgment possible. He is not likely to be seen as the FDR or LBJ transformative president he hoped to be. And this is partly because he looked at government as a change agent and source of remedy at a time when most Americans feared, worried, or were in conflict about its efficacy and value.

Nor can he claim the persona of Kennedy, who captured a nation's imagination; nor even the mantle of Reagan, who altered the debate or, as Obama himself admitted, changed the trajectory of the country. Unlike Kennedy and Reagan, who helped inspire countless future politicians to seek elected office, Obama has seemingly failed to inspire a new generation to choose that path.[21] Obama was more likely closest to Bill Clinton, a fact historian David Greenberg took note of a year into his presidency. Both men were elected with strikingly similar mandates in the Electoral College and popular vote. Both faced strong opposition from Republicans who imagined the president to be far more radical than he was, and both concentrated on the economy. In one respect, Obama was Clinton Plus—he succeeded in health care and avoided personal scandal. But in another big way he was Clinton Minus—he was not nearly as likeable or as good a pol. Obama will be lucky if he can leave office with approval ratings as high as Clinton's or with an economy in as good a shape.

That would have been hard under any circumstance, even if the remainder of his presidency comes off without a flaw. His *crisis,* a complex banking/financial and housing sector recession, was sufficiently nasty and deep that he could not break it easily or quickly, but not adequately encumbering enough that it enabled him to tame the politics in Washington as FDR or Johnson had done. As for Obama's *capacity*—his ability to extract out of his crisis some long-term transformative change through political smarts, persuasion, hands-on working with Congress, and deal making—the president did not so much miss his FDR/LBJ moment as misread it. Most of the voting public seemed to want a way out of a terrible recession and two long, unwinnable, and costly wars in Afghanistan and Iraq; if they could get it, they wanted a renewed faith in their government's competence. The public didn't seek transformation or a reformulation of the social contract. And Obama neither had the huge partisan dominance (of an FDR or LBJ) nor even the working bipartisanship with the Republicans to bring it about in any event. The Affordable Care Act of 2010 will be his legacy issue, and in years to come it may well be seen as a moral, economic, and practical good. But there are too many complexities, uncertainties, and unknowns to call it transformative now. Medicare and Medicaid and two civil rights bills could not save Johnson's reputation and make him a great president. And 2008 was not 1964/1965, let alone 1932. Not even close.

Finally, while the presidential historians remind us that *character* trumps all, no president—no matter how smart, determined, or gifted—does well in the face of a severe economic recession. Those who do survive these crises are rare (FDR or Reagan). And why do they survive, even prosper? Because enough Americans not only like and trust the president, but they also think they know who he is and what he is willing to fight for. Here, Obama had a Jekyll and Hyde problem. The *Washington Post*'s Michael Gerson argues that Obama's personality has an aspirational and transformational side that is in conflict with his personal sense of complexity and limits, what David Remnick describes as the "calm, professorial immersion in complexity."[22] Part pragmatist, part believer, but always capable of seeing all sides to the argument, in his first six years in office, he seemed too often at war with himself and emotionally detached. And in such a state, it was too hard for him to be at peace with his public.

The president wanted greatness but often seemed unsure of what he was prepared to risk for it. Perhaps because even as he articulated the desire for transformative change, he knew intellectually he could not attain it. And even if he knew his own mind, he lacked the circumstances that would have enabled him to produce change and the clear and compelling message to convince the public to follow. By nature, Barack Obama is not a partisan, a populist, or a revolutionary. Instead, he finds his comfort zone in conciliation and accommodation, and in the rational, empirical, logical world of policy analysis. In his first six years in office, President Obama promised transformation but could not be a transformer. His crisis and his own character would not allow it. Nor would his Republican opponents who were determined to just say no. Given what he hoped to achieve, the irony is that the president may well have been his own worst enemy.

The *New York Times*' David Brooks, an admirer of the president, wrote that to be an Obama supporter was "to toggle from being uplifted to feeling used."[23] Barack Obama's supporters misread him. We all house contradictory tendencies in our personalities that must coexist, sometimes very uneasily. He proved to be enough of a transformer to scare independents, but not enough of one to avoid disappointing his base. Obama is, by nature, a gradualist, yet he espoused ambitious goals because he actually wanted a transformation even though he lacked the persona and times to effect one. He believed in postpartisanship because by nature and instinct he is a conciliator who sought common ground, and yet he was forced to operate in an intensely partisan environment in which he never felt comfortable and in which he had trouble competing. Valerie Jarrett, perhaps his closest adviser, noted that Obama has little patience for the "inevitable theatrics of Washington. He's never gotten comfortable here."[24] In the end, having failed to adequately define himself, he let his supporters and opponents do it for him. "I am like a Rorschach test," he told the *New York Times* way back in 2008. "Even if people find me disappointing ultimately, they might gain something."[25] And the country did. Obama could not be the savior or the redeemer he and his supporters hoped he would be. But neither was he the catastrophic incompetent his critics imagined. In the end, he has made mistakes. And he has achieved much of value too. Being a Rorschach test can get a president reelected, with some favorable marks too. But it cannot get you an exclusive membership in the presidential Hall of Fame. In Obama's case, neither the times nor his own character or capacity would allow it.

CONCLUSION

Greatness with
a Small g

IN 1932, THREE YEARS INTO THE GREAT DEPRES-
sion, Walter Lippmann, the most influential columnist of his day, speculated about what Americans were searching for in their leaders: "They
are looking for new leaders, for men who are trusted and resolute and
eloquent in the conviction that the American destiny is to be free and
magnanimous . . . they are looking for leaders who will talk to the
people . . . about the sacrifices they must make, and about the discipline
they must impose upon themselves and about their responsibility to the
world and to posterity, about all the things which make a people self-
respecting, serene, and confident. May they not look in vain."[1]

Within a year, Franklin Roosevelt—whom Lippmann had described four months earlier (in what must have been one of the worst
predictions in modern politics) as a "pleasant man who without any
important qualifications for the office would very much like to be
president"—took the inaugural oath.[2]

So, why all the pessimism? Surely we can still produce another great
leader. As Lippmann suggested, nobody in 1932 was expecting an FDR,
let alone a president who would be elected four times. Indeed, our own
history shows that leaders emerge when you least expect them but when

you most need them. So, surely we can have another great president, right?

The best answer comes not from politics or history but from Gilbert and Sullivan. In their musical *H.M.S. Pinafore,* one of the catchiest tunes finds Captain Corcoran singing about his virtues in a lively back and forth with the chorus/crew:

> *And I'm never, never, sick at sea!*
> *What never?*
> *No, never!*
> *What never?*
> *Hardly ever!*[3]

Hardly ever. There you have it. And it's as good an answer as any. None of us can divine the future. Who knows what 2016, 2020, and beyond will bring? Good times or black swans; great presidents or average ones?

But politics is as much about probabilities as it is possibilities. And the trend line running against greatness in the presidency (twelve presidents and counting since FDR) seems pretty strong. The alignment of the right crisis, together with the right character and capacity necessary for greatness is rare under any circumstance; it has become much more so in the past 70 years. To compare 1932 to 2008 or FDR to Obama (as many did) is to fundamentally misunderstand the differences in their characters, personalities, and most important, their times. FDR's economic crisis was more severe, which broadened his options; Obama's political time, particularly the structural polarization of Washington's politics, severely narrowed his and made Rooseveltian transformational change impossible.

But the reality of long odds tells only part of the story. Times really have changed. Our challenges today are varied and diffused, our politics too broken and dysfunctional and unforgiving to be resolved by a single or a series of heroic presidential actions. Our crises are deadly, to be sure, but mostly for the longer term, not for the moment. And it is the urgency and clarity of the moment (even while keeping an eye on the future) that has always offered up the best chance for dramatic and effective presidential action. The relentlessness of crisis gives the right president the opportunity to tame American politics enough to create a consensus for effective action, and even to unify the country. The last such opportunity was 9/11. But that was a hard moment to exploit. In any event, the real crisis was wasted in the mix of unrealistic hopes and fears of two costly and unwinnable wars. And one of them—Iraq—led the nation down a dead-end path based on bad analysis and worse policy making. Today's problems—from debt to deficits—make Washington an even more unruly place and a president's job next to impossible.

Today an American president simultaneously confronts an economy that is impervious to remedial government actions (at least on jobs) and unwinnable wars abroad. Barack Obama has withdrawn American military forces from one war in Iraq (a country still horribly marred by violence and sectarian division) and presides over another unwinnable one in Afghanistan, where "victory" will be determined not by whether we win decisively but by when we can leave and what we leave behind. And if Iraq is any indication, while the future in Afghanistan may not be calamitous it won't be a terribly happy one either. At the same time, he grapples with a globalized financial system critical to America's own economic well-being, yet he is without much capacity to influence it. In the president's world these days, there's little finality, certainty, sense of completion, or slam-dunk successes.

Nor can any president dominate the day in quite the same way the greats seemed to dominate theirs. The national stage was smaller, the number of competing voices fewer, and the challenges they faced so irrepressible that they were able to focus and concentrate on them in a way that simply is not possible today. Personal and professional failings notwithstanding, they were by any standard extraordinary leaders of substance and depth, hardened and deepened by life's experiences, tragic loss, catastrophic illness, and, in Washington's case, even by battle. A remarkable mix of pragmatism and vision, prudence and risk-readiness made them great leaders who gained the public's trust. Their enemies and adversaries mocked and pilloried them publicly, yet each projected authority, confidence, and, in Lincoln's case, compassion; in doing so, they created unique bonds with the American people.

And they lived in extraordinary and formative times. Consider the fact that of the 27 amendments to the Constitution, more than half (15 to be exact) were passed between 1791 and 1870, roughly from Washington's to Lincoln's time. But these early amendments defined so much about the American enterprise: the limitation of centralized power, expansion of democracy, civil and protected freedoms, and the expansion of federal power at the expense of the states. Former secretary of state Dean Acheson called his memoir of his life in diplomacy *Present at the Creation*. The term seems much better suited to an even earlier time. How much more essential can times and leadership be? Washington created the basis for the presidency. Lincoln's election started the Civil War; his wartime leadership ended it, and his commitment to ending slavery would provide the basis for passage of the Thirteenth, Fourteenth (due process), and Fifteenth (right to vote without regard to race, color) Amendments, constitutional changes that would over time profoundly change the character of America, how we look at and govern ourselves too.

Today there are times when it seems that the president is just another voice, another politician talking in the cacophonous and divisive arena of American politics. He's often "just another guy talking," CNN's John King quipped during a chat we had on the presidency.[4] The combination of an increasingly personalized presidency and a teardown, nonstop media is a deadly one. The president lives in a fishbowl (partly because he needs and wants to) and is constantly on display, trying to reconcile impossible expectations with a diminished capacity to deliver. And even if he delivers, unless his politics and persona are right, he won't get much credit in the take-no-prisoners arena that's American politics today. It is hard to imagine in today's politics a truly popular and beloved president, or even one like a Kennedy or Reagan who embodies his time and captures the public's imagination.

Those politics, fractured and polarized as they are, also undermine a president's capacity to produce a consensus on big, controversial issues. The old saw that we have an eighteenth-century political system designed by geniuses and now run by idiots is only partially true. Our governing system was designed to resist, or at least constrain, comprehensive change. In America, power is too fragmented and diffuse to produce big change in all but the most exigent circumstances. As we have seen, there have been few truly transforming moments in American history, when presidents took decisions that would fundamentally alter the course of the nation.

Instead, American governance has sought redress in gradual, incremental reforms. These days, even that's difficult. Today, in the face of our tribalized politics, presidents can't put together the large majorities that FDR or LBJ fashioned; even bipartisan cooperation has become, at best, forced and grudging, a game of political hot potato to avoid public censure and the blame for gridlock. Pushing big reforms with a narrow edge can stress the system, make a president politically vulnerable, and may not even guarantee that reforms endure. Jefferson's warning that transformative change shouldn't rest on slender majorities may yet prove true for President Obama's health-care reform, an initiative passed by a Democratic Congress with no Republican support against the backdrop of a divided public worried about big deficits and bigger government. That accomplishment, historic though it surely is, still faces a very uncertain future.

Waiting to be rescued by another FDR may be understandable, but it is also misplaced. The demand for effective leaders, let alone great ones, has always exceeded the supply. And hoping for another FDR takes the rest of us off the hook. Leaders of that caliber cannot exist in our system without followers who are willing to sacrifice and invest in leadership and in themselves as well.

Forget great presidents for a minute. What if our current leadership deficit is partly related to a loss of confidence and faith in ourselves, and to the realization that we cannot imagine that a touch of greatness can be rooted in national purpose in our own lives? To imagine being great means to be identified and associated with some broader enterprise or cause, a reason to look beyond your narrow concerns and to sacrifice and serve. Today, there is no such national enterprise and common cause, little sense of shared sacrifice or burden. We have a volunteer military and a surrogate political class to do our national service and politics for us. Occupy Wall Street—the closest thing to a sustained protest movement in America since the 1960s—was always too diffuse, unorganized, and unrepresentative to reflect the need or capacity to drive change on the national level. And the Tea Party, the putative Republican insurgency on the right, is too partisan and polarizing to appeal to Americans outside of a narrow range.

Leaders cannot exist without followers in the best sense of the word. And both need to believe in themselves and each other and be linked in a broader cause they both share. "In 1934, the government was us," Theodore Marmor and Jerry Mashaw write. "We had shared circumstances, shared risks and shared obligations. Today the government is the other—not an institution for the achievement of our common goals, but an alien presence that stands between us and the realization of our individual ambitions. Programs of social insurance have become 'entitlements,' a word apparently meant to signify not a collectively provided and cherished basis for family-income security, but a sinister threat to our national well-being."[5]

This sense of distance, detachment, and otherness is best reflected in our bizarre relationship and attitude toward our government. On one hand, we have a significantly diminished faith and trust in Washington. A September 2013 Pew poll showed that 77 percent of Americans were either angry or frustrated with the federal government.[6] Right now, the level of trust in Washington, declining for years with several notable exceptions, is lower than at any point since the 1970s.

At the same time, we are more dependent on federal and state programs than at any time in our history. A 2008 Cornell University poll even suggested that we do not even realize how dependent we are.[7] Ninety-four percent of those polled initially denied using government programs, but when shown a list of possible services, they admitted to benefiting from at least one; the average respondent had used four federal programs. Public polling continues to reveal strong opposition to the way the nation is governed and great frustration with Congress and with a federal government that's perceived to be doing too much. Still, those same surveys show a pretty even split on the issue of whether government should only provide basic functions and services or whether it should try to be more proactive to improve the lives of its citizens. Americans clearly want less, but more effective, government.

For a president who wants to change things, the issue of the government as friend or adversary comes with serious consequences. In the 1930s there was clearly a sense that the federal government was effective, necessary, and benefited the lives of individuals in need. The war years shaped a sense of national purpose, power, and success in war making, national security, and economic growth and prosperity. And Washington, DC, stood at the center of those successes. Today, many Americans view Washington as a separate planet inhabited by alien creatures who have only a vague understanding of what life is like on Earth and what many Americans want or need. For a president facing challenges and crises that can only be addressed, at least partially, through effective federal policies, this represents a serious problem. How does a president legitimize his policies if the public and much of the political class oppose many of the instruments at his disposal (federal spending, programs, bureaucracy) to carry them out? A president can run effectively against a Congress with an 11 percent approval rating, but he can't run against himself as head of the very government that's trying to fix what ails the nation. At a moment when many Americans are at best ambivalent, and at worst hostile, to big government, a big government president (which is how Barack Obama is perceived) has a major problem.

So where does all of this leave us and the future of the presidency? If we cannot have, seldom need, and do not want another great president, what do we want?

"Maybe you should consider the notion of greatness with a small g," CNN's John King observed later in our conversation. "Not likely we're going to see another Washington, Lincoln, or FDR anytime soon."[8]

The very concept offends, but King is on to something. The undeniably great presidents who wrestled decisively and successfully with the nation-encumbering challenges that defined us as Americans have come and gone. But does that mean we cannot have presidents who are capable of great acts and moments; presidents who inspire us both in their words and deeds; leaders who through wise judgment, boldness, prudence, and restraint help get us closer to solutions to our problems? After all, had the story of the presidency only been a record of the greats and their crises, the institution would have lost its salience in our politics long ago. A half a dozen other presidents who left honorable, consequential, and memorable legacies fill out a considerable part of the story. But the far larger part is a story of competent men, most of whom discharged their duties ably and without personal scandal, respected both the law and the Constitution, and, while making their fair share of mistakes, managed to accomplish a thing or two that benefited the nation. They were certainly not great leaders, but good ones carrying out a difficult job in tough and sometimes impossible circumstances.

Historian David Greenberg has written a wonderful essay on why last chapters almost always disappoint.[9] They do so, he argues, largely because writers of books on complex social or political issues are weak in the "to do" category and usually come up with "utopian, banal, or unhelpful or out of tune with the rest of the book" solutions for the problem at hand.

When it comes to fixing the presidency—to mixing up some magic potion to create another great one, or to addressing our broken politics—honest analysis almost always leads to frustrating paralysis. I will spare you the obligatory civics lesson about how to reform the American presidency and our political system by abolishing the Electoral College; imposing mandatory voting or term limits; changing the president's four-year terms to one six-year administration; bringing back the draft; or creating a competitive third party. The Constitution has been amended 27 times in 236 years. (The first ten—the Bill of Rights—came as a package in 1791; the last was in 1992—compensation for senators and representatives). There are no quick or easy fixes, and it is likely that no major transformations in our political system are coming. The system we have is basically the one we're stuck with. Get over it.

Solving the nation's problems, including the dysfunction in our politics, is not about just seeing and accepting the world the way it is. Going down that road would lead to no change at all, and to despair or even cynicism to boot. It also makes no sense just to see the world the way you want it to be. That would invariably lead to overreach and failure. And since no one in life gets 100 percent of anything, that means finding the balance between the two. Jack Kennedy squared the circle by describing himself as an idealist without illusion. And that might apply to how we see the presidency too. Toward that end, let me offer several suggestions, most of which have much more to do with altering our own expectations and how we look at our presidents, and the presidency, than redesigning the architecture of our political system, the presidency, or who holds the job.

First, read more presidential history. Studying the American past is not so much about learning specific lessons, though there is

still much value in George Santayana's warning that "those who cannot remember the past are condemned to repeat it."[10] I like the notion
ascribed to Mark Twain instead: history does not so much repeat as
it rhymes. Look for the broader rhythmic patterns of the past rather
than the strict repetitions or parallels when it comes to presidential
performance. Historian Stephen Skowronek's notion of shared political time is instructive here.[11] Presidential success is neither random nor
necessarily driven by certain personality traits or skill sets. Certain
presidencies—Andrew Jackson and Franklin Roosevelt, or James Polk
and John Kennedy—shared similar political circumstances that shaped
what could be achieved and what could not, and shaped how presidents
were also able to make their own politics as a consequence.

The world did not begin yesterday. And romping through the past
may help reduce the odds that wrongheaded and simple comparisons
will be made between past and current presidents, or misleading notions
that our times are similar and ripe for the kinds of big changes some of
the greats produced in theirs. That Barack Obama was compared to our
three greatest presidents in the aftermath of his election is a very cautionary tale. Studying the past offers up perspective, prudence, and humility.
And it should be a guard, particularly for great powers and for presidents,
against the two transgressions that can get them into big trouble—the
hubris of thinking that they know the world, their own country's political
reality included, and the arrogance of believing that they can somehow
dominate or transform it. Finally, looking at how presidents dealt with
the challenges of their own times can in fact provide perspective in how
we deal with ours, specifically in regard to how and under what circumstances presidents are able to succeed and how they do it.

Second, think transaction, not transformation. Most presidents
do not govern and lead in extraordinary times. They are not faced with
a single overriding issue that threatens the nation and creates the kind
of urgency and relentlessness than can lead to catastrophe or genius
accomplishment. Instead today they face many issues: unruly politics

that put a premium on achieving a consensus, and powers that, however formidable, are really quite constrained. And yet we often judge our presidents as if we expected transformation, partly because we have expectations that they themselves have helped raise in the course of winning the White House.

The problems that confront America today cannot be addressed through unilaterally conceived presidential grand designs, plans, and solutions. Climate change, improving economic competitiveness, structural unemployment, debt, dependence on hydrocarbons, educational reform—these are systemic challenges. And the challenge of systemic change is relevant in foreign policy too, where big schemes and visions not only usually fail, but can get the nation into serious trouble. Despite his rhetoric and image, Ronald Reagan was a careful and pragmatic transactor, certainly in his approach to the former Soviet Union, and he had a partner in its leader, Mikhail Gorbachev. His successor, George H. W. Bush, perhaps the last highly effective foreign policy president we've had, was also a skilled transactor. George W. Bush, on the other hand, tried to be a transformer, not even of his own country, but of Iraq and Afghanistan in the wake of 9/11, and paid the price for reaching too far.

The fact that government is not seen as an effective source of remedy, that our politics are so polarized, and the problems so complex, raises the fascinating question of just what kind of leader can operate in these circumstances. What we cannot afford, however, is to cling to the cardboard view of leadership in which the charismatic leader constructs the powerful narrative and then willfully persuades Congress, the media, the public, and the rest of the world to go along with it. It just does not work. What it does do is to raise expectations and increase frustration. Indeed, these days the capacity of presidents to sway public opinion rests at the margins.

No one is arguing that the president should give up on persuasion or craft messages that leave the public down and dispirited. Optimism is the key currency of great presidents. But that faith in the future and in America's capacity to solve problems must be grounded and real too. Most presidents are not visionaries, nor do they govern in times that allow those transformations to become real. My sense is that for the foreseeable future, presidents will succeed or fail—as most have in the past—by whether they can make the most of the circumstances they confront and can add political direction to the chaos and confusion they inherit. Big speeches are fine, even visions of a better America. But more important are the political skills that are required to build coalitions and control their own parties, and even in the tribalized world of politics, find ways to reach out to the opposing party to build bipartisan support. Indeed, however fanciful it appears today, sustainable solutions to the nation's problems will require Republican and Democratic buy-in. And that will require future presidents to put in the time and the hands-on effort to work with Congress and to develop a more collective and collegial approach to effective governance. Forget heroic action in the presidency for a moment. Solutions to the nation's problems will be rooted in getting Congressional, public, and interest group support and in securing the inevitable compromises that will entail.

Third, think good, not great. *Good* is not how we would like to think of our presidents. The word is just too ordinary, common, even banal. *Good* is a word someone might use in a eulogy at a funeral: *He was a good father and friend.* We do not want presidents who are haughty, arrogant, or self-absorbed, but we do want presidents who are special, talented, even unique. We certainly are not looking for average, conventional, above average, or good candidates. We want exceptional, great presidents. And yet there is a case to be made for goodness as a desirable standard for presidents, particularly in an era when heroic leadership is not in ready supply—and maybe even if it were. In a fascinating discussion of the differences between goodness and greatness, presidential scholar Lara Brown reminds us that goodness is rooted in the concepts of proportionality and moderation.[12] Achieving greatness, on the other hand, might demand a single-minded focus, ambition, and ruthlessness, that could easily produce all kinds of bad behaviors, not to mention the conduct of leaders like Adolf Hitler or Joseph Stalin. Sometimes greatness and goodness are compatible. Lincoln was a great president; his humanity and compassion made him a good man too. Roosevelt was also a great president. But his manipulative nature, arrogance, and adulterous behavior couldn't make him a good man in quite the same way.

We should not dismiss the idea of goodness and good presidents, because given the troubled history of the modern presidency, undeniably good presidents are not that easy to come by; it's still a high expectation to meet. And by good we can suggest at least three distinct qualities: first, good presidents in the sense that they are effective, know what they are doing, and can be productive leaders; second, good presidents in regard to having a moral and ethical compass; and finally, good emotional intelligence too, in the sense that they are emotionally capable and intelligent, with a balanced sense of themselves and others.[13] In discussing a strong president more than half a century ago, presidential scholar Clinton Rossiter essentially identified the qualities that we should want to see in a good one: "A strong president is a bad president, a curse upon the land, unless his means are constitutional, and his ends democratic, unless he acts in ways that are fair, dignified, and familiar, and pursues policies to which a 'persistent and undoubted' majority of the people has given support."[14] Good presidents are those who remain within sound moral parameters and constitutional ones too and can go about the business of leading and governing the nation with prudence, capacity, and resolve.

The disappearance of our greatest presidents is no cause for despair and cynicism about our politics; nor is it reason to give in to the declinist tropes that America's best days are behind it, or that we cannot have successful leaders. But it does mean that we need to come to terms with the limits of a president's capacity to fix things and with our own desire to find comprehensive solutions to all our problems. We must also abandon any notion that the One is coming to rescue us. And we must assume our own responsibilities as citizens to educate ourselves, to participate in our politics, and to strive to strike the right balance that allows us not just to be partisans but also be advocates of America's national interest too.

It is worth repeating: America rarely needs great presidents. But we need, and must have, good ones who can lead effectively, respect the law and the Constitution, and keep us ever focused on the America that can be even while working steadily and doggedly to better the America that is. The time has come for us to abandon our illusions and have a more realistic appreciation of the person, the office, and the job we have elected our presidents to do. Maybe then, perhaps only then, can we allow and enable our presidents to be truly good without always expecting them to be great.

NOTES

INTRODUCTION

1. John Keegan, "Sir Winston Churchill," *Time,* April 13, 1998, http://content.time
    .com/time/magazine/article/0,9171,988157,00.html.
2. Micah Zenko, "The L Word," *Foreign Policy,* April 2, 2013, http://www.foreign
    policy.com/articles/2013/04/02/the_l_word.
3. "Leadership Program Directory," International Leadership Association, accessed
    May 5, 2014, http://www.ila-net.org/Resources/LPD/index.htm.
4. Barbara Kellerman, *The End of Leadership* (New York: Harper, 2012), 159–63.
5. Ezra Klein, "Who Listens to a President," *New Yorker,* March 19, 2012, http://
    www.newyorker.com/reporting/2012/03/19/120319fa_fact_klein.
6. Karl Marx, "The Eighteenth Brumaire of Louis Bonaparte," quoted in Paul Ken-
    nedy, "Do Leaders Make History, or Is It Beyond Their Control?," *New York
    Times,* May 21, 2010, http://www.nytimes.com/2010/05/22/opinion/22iht-ed
    kennedy.html.
7. "Freedom in the World 2014," Freedom House, January 23, 2014, http://freedom
    house.org/report/freedom-world/freedom-world-2014.
8. Moises Naim, *The End of Power: From Boardrooms to Battlefields and Churches
    to States, Why Being in Charge Isn't What It Used to Be* (New York: Basic Books,
    2013), 5.
9. Ibid., 13.
10. Joseph S. Nye Jr., "The Future of American Power," *Foreign Affairs,* November/
    December 2010, http://www.foreignaffairs.com/articles/66796/joseph-s-nye-jr
    /the-future-of-american-power.
11. Bret Stephens, "Nobels and National Greatness," *Wall Street Journal,* October 14,
    2013, http://online.wsj.com/news/articles/SB10001424052702303376904579135
    283429301854.
12. "Americans' Approval of Congress Drops to Single Digits," *New York Times,*
    October 25, 2011, http://www.nytimes.com/interactive/2011/10/25/us/politics
    /approval-of-congress-drops-to-single-digits.html.
13. "Congress Less Popular than Cockroaches, Traffic Jams," Public Policy Polling,
    January 8, 2013, http://www.publicpolicypolling.com/main/2013/01/congress
    -less-popular-than-cockroaches-traffic-jams.html.
14. George Packer, "The Empty Chamber," *New Yorker,* August 9, 2010, 14.
15. Thomas E. Mann and Norman J. Ornstein, *The Broken Branch: How Congress Is
    Failing America and How to Get It Back on Track* (New York: Oxford University
    Press, 2006).

16. Rachel Weiner, "McCain Calls Paul, Cruz, Amash 'wacko birds,'" *Washington Post,* March 8, 2013, http://www.washingtonpost.com/blogs/post-politics/wp/2013/03/08/mccain-calls-paul-cruz-amash-wacko-birds/.

17. Dean Keith Simonton, *Greatness: Who Makes History and Why* (New York: Guilford, 1994), 340.

18. Robert Dallek, *Harry S. Truman: The American Presidents Series: The 33rd President, 1945–1953* (New York: Macmillan, 2008), 68.

19. Thomas Andrew Bailey, *Presidential Greatness: The Image and the Man from George Washington to the Present* (New York: Irvington Publishers, 1978), 3.

20. Jeffrey M. Jones, "History Usually Kinder to Ex-Presidents," Gallup, April 25, 2013, http://www.gallup.com/poll/162044/history-usually-kinder-presidents.aspx.

21. James Warren, "After 50 Years, How We Remember the Legacy of President John F. Kennedy," *New York Daily News,* May 5, 2014, http://www.nydailynews.com/news/national/jfk-legacy-article-1.1514763#ixzz30rZcjSx0.

22. Andrew Dugan and Frank Newport, "Americans Rate JFK as Top Modern President," Gallup, November 15, 2013, http://www.gallup.com/poll/165902/americans-rate-jfk-top-modern-president.aspx.

23. Larry Sabato, *The Kennedy Half Century: The Presidency, Assassination, and Lasting Legacy of John F. Kennedy* (New York: Bloomsbury, 2013).

PART I

1. Bill Moyers, interview by Robin Lindley, History News Network, December 17, 2013, http://hnn.us/article/141337.

2. Michael R. Beschloss, "Annals of the Presidency: Seven Ways to Win Friends," *New Yorker,* January 30, 1995, http://www.newyorker.com/archive/1995/01/30/1995_01_30_043_TNY_CARDS_000369330.

3. Jon Meacham, *American Lion: Andrew Jackson in the White House* (New York: Random House, 2008).

4. Arthur H. Vandenberg, *The Greatest American, Alexander Hamilton: An Historical Analysis of His Life and Works Together with a Symposium of Opinions by Distinguished Americans* (New York: G.P. Putnam's Sons, 1921).

5. William L. Hamilton, "Calling Up the P.R. Troops For the Father of His Country," *New York Times,* February 8, 1999, http://www.nytimes.com/1999/02/08/us/calling-up-the-p-r-troops-for-the-father-of-his-country.html.

6. Barack Obama, interview with Diane Sawyer, *ABC World News,* January 25, 2010, http://abcnews.go.com/WN/Obama/abc-world-news-diane-sawyer-diane-sawyer-interviews/story?id=9659064&singlePage=true.

7. "Presidential Elections Data," American Presidency Project, accessed April 11, 2014, http://www.presidency.ucsb.edu/elections.php.

8. Pieter Geyl, *Napoleon, For and Against* (New Haven: Yale University Press, 1949), 15.

CHAPTER 1

1. Jean Edward Smith, *FDR* (New York: Random House, 2008), 296–98.

2. James A Hagerty, "Special to the New York Times: Assassin Shoots 5 Times," *New York Times,* February 16, 1933; retrieved from http://search.proquest.com/docview/100770597. See also: Kenneth S. Davis, *FDR: The New York Years* (New York: Random House, 1985), 427–32; Nathan Miller, *FDR: An Intimate History*

(Garden City, NY: Doubleday, 1983), 297–300; Conrad Black, *Franklin Delano Roosevelt: Champion of Freedom* (New York: Public Affairs, 2003), 263–64; Arthur M. Schlesinger, *The Crisis of the Old Order* (Boston: Houghton Mifflin, 1957), 465–66; Michael F. Reilly and William J. Slocum, *Reilly of the White House* (New York: Simon and Schuster, 1947), 48–52; Jean Edward Smith, *FDR*, 296–98.

3. Raymond Moley, *After Seven Years* (New York: Da Capo, 1972), 139.
4. Ira Berlin, "Book review: 'The Scorpion's Sting: Antislavery before the Civil War' by James Oakes," *Washington Post*, May 30, 2014, http://www.washingtonpost .com/opinions/book-review-the-scorpions-sting-antislavery-before-civil-war-by -james-oakes/2014/05/30/4ac8be44-c972-11e3-95f7-7ecdde72d2ea_story.html.
5. Blaise Pascal, *Pensées de M. Pascal sur la religion et sur quelques autres sujets* (1670), Fragment 162.
6. H.W. Brands, "Review: 'No End Save Victory: How FDR Led the Nation into War' by David Kaiser," *Washington Post*, May 9, 2014, http://www.washington post.com/opinions/no-end-save-victory-how-fdr-led-the-nation-into-war-by -david-kaiser/2014/05/09/d5e265fa-c66d-11e3-bf7a-be01a9b69cf1_story.html.
7. Robert S. McElvaine, *The Great Depression: America, 1929–1941* (New York: Three Rivers Press, 2009), 93.
8. James Thomas Flexner, *Washington: The Indispensable Man* (Boston: Little, Brown, 1974).
9. Karen Tumulty, "Today's Republicans, Staying in the Shadow of Ronald Reagan," *Washington Post*, February 4, 2011, http://www.washingtonpost.com/wp-dyn /content/article/2011/02/04/AR2011020403051_pf.html.
10. Deane W. Merrill, "Population of Counties, Earliest Census to 1990: Kentucky– Oklahoma," accessed April 10, 2014, http://merrill.olm.net/pdocs/feas/pop /pop1790_1990/piiikyok.txt.

CHAPTER 2

1. Clinton Rossiter, *The American Presidency* (Baltimore: Johns Hopkins University Press, 1987), 129.
2. "America's Wars," Department of Veterans Affairs, May 2013, http://www.va.gov /opa/publications/factsheets/fs_americas_wars.pdf.
3. Rick Beard, "America's Bloodiest Day," *New York Times*, September 17, 2012, http://opinionator.blogs.nytimes.com/2012/09/17/americas-bloodiest-day.
4. "Public Sees U.S. Power Declining as Support for Global Engagement Slips," Pew Research Center for the People and the Press, December 3, 2013, http:// www.people-press.org/2013/12/03/public-sees-u-s-power-declining-as-support -for-global-engagement-slips/.
5. Godfrey Hodgson, *All Things to All Men: The False Promise of the Modern American Presidency* (New York: Simon and Schuster, 1980), 60.
6. Eric Foner, *Reconstruction: America's Unfinished Revolution, 1863–1877* (New York: Harper & Row, 1988), 32.
7. H. W. Brands, *Traitor to His Class: The Privileged Life and Radical Presidency of Franklin Delano Roosevelt* (New York: Doubleday, 2008).
8. Jean Edward Smith, "Roosevelt: The Great Divider," *New York Times*, September 2, 2009, http://www.nytimes.com/2009/09/03/opinion/03smith.html.
9. Lydia Saad, "Bush Presidency Closes with 34% Approval, 61% Disapproval," Gallup, January 14, 2009, http://www.gallup.com/poll/113770/bush-presidency -closes-34-approval-61-disapproval.aspx.

10. "Quotes on Character from Former Presidents of the United States," Public Broadcasting Service, accessed May 6, 2014, http://www.pbs.org/newshour/character/quotes/.
11. George C. Rable, "Lincoln's Civil Religion," *History Now* 1, no. 6, December 2005, https://www.gilderlehrman.org/history-by-era/lincoln/essays/lincoln%E2%80%99s-civil-religion.
12. Ron Chernow, *Washington: A Life* (New York: Penguin Press, 2010), 467.
13. Ibid., 30; John E. Ferling, *The Ascent of George Washington: The Hidden Political Genius of an American Icon* (New York: Bloomsbury Press, 2009), 13.
14. Geoffery C. Ward, *A First-Class Temperament* (New York: Harper & Row, 1989), 630.
15. Ian Jackman, *Ronald Reagan Remembered: CBS News* (New York: Simon & Schuster, 2004), 7.
16. Geoffery C. Ward, *A First-Class Temperament*, 280–83.
17. David Herbert Donald, *Lincoln* (New York: Simon & Schuster, 1995), 158.
18. Frank J. Williams and Michael Burkhimer, *The Mary Lincoln Enigma: Historians on America's Most Controversial First Lady* (Carbondale: Southern Illinois University Press, 2012), 127. (The quote is from William H. Herndon's interview with Mary Lincoln, published as "Lincoln's Religion" in the *Illinois State Register,* December 13, 1873.)
19. Jean Edward Smith, *FDR* (New York: Random House, 2008), 24.
20. Waller Randy Newell, *The Soul of a Leader: Character, Conviction, and Ten Lessons in Political Greatness* (New York: Harper, 2009), 53.

CHAPTER 3

1. Warren G. Harding, "Dedication of the Lincoln Memorial," May 30, 1922, https://archive.org/details/presidentharding00hard.
2. John Ray, "George Washington's Pre-Presidential Statesmanship, 1783–1789," *Presidential Studies Quarterly* 27, no. 2 (Spring 1997), 207.
3. Fred I. Greenstein, *Inventing the Job of President: Leadership Style from George Washington to Andrew Jackson* (Princeton: Princeton University Press, 2009), 9.
4. "April 5, 1792," Center for the Study of the Presidency and Congress, http://www.thepresidency.org/publications/presidential-fellows-works/33-on-this-day/739-april-5-1792.
5. Ron Chernow, *Washington: A Life* (New York: Penguin Press, 2010), 726.
6. Robert Dallek, *Hail to the Chief: The Making and Unmaking of American Presidents* (Oxford: Oxford University Press, 2001), 10–12.
7. Mark Greenbaum, "Lincoln's Do Nothing Generals," *New York Times,* November 27, 2011, http://opinionator.blogs.nytimes.com/2011/11/27/lincolns-do-nothing-generals/.
8. "Wanted: A Policy," *New York Times,* April 3, 1861, http://www.nytimes.com/1861/04/03/news/wanted-a-policy.html.
9. James M. McPherson, *Battle Cry of Freedom: The Civil War Era* (New York: Oxford University Press, 1988), 589.
10. Owen Edwards, "Inventive Abe," *Smithsonian Magazine,* October 2006, http://www.smithsonianmag.com/history/inventive-abe-131184751.
11. Tom Wheeler, *Mr. Lincoln's T-Mails: The Untold Story of How Abraham Lincoln Used the Telegraph to Win the Civil War* (New York: Collins, 2006); see also http://www.mrlincolnstmails.com/.

12. Tom Wheeler, "The First Wired President," *New York Times,* May 24, 2012, http://opinionator.blogs.nytimes.com/2012/05/24/the-first-wired-president/.

13. Gary W. Gallagher, *The Shenandoah Valley Campaign of 1864* (Chapel Hill: University of North Carolina Press, 2006), 257–58.

14. Joel D. Aberbach and Mark Allen Peterson, *The Executive Branch* (Oxford: Oxford University Press, 2005), 45.

15. "Death and the Civil War," Public Broadcasting Service, accessed June 9, 2014, http://www.pbs.org/wgbh/americanexperience/films/death/.

16. Robert Hicks, "Why the Civil War Still Matters," *New York Times,* July 2, 2013, http://www.nytimes.com/2013/07/03/opinion/why-the-civil-war-still-matters.html.

17. Robert S. McElvaine, *The Great Depression: America, 1929–1941* (New York: Three Rivers Press, 2009), 92.

18. David W. Dunlap, "From the Archive: Dealing with Foreclosure (1933)," *New York Times,* May 18, 2009, http://lens.blogs.nytimes.com/2009/05/18/from-the-archive-how-we-used-to-deal-with-foreclosures-in-this-country-1933/.

19. H. W. Brands, *Traitor to His Class: The Privileged Life and Radical Presidency of Franklin Delano Roosevelt* (New York: Doubleday Publishing Group, 2008), 286.

20. Jean Edward Smith, *FDR* (New York: Random House, 2008), 308.

21. Ibid., 288.

22. "National Economic Accounts: Gross Domestic Product," US Bureau of Commerce: Bureau of Economic Analysis, accessed April 14, 2014, http://www.bea.gov/national/index.htm#gdp; "U.S. Unemployment Rate Hits 25%," *Econ Review,* accessed April 14, 2014, http://www.econreview.com/events/ur1932b.htm.

23. Richard Hofstadter, *The American Political Tradition and the Men Who Made It* (New York: Vintage Books, 1989), 411.

24. Franklin D. Roosevelt, "Radio Address on Unemployment and Social Welfare from Albany, New York," October 13, 1932, http://www.presidency.ucsb.edu/ws/?pid=88398.

25. "1935 Congressional Debates on Social Security," Social Security Administration, accessed April 14, 2014, http://www.ssa.gov/history/tally.html.

26. Franklin D. Roosevelt, "Message to Congress Reviewing the Broad Objectives and Accomplishments of the Administration," June 8, 1934, http://www.ssa.gov/history/fdrstmts.html.

27. Franklin D. Roosevelt, "Fireside Chat," June 28, 1934, http://www.ssa.gov/history/fdrstmts.html.

28. "Presidential Elections Data," American Presidency Project, accessed April 11, 2014, http://www.presidency.ucsb.edu/elections.php.

29. Jean Edward Smith, *FDR,* 396.

30. Franklin D. Roosevelt, "Acceptance Speech for the Renomination for the Presidency, Philadelphia, Pa.," June 27, 1936, http://www.presidency.ucsb.edu/ws/?pid=15314.

31. Jean Edward Smith, *FDR,* 396.

32. Carol W. Gelderman, *All the Presidents' Words: The Bully Pulpit and the Creation of the Virtual Presidency* (New York: Walker and Company, 1997), Chapter 1; excerpted from review at *New York Times,* accessed May 6, 2014, http://www.nytimes.com/books/first/g/gelderman-presidents.html.

33. Martin Gilbert, *Churchill and America* (New York: Free Press, 2008), 234.

34. Jean Edward Smith, *FDR,* 483–84.

35. "Presidential Elections Data," American Presidency Project.

36. Jean Edward Smith, *FDR,* 504; "A Brief History of U.S. Navy Destroyers, Part II: World War II (1941–1943)," Department of the Navy, accessed April 14, 2014, http://www.navy.mil/navydata/nav_legacy.asp?id=142.

37. Franklin Delano Roosevelt, "Address to Congress Requesting a Declaration of War," December 8, 1941; Miller Center at University of Virginia, http://miller center.org/president/speeches/detail/3324.

38. Franklin Delano Roosevelt, "Fireside Chat 19: On the War with Japan," December 9, 1941; at Miller Center at University of Virginia, http://millercenter.org /president/speeches/detail/3325.

39. Jean Edward Smith, *FDR,* 586.

40. Ibid., 549.

41. Richard Breitman and Allan J. Lichtman, *FDR and the Jews* (Cambridge, MA: Harvard University Press, 2013).

42. "Presidential Elections Data," American Presidency Project.

43. Andrew Goldman, "Cornel West Flunks the President," *New York Times,* July 22, 2011, http://www.nytimes.com/2011/07/24/magazine/talk-cornel-west.html.

44. Archie Brown, *The Myth of the Strong Leader: Political Leadership in Modern Politics* (New York: Basic Books, 2014), 8.

45. Marc Karnis Landy and Sidney M. Milkis, *Presidential Greatness* (Lawrence: University Press of Kansas, 2000), 4.

CHAPTER 4

1. Robert W. Merry, *Where They Stand: The American Presidents in the Eyes of Voters and Historians* (New York: Simon & Schuster, 2012).

2. Arthur M. Schlesinger, "Historians Rate the U.S. Presidents," *Life,* November 1, 1948.

3. Arthur M. Schlesinger, "Our Presidents: A Rating by 75 Historians," *New York Times Magazine,* July 29, 1962.

4. Arthur M. Schlesinger Jr., "Rating the Presidents: Washington to Clinton," *Political Science Quarterly* 112, no. 2 (1997).

5. Merrill D. Peterson, *The Jefferson Image in the American Mind* (New York: Oxford University Press, 1960), 457.

6. "Andrew Jackson: Good, Evil & the Presidency," Public Broadcasting Service, accessed April 14, 2014, http://www.pbs.org/kcet/andrewjackson/.

7. Richard F. Haynes, *The Awesome Power: Harry S. Truman as Commander in Chief* (Baton Rouge: Louisiana State University Press, 1973), 24.

8. Gordon S. Wood, "Thomas Jefferson, Equality, and the Creation of a Civil Society," *Fordham Law Review* 64, no. 5 (1996), 2137.

9. James P. Pfiffner, "George Washington's Character and Slavery," *White House Studies* 1, no. 4 (2001): 351–461; Gordon S. Wood, *The Idea of America* (New York: Penguin Press, 2011), 226–28.

10. "Louisiana Purchase Treaty," National Archives, accessed April 14, 2014, http:// www.archives.gov/historical-docs/document.html?doc=5&title.raw=Louisiana %20Purchase%20Treaty.

11. Clinton Rossiter, *The American Presidency* (Baltimore: Johns Hopkins University Press, 1987), 83.

12. Jon Meacham, "Rocking the Vote, in the 1820s and Now," *New York Times,* October 21, 2010, http://www.nytimes.com/2010/10/24/theater/24meacham.html.

13. Ibid.

14. "The Power of the Presidency: The Veto," Public Broadcasting Service, http://www.pbs.org/kcet/andrewjackson/features/the_veto.html.

15. "Presidential Elections Data," American Presidency Project, accessed April 11, 2014, http://www.presidency.ucsb.edu/elections.php.

16. "The Trail of Tears," Public Broadcasting Service, accessed April 14, 2014, http://www.pbs.org/wgbh/aia/part4/4h1567.html.

17. James MacGregor Burns, Arthur M. Schlesinger Jr., and Fred I. Greenstein, "Rating the Presidents: Purpose, Criteria, Consequences," *White House Studies* 3.1 (Winter 2003).

18. Dixon Wecter and Woodi Ishmael, *The Hero in America: A Chronicle of Hero-Worship* (Ann Arbor: University of Michigan Press, 1963), 374.

19. "Theodore Roosevelt—Facts," Nobel Peace Prize, accessed April 14, 2014, http://www.nobelprize.org/nobel_prizes/peace/laureates/1906/roosevelt-facts.html.

20. David Greenberg, "Beyond the Bully Pulpit," *Wilson Quarterly* (Summer 2011), http://www.wilsonquarterly.com/essays/beyond-bully-pulpit.

21. Milton Meltzer, *Mark Twain Himself: A Pictorial Biography* (Columbia: University of Missouri Press, 2002), 258.

22. "Theodore Roosevelt and Conservation," National Park Service, accessed April 14, 2014, http://www.nps.gov/thro/historyculture/theodore-roosevelt-and-conservation.htm.

23. "Presidential Elections Data," American Presidency Project.

24. John Milton Cooper, *Reconsidering Woodrow Wilson: Progressivism, Internationalism, War, and Peace* (Washington, DC: Woodrow Wilson Center Press, 2008), 10–13.

25. "Presidential Elections Data," American Presidency Project; "Party Divisions of the House of Representatives, 1789–Present," United States House of Representatives, accessed April 14, 2014, http://history.house.gov/Institution/Party-Divisions/Party-Divisions/; "Party Division in the Senate, 1789–Present," United States Senate, accessed April 14, 2014, http://www.senate.gov/pagelayout/history/one_item_and_teasers/partydiv.htm.

26. Lydia Saad, "Bush Presidency Closes with 34% Approval, 61% Disapproval," Gallup, January 14, 2009, http://www.gallup.com/poll/113770/bush-presidency-closes-34-approval-61-disapproval.aspx.

PART II

1. "Watergate and the Presidency: Should We Abolish the Presidency?," in Barbara W. Tuchman, *Practicing History: Selected Essays* (New York: Random House, 2011), 294–303.

2. Suzanne Mettler and Andrew Milstein, "American Political Development from Citizens' Perspective: Tracking Federal Government's Presence in Individual Lives over Time," *Studies in American Political Development* 21, no. 1 (2007): 110–30.

3. Terrence P. Jeffrey, "Census: 49% of Americans Get Gov't Benefits; 82M in Households on Medicaid," CNSNews, October 23, 2013, http://cnsnews.com/news/article/terence-p-jeffrey/census-49-americans-get-gov-t-benefits-82m-households-medicaid.

4. Martin E. Goldstein, *America's Foreign Policy: Drift or Decision* (Wilmington, DE: Rowman & Littlefield, 1984), 113.

5. Jerel Rosati and James Scott, *Cengage Advantage Books: The Politics of United States Foreign Policy* (Cengage Learning, 2013), 57.

CHAPTER 5

1. Robert E. Sherwood, *Roosevelt and Hopkins: An Intimate History* (New York: Harper, 1950), 881.
2. William E. Leuchtenburg, *In the Shadow of FDR: From Harry Truman to George W. Bush* (Ithaca, NY: Cornell University Press, 2001), 3.
3. Ibid.
4. Ronald Reagan, "Address Accepting the Presidential Nomination at the Republican National Convention in Detroit," July 17, 1980, http://www.presidency.ucsb .edu/ws/?pid=25970; Ronald Steel, "Franklin D. Reagan," *New York Times,* January 18, 1981, http://www.nytimes.com/1981/01/18/opinion/franklin-d-reagan .html.
5. William E. Leuchtenburg, *In the Shadow of FDR,* 33.
6. Ibid., 145.
7. William J. Clinton, "Remarks at the Dedication of the Franklin Delano Roosevelt Memorial," May 2, 1997, http://www.presidency.ucsb.edu/ws/index.php ?pid=54081.
8. "Background: Franklin Delano Roosevelt Memorial," National Park Service, accessed May 6, 2014, http://www.nps.gov/ncro/publicaffairs/FDRMemorial.htm.
9. William E. Leuchtenburg, *In the Shadow of FDR,* 240.
10. Sandy Grady, "Clinton Fell Victim to His '100 Days' Hype," *Wilmington Morning Star,* April 30, 1993, 12A.
11. George F. Will, "James Q. Wilson, Honored Prophet," *Washington Post,* March 2, 2012, http://www.washingtonpost.com/opinions/james-q-wilson-americas-pro phet/2012/03/02/gIQAtEWGnR_story.html.

CHAPTER 6

1. Guy Gugliotta, "New Estimate Raises Civil War Death Toll," *New York Times,* April 2, 2012, http://www.nytimes.com/2012/04/03/science/civil-war-toll-up -by-20-percent-in-new-estimate.html.
2. Andrew Dugan, "In U.S., Big Gap between Personal and National Satisfaction," Gallup, December 18, 2013, http://www.gallup.com/poll/166517/big-gap -personal-national-satisfaction.aspx.
3. George W. Bush, "President Bush Addresses the Nation," *Washington Post,* September 20, 2001, http://www.washingtonpost.com/wp-srv/nation/specials/attacked /transcripts/bushaddress_092001.html.
4. "Most Members of Congress Have Little Direct Military Experience," Pew Research Center for the People and the Press, September 4, 2013, http://www.pew research.org/fact-tank/2013/09/04/members-of-congress-have-little-direct-military -experience/.
5. Robert M. Gates, "Lecture at Duke University (All-Volunteer Force)," September 29, 2010, http://www.defense.gov/speeches/speech.aspx?speechid=1508.
6. Chris Kenrick, "Stanford Historian Sees Hazard in U.S. Military-Civilian Gap," *Palo Alto Weekly,* November 12, 2013, http://www.paloaltoonline.com /news/2013/11/12/dangerous-gap-between-us-military-and-civilian-spheres-stan ford-historian-says.
7. Jimmy Carter, interview with author, April 16, 2009.
8. Jeff Zeleny and Megan Thee-Brenan, "New Poll Finds a Deep Distrust of Government," *New York Times,* October 25, 2011, http://www.nytimes.com/2011/10/26

/us/politics/poll-finds-anxiety-on-the-economy-fuels-volatility-in-the-2012-race
.html.

9. "Trust in Government 1958–2013," Pew Research Center for the People and
the Press, October 18, 2013, http://www.people-press.org/2013/10/18/trust-in
-government-interactive/.

10. Richard E. Neustadt, *Presidential Power and the Modern Presidents: The Politics of
Leadership from Roosevelt to Reagan* (New York: Free Press, 1990), ix.

CHAPTER 7

1. Frederick C. Mosher, *Basic Documents of American Public Administration, 1776–
1950* (New York: Holmes & Meier, 1976).

2. "Partisan Polarization Surges in Bush, Obama Years," Pew Research Center for
the People and the Press, June 4, 2012, http://www.people-press.org/2012/06/04
/partisan-polarization-surges-in-bush-obama-years/.

3. Norman Ornstein, "A Very Productive Congress, Despite What the Approval Ratings Say," *Washington Post,* January 31, 2010, http://www.washingtonpost.com
/wp-dyn/content/article/2010/01/29/AR2010012902516.html.

4. Ezra Klein, "Goodbye and Good Riddance, 112th Congress," *Washington Post,* January 4, 2013, http://www.washingtonpost.com/blogs/wonkblog/wp/2013/01/04
/goodbye-and-good-riddance-112th-congress/.

5. Sarah A. Binder, "Polarized We Govern?," Center for Effective Public Management
at Brookings Institution, May 2014, http://www.brookings.edu/research/papers
/2014/05/27-polarized-we-govern-congress-legislative-gridlock-polarized-binder.

6. John Harwood, "When a 2nd-Term President and a Divided Congress Made
Magic," *New York Times,* January 2, 2014, http://www.nytimes.com/2014/01/03
/us/politics/when-a-2nd-term-president-and-a-divided-congress-made-magic
.html.

7. John Harwood, "When a Second-Term President Nears the Midterm Shoals,"
New York Times, December 11, 2013, http://www.nytimes.com/2013/12/12/us
/politics/obama-midterm-election.html.

8. Sarah A. Binder, "Going Nowhere: A Gridlocked Congress?," *Brookings Review* 18,
no. 1 (Winter, 2000): 19; Sarah A. Binder, "The Disappearing Political Center:
Congress and the Incredible Shrinking Middle," *Brookings Review* 14, no. 4 (fall
1996): 36.

9. Jeffrey M. Jones, "Obama Ratings Historically Polarized," Gallup, January 27,
2012, http://www.gallup.com/poll/152222/obama-ratings-historically-polarized
.aspx.

10. Ibid.

11. Frank Newport, "Congressional Approval Sinks to Record Low," Gallup, November 12, 2013, http://www.gallup.com/poll/165809/congressional-approval-sinks
-record-low.aspx.

12. Carl Hulse, "Lawmakers' Modest Proposal: To Pass Spending Bills on Time," *New
York Times,* May 29, 2014, http://www.nytimes.com/2014/05/30/us/politics/from
-2-lawmakers-a-modest-proposal-to-pass-spending-bills-on-time.html.

13. "Public Trust in Government 1958–2013," Pew Research Center for the People
and the Press, October 18, 2013, http://www.people-press.org/2013/10/18
/trust-in-government-interactive/.

14. Jeff Zeleny and Megan Thee-Brenan, "New Poll Finds a Deep Distrust of Government." *New York Times,* October 25, 2011, http://www.nytimes.com/2011/10/26

/us/politics/poll-finds-anxiety-on-the-economy-fuels-volatility-in-the-2012-race
.html.

15. "CNN Poll: Obama Approval Falls Amid Controversies," CNN, June 17, 2013,
http://politicalticker.blogs.cnn.com/2013/06/17/cnn-poll-obama-approval
-falls-amid-controversies/. "President's Marks as Manager Take Hit in New
CNN/ORC Poll," CNN, November 25, 2013, http://politicalticker.blogs.cnn
.com/2013/11/25/presidents-marks-as-manager-take-hit-in-new-cnnorc-poll/.

16. Michael Gerson, "Tone Down the Hatefulness in Politics," *Washington Post,* April
9, 2010, http://www.washingtonpost.com/wp-dyn/content/article/2010/04/08
/AR2010040803738.html.

17. Francis Fukuyama, "Oh for a Democratic Dictatorship and Not a Vetocracy," *Financial Times,* November 22, 2011, http://www.ft.com/cms/s/0/d82776c6-14fd
-11e1-a2a6-00144feabdc0.html.

CHAPTER 8

1. On the personalized presidency, see Theodore J. Lowi, *The Personal President:
Power Invested, Promise Unfulfilled* (Ithaca: Cornell University Press, 1985). On
Washington's love of hoopla, see John E. Ferling, *The Ascent of George Washington:
The Hidden Political Genius of an American Icon* (New York: Bloomsbury Press,
2009), 280.

2. Sidney Blumenthal, *The Permanent Campaign* (New York: Simon and Schuster,
1982).

3. William J. Clinton, "Interview on MTV's 'Enough is Enough' Forum," April 19,
1994, http://www.presidency.ucsb.edu/ws/?pid=49995.

4. Elizabeth Kolbert, "Frank Talk by Clinton to MTV Generation," *New York
Times,* April 20, 1994, http://www.nytimes.com/1994/04/20/us/frank-talk-by
-clinton-to-mtv-generation.html.

5. Jerry Adler with Eleanor Clift and Bob Cohn, "Clinton: A Brief History," *Newsweek,* May 2, 1994, 2.

6. "Barack Obama Gets the Boxers vs. Briefs Question," *Los Angeles Times,* March
1, 2008, http://latimesblogs.latimes.com/washington/2008/03/barack-obama-ge
.html.

7. Michael James, "President Obama Jokes about Being a Bad Bowler: 'It's Like the
Special Olympics,'" *ABC News,* March 19, 2009, http://abcnews.go.com/blogs
/politics/2009/03/president-ob-15-3/.

8. Martha Joynt Kumar, "The Kennedy White House and the Press," White House
Historical Association, May 16, 2011, http://www.whitehousehistory.org/history
/white-house-facts-trivia/facts-press-presidential-press-conferences.html.

9. Gerhard Peters, "State of the Union Addresses and Messages," American Presidency Project, accessed May 6, 2014, http://www.presidency.ucsb.edu/sou
.php.

10. Clifford Krainik, "Face the Lens, Mr. President: A Gallery of Photographic Portraits of 19th-Century U.S. Presidents," *White House History* 16 (2005): 28.

11. "Calvin Coolidge Delivers First Presidential Address on Radio," *New York
Times,* December 6, 2011, http://learning.blogs.nytimes.com/2011/12/06
/dec-6-1923-calvin-coolidge-delivers-first-presidential-address-on-radio/.

12. "Hughes Deplores Our Speed Mania," *New York Times,* October 10, 1923.

13. "Historical Timeline: 1939," Public Broadcasting Service, accessed May 6, 2014,
http://www.pbs.org/30secondcandidate/timeline/years/1939.html.

14. Hedrick Smith, *The Power Game: How Washington Works* (New York: Random House, 1988), 36.
15. David Kirkpatrick, "Does Corporate Money Lead to Political Corruption?," *New York Times,* January 23, 2010, http://www.nytimes.com/2010/01/24 /weekinreview/24kirkpatrick.html.
16. Kate Kenski, Bruce W. Hardy, and Kathleen Hall Jamieson, *The Obama Victory: How Media, Money, and Message Shaped the 2008 Election* (Oxford: Oxford University Press, 2010).
17. Ken Auletta, "With Cable, the Web, and Tweets, Can the President—or the Press—Still Control the Story?," *New Yorker,* January 25, 2010, 38.
18. David Carr, "The Battle between the White House and Fox News," *New York Times,* October 17, 2009, http://www.nytimes.com/2009/10/18/weekin review/18davidcarr.html.
19. Ibid.
20. Ibid.
21. "Online and Digital News," Pew Research Center for the People and the Press, September 27, 2012, http://www.people-press.org/2012/09/27/section-2-online -and-digital-news-2/.
22. Walt Whitman, "Visit to Plumbe's Gallery," *Brooklyn Daily Eagle* 5, No. 160, July 2, 1846, http://www.daguerre.org/resource/texts/whitman.html.
23. Clifford Krainik, "Face the Lens, Mr. President," 28.
24. David Culbert, "Presidential Images," *Wilson Quarterly* (New Year's 1983): 166–67.
25. "Adult Obesity Facts," Centers for Disease Control and Prevention, accessed May 6, 2014, http://www.cdc.gov/obesity/data/adult.html; Jeremy D. Mayer, "The Contemporary Presidency: The Presidency and Image Management: Discipline in Pursuit of Illusion," *Presidential Studies Quarterly* 34, no. 3 (September 2004): 620–31.
26. Joe Bauer, "A Hoosier in the White House?," *Examiner,* January 27, 2011, http:// www.examiner.com/article/a-hoosier-the-white-house.
27. Steve Rushin, "The Bald Truth," *Time,* November 5, 2007, 76.
28. Lou Cannon, "At 40th D-Day Tribute, Reagan Took the Occasion by Storm," *Washington Post,* June 7, 2004, A06, http://www.washingtonpost.com/wp-dyn /articles/A20780-2004Jun6.html.
29. Larry Sabato, *Feeding Frenzy: Attack Journalism and American Politics* (Baltimore: Lanahan Publishers, 2000), 18.
30. Robert Dallek, *An Unfinished Life: John F. Kennedy, 1917–1963* (Boston: Little, Brown, 2003), 281.
31. Alden Whitman, "De Gaulle Rallied France in War and Strove to Lead Her to Greatness," *New York Times,* November 11, 1970, https://www.nytimes.com /learning/general/onthisday/bday/1122.html.
32. John F. Burns, "A Royal Wedding, a Tarnished Crown," *New York Times,* April 23, 2011, http://www.nytimes.com/2011/04/24/weekinreview/24burns.html.
33. Howard Kurtz, interview with author, February 18, 2010.
34. Joshua Meyrowitz, *No Sense of Place: The Impact of Electronic Media on Social Behavior* (New York: Oxford University Press, 1985).
35. Martha Joynt Kumar, email to author, February 13, 2012.
36. Ken Auletta, "Can the President—or the Press—Still Control the Story?," 43.
37. Michael Gerson, "The Internet: Enabling Pastor Terry Jones and Crazies Everywhere," *Washington Post,* September 14, 2010, http://www.washingtonpost.com /wp-dyn/content/article/2010/09/13/AR2010091305289.html.

38. Dana Milbank, "America Doesn't Need a Lame-Duck President," *Washington Post*, January 30, 2014, http://www.washingtonpost.com/opinions/dana-milbank-america-doesnt-need-a-lame-duck-president/2014/01/30/110c90ac-8a04-11e3-916e-e01534b1e132_story.html.
39. Ken Auletta, "Can the President—or the Press—Still Control the Story?," 38.

CHAPTER 9

1. "The Kennedy Half Century National Polling Results," October 25, 2013, http://www.thekennedyhalfcentury.com/pdf/Kennedy-Half-Century-National-Polling-Results.pdf.
2. Robert Dallek, *Flawed Giant: Lyndon Johnson and His Times, 1961–1973* (New York: Oxford University Press, 1998).
3. Lyndon B. Johnson, "Address before a Joint Session of the Congress," November 27, 1963; American Presidency Project, http://www.presidency.ucsb.edu/ws/?pid=25988.
4. Robert Dallek, *Lyndon B. Johnson: Portrait of a President* (Oxford: Oxford University Press, 2005), 37.
5. Robert Dallek, *Flawed Giant*, 4.
6. Joseph A. Califano Jr., "It Took a Partnership," *Washington Post*, January 15, 2008, http://www.washingtonpost.com/wp-dyn/content/article/2008/01/14/AR2008011402079.html.
7. David J. Garrow, "The Obscure Heroes behind Congress's Great Moment," *American Prospect*, April 3, 2014, http://prospect.org/article/obscure-heroes-behind-congress%E2%80%99s-great-moment; Eric Arnesen, "The Bill of the Century: The Epic Battle for the Civil Rights Act by Clay Risen," *Washington Post*, April 25, 2014, http://www.washingtonpost.com/opinions/the-bill-of-the-century-the-epic-battle-for-the-civil-rights-act-by-clay-risen/2014/04/25/50846c7c-c7d6-11e3-9f37-7ce307c56815_story.html.
8. Lyndon B. Johnson, "Remarks on the Accomplishments of the 89th Congress," October 15, 1966; American Presidency Project, http://www.presidency.ucsb.edu/ws/?pid=27931.
9. Robert Dallek, "Lyndon B. Johnson," Public Broadcasting Service, http://www.pbs.org/newshour/spc/character/essays/johnson.html.
10. Robert Dallek, *Flawed Giant*, 4.
11. Robert Dallek, *Lone Star Rising: Lyndon Johnson and His Times, 1908–1960* (New York: Oxford University Press, 1991), 44–45.
12. Robert Dallek, "Lyndon Baines Johnson," in *Presidential Leadership: Rating the Best and the Worst in the White House,* James Taranto and Leonard Leo (New York: Wall Street Journal Books, 2004), 176.
13. Charles Peters, "President Johnson's Record: Vietnam and Domestic Policies," *Command Posts*, August 27, 2011, http://www.commandposts.com/2011/08/president-johnsons-record-vietnam-and-domestic-policies/.
14. Hugh Heclo, "The Mixed Legacies of Ronald Reagan," *Presidential Studies Quarterly* 38, no. 4, December 1, 2008.
15. Peter B. Sperry, "The Real Reagan Economic Record: Responsible and Successful Fiscal Policy," Heritage Foundation, March 1, 2001, http://www.heritage.org/research/reports/2001/03/the-real-reagan-economic-record. "Reagan's Legacy: Our 25-Year Boom," *Real Clear Markets,* April 10, 2009, http://www.realclearmarkets.com/articles/2009/04/reagans_legacy_our_25year_boom.html.

16. Will Bunch, "Five Myths about Ronald Reagan's Legacy," *Washington Post,* February 4, 2011, http://www.washingtonpost.com/wp-dyn/content/article/2011/02/04/AR2011020403104.html.

17. "Presidential Elections Data," American Presidency Project, accessed April 11, 2014, http://www.presidency.ucsb.edu/elections.php.

PART III

1. Kenneth T. Walsh, "How History Shapes Barack Obama's Inauguration: As He Assumes the Presidency, Obama Will Draw Inspiration from Lincoln, FDR And Kennedy," *US News & World Report,* December 22, 2008, http://www.usnews.com/news/obama/articles/2008/12/22/how-history-shapes-barack-obamas-inauguration.

2. "The New New Deal," *Time,* November 24, 2008, http://content.time.com/time/covers/0,16641,20081124,00.html.

3. *New Yorker,* Cover, January 26, 2009, http://www.newyorker.com/magazine/toc/2009/01/26/toc.

4. Robert Sullivan, *100 People Who Changed the World* (New York: Life Books, 2010).

5. "The Top 100 Influential Figures in American History," *Atlantic,* December 1, 2006, http://www.theatlantic.com/magazine/archive/2006/12/the-top-100-influential-figures-in-american-history/305384/.

6. W. J. C. Meighan, "Odd Facts about Our Presidents," *New York Times,* January 25, 1903, http://search.proquest.com/docview/96354001.

7. Lawrence K. Altman, "Being President Is Tough but Usually Not Fatal, a Study Concludes," *New York Times,* December 6, 2011, http://www.nytimes.com/2011/12/07/health/american-presidents-outlive-other-men-their-age-study-finds.html.

8. Calvin Coolidge, "Address at the Opening of Work on Mount Rushmore in Black Hills, SD," August 10, 1927; American Presidency Project, http://www.presidency.ucsb.edu/ws/?pid=24175.

9. William J. Clinton, "Remarks at the Dedication of the Franklin Delano Roosevelt Memorial," May 2, 1997; American Presidency Project, http://www.presidency.ucsb.edu/ws/index.php?pid=54081&st=&st1.

10. David P. Phillips and Kenneth A. Feldman, "A Dip in Deaths before Ceremonial Occasions: Some New Relationships between Social Integration and Mortality," *American Sociological Review* 38, no. 6 (December 1973): 678–96.

CHAPTER 10

1. John Steinbeck, *America and Americans* (New York: Viking Press, 1966), 46.

2. Joseph J. Ellis, *American Creation: Triumphs and Tragedies at the Founding of the Republic* (New York: A.A. Knopf, 2007), 6.

3. Edwin S. Gaustad, *Benjamin Franklin: Inventing America* (Oxford: Oxford University Press, 2004), 8.

4. "Swearing in Ceremony for President George Washington," Joint Congressional Committee on Inaugural Ceremonies, accessed April 18, 2014, http://www.inaugural.senate.gov/swearing-in/event/george-washington-1789.

5. "Swearing in Ceremony for President Thomas Jefferson," Joint Congressional Committee on Inaugural Ceremonies, accessed April 18, 2014, http://www.inaugural.senate.gov/swearing-in/event/thomas-jefferson-1801.

6. "Swearing in Ceremony for President John Quincy Adams," Joint Congressional Committee on Inaugural Ceremonies, accessed April 18, 2014, http://www.inaugural.senate.gov/swearing-in/event/john-quincy-adams-1825.

7. Alexis de Tocqueville, John Stone, and Stephen Mennell, *Alexis De Tocqueville on Democracy, Revolution, and Society: Selected Writings* (Chicago: University of Chicago Press, 1980), 131.

8. Viscount James Bryce, *The American Commonwealth* (New York: Macmillan, 1919), 77.

9. Henry Adams, *The Education of Henry Adams: An Autobiography* (Boston: Houghton Mifflin, 1918), 266.

10. Matthew Algeo, "Harry Truman, Leader of the Freeway," *New York Times,* April 4, 2009, http://www.nytimes.com/2009/04/05/opinion/05algeo.html.

11. Matthew Algeo, *Harry Truman's Excellent Adventure: The True Story of a Great American Road Trip* (Chicago: Chicago Review Press, 2009).

12. Tevi Troy, *What Jefferson Read, Ike Watched, and Obama Tweeted* (Washington, DC: Regnery, 2013), 211–39.

13. Daniel J. Boorstin, *The Image: A Guide to Pseudo-Events in America* (New York: Vintage Books, 2012), 50.

14. James M. McPherson, *Battle Cry of Freedom: The Civil War Era* (New York: Oxford University Press, 1988), 364, 594; Ted Widmer, "Yacht for Sale," *New York Times,* April 21, 2011, http://opinionator.blogs.nytimes.com/2011/04/21/yacht-for-sale/.

15. John E. Ferling, *The Ascent of George Washington: The Hidden Political Genius of an American Icon* (New York: Bloomsbury Press, 2009), 344.

16. William Edward Leuchtenburg, *The FDR Years: On Roosevelt and His Legacy* (New York: Columbia University Press, 1997), 2.

17. Andrew Glass, "Jackson Escapes Assassination Attempt Jan. 30, 1835," *Politico,* January 30, 2008, http://www.politico.com/news/stories/0108/8184.html.

18. Patricia O'Toole, "The Speech That Saved Teddy Roosevelt's Life," *Smithsonian Magazine,* November 2012, http://www.smithsonianmag.com/history/the-speech-that-saved-teddy-roosevelts-life-83479091/.

19. Lisa Anderson, "The Ex-Presidents," *Journal of Democracy* 21, no. 2 (2010): 64–78.

20. "Federal Holidays: Evolution and Application," Congressional Research Service, February 8, 1999, accessed April 18, 2014, http://www.senate.gov/reference/resources/pdf/Federal_Holidays.pdf.

21. Barry Schwartz, "Collective Memory and Abortive Commemoration: Presidents' Day and the American Holiday Calendar," *Social Research* 75, no. 1 (spring 2008): 75–110.

22. Edward G. Lengel, *Inventing George Washington: America's Founder, in Myth and Memory* (New York: Harper, 2011), 28–32.

23. Andrew Ferguson, *Land of Lincoln: Adventures in Abe's America* (New York: Grove Press, 2008), 137.

24. Eric Pfeiffer, "George Washington–Shaped Chicken McNugget Sells for $8,100 on eBay," *Yahoo! News,* March 6, 2012, http://news.yahoo.com/blogs/sideshow/george-washington-shaped-chicken-mcnugget-sells-8-100-215736625.html.

25. Stefanie Cohen, "Fourscore and 16,000 Books," *Wall Street Journal,* October 12, 2012, http://online.wsj.com/news/articles/SB10000872396390444024204578044403434070838.

26. Jacques Steinberg, "Animatronic Obama Going to Disney World with High-Tech Style," *New York Times,* May 21, 2009, http://www.nytimes.com/2009/05/22/us/politics/22obamatron.html.

27. "Presidential $1 Coin Act of 2005," US Government Printing Office, December 22, 2005, accessed April 18, 2014, http://www.gpo.gov/fdsys/pkg /PLAW-109publ145/pdf/PLAW-109publ145.pdf; Roberta Benincasa and David Kestenbaum, "$1 Billion That Nobody Wants," National Public Radio, June 28, 2011, http://www.npr.org/2011/06/28/137394348/-1-billion-that-nobody -wants; Stephanie Condon, "Obama Administration Halts Production of $1 Presidential Coin," CBS News, December 13, 2011, http://www.cbsnews.com/news /obama-administration-halts-production-of-1-presidential-coin/.

28. Andrew Romano, "How Ignorant Are Americans?," Newsweek, March 20, 2011, http://www.newsweek.com/how-ignorant-are-americans-66053.

29. Hendrik Hertzberg, "Too Many Chiefs," New Yorker, February 19, 2007, http:// www.newyorker.com/talk/comment/2007/02/19/070219taco_talk_hertzberg.

30. Scott T. Allison and George R. Goethals, Heroes: What They Do and Why We Need Them (Oxford: Oxford University Press, 2011), 26.

CHAPTER 11

1. Sarah Parnass, "Obama Biography: 'I'm LeBron, Baby,'" ABC News, June 13, 2011, http://abcnews.go.com/blogs/politics/2011/06/obama-biography-im-lebron-baby/.

2. Todd Purdum, "Washington, We Have a Problem," Vanity Fair, September 2010, http://www.vanityfair.com/politics/features/2010/09/broken-washington-201009.

3. Abraham Lincoln, "Abraham Lincoln to Albert G. Hodges," April 4, 1864, at Library of Congress, accessed April 18, 2014, http://www.loc.gov/teachers/class roommaterials/connections/abraham-lincoln-papers/thinking2.html.

4. Jonathan Alter, "The Obama Dividend," Newsweek, March 22, 2008, http:// www.newsweek.com/alter-obama-dividend-84253.

5. John Harold Plumb, The Death of the Past (Basingstoke: Palgrave Macmillan, 2004), 14.

6. Factcheck.org, "Bum Rap for Rahm," January 13, 2011, http://www.factcheck .org/2011/01/bum-rap-for-rahm/.

7. Arthur M. Schlesinger, "What Makes a President Great? Or a Failure? The Verdict of History Provides Some Answers," LIFE Magazine, November 1, 1948.

8. Akhil Reed Amar, America's Constitution: A Biography (New York: Random House, 2005), 141.

9. Ibid., 143–44.

10. Clinton Rossiter, The American Presidency (Baltimore: Johns Hopkins University Press, 1987), 67.

11. James Madison, "The Federalist Papers: No. 48," February 1, 1788; at Avalon Project, http://avalon.law.yale.edu/18th_century/fed48.asp.

12. Scott Lilly, "Communication Is Destiny," in Obama in Office, James A. Thurber ed. (Boulder, CO: Paradigm, 2011), 166.

CHAPTER 12

1. Yair Rosenberg, "Why 'The West Wing' Is a Terrible Guide to American Democracy," Atlantic, October 1, 2012, http://www.theatlantic.com/politics/archive/2012/10 /why-the-west-wing-is-a-terrible-guide-to-american-democracy/263084/.

2. "Geroge H. W. Bush, 43rd Vice President (1981–1989)," United States Senate, accessed April 18, 2014, http://www.senate.gov/artandhistory/history/common /generic/VP_George_Bush.htm.

3. Arthur M. Schlesinger Jr., "Rating the Presidents: Washington to Clinton," *Political Science Quarterly* 112, no. 2 (1997): 179.

4. Clinton Rossiter, *The American Presidency* (Baltimore: Johns Hopkins University Press, 1987), 243.

5. James MacGregor Burns, *Transforming Leadership: A New Pursuit of Happiness* (New York: Atlantic Monthly Press, 2003).

6. David R. Gergen, *Eyewitness to Power: The Essence of Leadership: Nixon to Clinton* (New York: Simon & Schuster, 2000), 347.

7. Marc Karnis Landy and Sidney M. Milkis, *Presidential Greatness* (Lawrence: University Press of Kansas, 2000), 198.

8. Ken Auletta, "With Cable, the Web, and Tweets, Can the President—or the Press—Still Control the Story?," *New Yorker,* January 25, 2010, 38.

9. Ross Douthat, "A Return to Normalcy," *New York Times,* December 26, 2010, http://www.nytimes.com/2010/12/27/opinion/27douthat.html.

10. Peter Baker, "Familiar Obama Phrase Being Groomed as a Slogan," *New York Times,* May 15, 2009, http://www.nytimes.com/2009/05/16/us/politics/16founda tion.html.

11. Jonathan Bernstein, "Campaign Promises: What They Say Is How They'll Govern," *Washington Monthly,* January/February 2012, http://www.washington monthly.com/magazine/january_february_2012/features/campaign_prom ises034471.php; Michael G. Krukones, *Promises and Performance* (Lanham, MD: University Press of America, 1984).

12. "Presidential Approval Ratings—Gallup Historical Statistics and Trends," Gallup, accessed May 8, 2014, http://www.gallup.com/poll/116677/presidential-approval -ratings-gallup-historical-statistics-trends.aspx; Jeffrey M. Jones, "Obama's Initial Approval Ratings in Historical Context," Gallup, January 26, 2009, http://www .gallup.com/poll/113968/obama-initial-approval-ratings-historical-context.aspx; Lydia Saad, "Bush Presidency Closes with 34% Approval, 61% Disapproval," Gallup, January 14, 2009, http://www.gallup.com/poll/113770/bush-presidency -closes-34-approval-61-disapproval.aspx.

13. George E. Reedy, *The Twilight of the Presidency: From Johnson to Reagan* (New York: New American Library, 1987), 15.

14. Barack Obama, *The Audacity of Hope: Thoughts on Reclaiming the American Dream* (New York: Crown, 2006), 54.

15. Abraham Lincoln, "Cooper Union Address," February 27, 1860; Miller Center at University of Virginia, http://millercenter.org/president/speeches/detail/3505.

16. Merrill D. Peterson, *Lincoln in American Memory* (New York: Oxford University Press, 1994), 324.

17. Richard Brookhiser, *What Would the Founders Do?: Our Questions, Their Answers* (New York: Basic Books, 2006), 3.

18. William E. Leuchtenburg, *In the Shadow of FDR: From Harry Truman to George W. Bush* (Ithaca, NY: Cornell University Press, 2001).

19. Theodore H. White, *America in Search of Itself: The Making of the President, 1956–1980* (New York: Harper & Row, 1982), 47.

20. Larry Sabato, *The Kennedy Half Century: The Presidency, Assassination, and Lasting Legacy of John F. Kennedy* (New York: Bloomsbury, 2013), 389.

21. Ibid., 370.

22. Lara M. Brown, "'The Contemporary Presidency': The Greats and the Great Debate: President William J. Clinton's Use of Presidential Exemplars," *Presidential Studies Quarterly* 37, no. 1, (March 2007), 124–38.

23. Larry Sabato, *The Kennedy Half Century*, 370.

24. Ibid., 379.

25. "In Their Own Words: Obama on Reagan," *New York Times*, accessed May 8, 2014, http://www.nytimes.com/ref/us/politics/21seelye-text.html.

26. Barack Obama, *The Audacity of Hope*, 38–39.

27. Ronald Wilson Reagan, "First Inaugural Address," January 20, 1981; Miller Center at University of Virginia, http://millercenter.org/president/speeches/detail/3407.

28. Ron Suskind, *Confidence Men: Wall Street, Washington, and the Education of a President* (New York: Harper, 2011), 156–57.

29. Barack Obama, *The Audacity of Hope*, 122–23.

30. Chris Hedges, "A Lincoln Scholar, Pulled Out of a Hat," *New York Times*, March 3, 2005, http://www.nytimes.com/2005/03/03/nyregion/03profile.html.

31. "Transcript: President Bush's Final News Conference," *New York Times*, January 12, 2009, http://www.nytimes.com/2009/01/12/us/politics/12text-bush.html.

32. Hans Nichols, "Obama Inaugural Strains Lincoln Comparisons While Inviting Them," *Bloomberg*, January 17, 2009, http://www.bloomberg.com/apps/news?pid=newsarchive&sid=az5HzIamy_NQ.

33. "Obama Takes Train Ride to History," *CBS News*/Associated Press, January 17, 2009, http://www.cbsnews.com/news/obama-takes-train-ride-to-history/.

34. "Transcript: Obama in Philadelphia," *New York Times*, January 17, 2009, http://www.nytimes.com/2009/01/17/us/politics/17text-obama.html.

35. Hans Nichols, "Obama Inaugural Strains Lincoln Comparisons While Inviting Them."

36. Ibid.

37. Richard E. Neustadt, *Presidential Power and the Modern Presidents: The Politics of Leadership from Roosevelt to Reagan* (New York: Free Press, 1990), ix.

38. Barack Obama, Interview by Steve Kroft, *60 Minutes*, November 4, 2010, http://www.cbsnews.com/news/transcript-president-barack-obama-part-2-07-11-2010/3/.

39. Stephen Hess, interview with author, January 11, 2010.

40. George C. Edwards III, "The Presidential Pulpit: Bully or Baloney," in *The Modern Presidency*, James P. Piffner ed. (Boston: Wadsworth Cengage Learning, 2011).

41. Ron Suskind, *Confidence Men*, 479.

42. Richard W. Stevenson, "From 'Change' Candidate to Changed Candidate," *New York Times*, February 10, 2012, http://thecaucus.blogs.nytimes.com/2012/02/10/from-change-candidate-to-changed-candidate/.

43. Barack Obama, "Inaugural Address," January 20, 2009; American Presidency Project, http://www.presidency.ucsb.edu/ws/index.php?pid=44.

44. John Harwood, "Woes of Obama Echo Those of Past Presidents," *New York Times*, January 16, 2014, http://www.nytimes.com/2014/01/17/us/politics/on-spying-obamas-woes-echo-those-of-past-presidents.html.

45. Franklin D. Roosevelt, "Inaugural Address," January 20, 1937; American Presidency Project, http://www.presidency.ucsb.edu/ws/index.php?pid=15349.

46. James MacGregor Burns, *Roosevelt: The Lion and the Fox* (New York: Harcourt, Brace, 1956).

47. George C. Edwards, *Overreach: Leadership in the Obama Presidency* (Princeton: Princeton University Press, 2012).

48. Jean Edward Smith, *FDR* (New York: Random House, 2008), 312–13.

49. Norm Ornstein, "The Myth of Presidential Leadership," *National Journal*, May 8, 2013, http://www.nationaljournal.com/washington-inside-out/the-myth-of-presidential-leadership-20130508.

50. Jackie Calmes, "A Dirty Secret Lurks in the Struggle over a Fiscal 'Grand Bargain,'" *New York Times,* November 18, 2013, http://www.nytimes.com/2013/11/19/us/politics/the-hidden-hurdles-to-a-fiscal-grand-bargain.html.

CHAPTER 13

1. Ron Suskind, *Confidence Men: Wall Street, Washington, and the Education of a President* (New York: Harper, 2011), 48.
2. "Barack Obama's Caucus Speech," *New York Times,* January 3, 2008, http://www.nytimes.com/2008/01/03/us/politics/03obama-transcript.html.
3. "2008 Voter Turnout," Factcheck.org, January 8, 2009, http://www.factcheck.org/2009/01/2008-voter-turnout/
4. Jeffrey M. Jones, "Obama's Initial Approval Ratings in Historical Context," Gallup, January 26, 2009, http://www.gallup.com/poll/113968/obama-initial-approval-ratings-historical-context.aspx.
5. "Obama Appeared on Half of *Time* Covers," *NBC News,* December 17, 2008, http://firstread.nbcnews.com/_news/2008/12/17/4432215-obama-appeared-on-half-of-time-covers.
6. Barack Obama, "Barack Obama's Inaugural Address," *New York Times,* January 20, 2009, http://www.nytimes.com/2009/01/20/us/politics/20text-obama.html?pagewanted=all.
7. Lydia Saad, "Obama Approval Advances to 47%, up from 43% Pre-Election," Gallup, November 8, 2010, http://www.gallup.com/poll/144347/obama-approval-advances-pre-election.aspx.
8. Lydia Saad, "Among Recent Bills, Financial Reform a Lone Plus for Congress," Gallup, September 13, 2010, http://www.gallup.com/poll/142967/among-recent-bills-financial-reform-lone-plus-congress.aspx.
9. Colleen J. Shogan, "The Contemporary Presidency: The Sixth Year Curse," *Presidential Studies Quarterly* 36, no. 1 (March 2006).
10. "Presidential Approval Ratings—Barack Obama," Gallup, accessed February 5, 2014, http://www.gallup.com/poll/116479/barack-obama-presidential-job-approval.aspx.
11. "President's Marks as Manager Take Hit in New CNN/ORC Poll," CNN, November 25, 2013, http://politicalticker.blogs.cnn.com/2013/11/25/presidents-marks-as-manager-take-hit-in-new-cnnorc-poll/.
12. David Remnick, "Annals of the Presidency: Going the Distance: On and Off the Road with Barack Obama," *New Yorker,* January 27, 2014, http://www.newyorker.com/reporting/2014/01/27/140127fa_fact_remnick.
13. Peter Baker, "Education of a President," *New York Times,* October 12, 2010, http://www.nytimes.com/2010/10/17/magazine/17obama-t.html.
14. Jeffrey M. Jones, "Obama Approval Most Polarized for First-Year President," Gallup, January 25, 2010, http://www.gallup.com/poll/125345/obama-approval-polarized-first-year-president.aspx.
15. Kevin Baker, "Barack Hoover Obama: The Best and the Brightest Blow It Again," *Harper's,* July 2009, http://harpers.org/archive/2009/07/barack-hoover-obama/.
16. Andrew Sullivan, "How Obama's Long Game Will Outsmart His Critics," *Newsweek,* January 16, 2012, http://www.newsweek.com/andrew-sullivan-how-obamas-long-game-will-outsmart-his-critics-64177.
17. Scott Horsley, "Obama Plugs Federal Oversight as Economic Fix," National Public Radio, September 17, 2008, http://www.npr.org/templates/story/story.php?storyId=94699099.

NOTES — 273

18. "The Obameter: Tracking Obama's Campaign Promises," Politifact, accessed April 20, 2014, http://www.politifact.com/truth-o-meter/promises/obameter/.
19. David Jackson, "Obama Echoes Reagan: 'Stay on Course,'" *USA Today,* October 1, 2010, http://content.usatoday.com/communities/theoval/post/2010/10/obama-channels-reagan-stay-on-course/1#.Uvv1R_ldWSo.
20. Carol E. Lee, "President Obama: 'Fear and Frustration' Drive Voters," *Politico,* October 16, 2010, http://www.politico.com/news/stories/1010/43706.html.
21. Jason Horowitz, "Obama Effect Inspiring Few to Seek Office," *New York Times,* April 13, 2014, http://www.nytimes.com/2014/04/14/us/obama-effect-inspiring-few-to-seek-office.html.
22. Michael Gerson, "Our Complex President," *Washington Post,* January 23, 2014, http://www.washingtonpost.com/opinions/michael-gerson-barack-obama-our-complex-president/2014/01/23/4ca45626-846a-11e3-8099-9181471f7aaf_story.html; David Remnick, "Annals of the Presidency: Going the Distance."
23. David Brooks, "Obama Rejects Obamaism," *New York Times,* September 19, 2011, http://www.nytimes.com/2011/09/20/opinion/brooks-obama-rejects-obamaism.html.
24. Peter Baker, "Education of a President."
25. Michael Powell, "Obama, the Self-described 'Rorschach Test,' Liberal but Inscrutable," *New York Times,* June 4, 2008, http://www.nytimes.com/2008/06/04/world/americas/04iht-obama.1.13459637.html.

CONCLUSION

1. David S. Broder, *The Party's Over: The Failure of Politics in America* (New York: Harper & Row, 1972), 167.
2. "American President: Franklin D. Roosevelt," Miller Center at University of Virginia, accessed April 20, 2014, http://millercenter.org/president/fdroosevelt/essays/biography/3.
3. Arthur Sullivan and W. S. Gilbert, *H.M.S. Pinafore: Or, The Lass That Loved a Sailor* (San Francisco: Bacon & Company, Book and Job Printers, 1879), 7.
4. John King, interview with the author, February 4, 2010.
5. Theodore R. Marmor and Jerry L. Mashaw, "How Do You Say 'Economic Security'?," *New York Times,* September 23, 2011, http://www.nytimes.com/2011/09/24/opinion/how-do-you-say-economic-security.html.
6. "Anger at Government Most Pronounced among Conservative Republicans," Pew Research Center for the People and the Press, September 30, 2013, http://www.people-press.org/2013/09/30/anger-at-government-most-pronounced-among-conservative-republicans/.
7. Suzanne Mettler, "Our Hidden Government Benefits," *New York Times,* September 19, 2011, http://www.nytimes.com/2011/09/20/opinion/our-hidden-government-benefits.html.
8. John King, interview with the author, February 4, 2010.
9. David Greenberg, "Why Last Chapters Disappoint," *New York Times,* March 18, 2011, http://www.nytimes.com/2011/03/20/books/review/why-last-chapters-disappoint-essay.html.
10. George Santayana, *The Life of Reason: Introduction and Reason in Common Sense* (Cambridge: MIT Press, 2011), 172.
11. Stephen Skowronek *Presidential Leadership in Political Time: Reprise and Reappraisal* (Lawrence: University Press of Kansas, 2008).

12. Lara M. Brown, "On Greatness & Masculinity," accessed May 8, 2014, http://www.larambrownphd.com/graphics/files/Greatness.pdf.
13. Joseph S. Nye, *Presidential Leadership and the Creation of the American Era* (Princeton, New Jersey: Princeton University Press, 2013), xii.
14. Clinton Rossiter, *The American Presidency* (Baltimore: Johns Hopkins University Press, 1987), 243.

INDEX